The Tour de France Complete Book of Cycling

Presse Sports photo

The Tour de France Complete Book of Cycling

David Chauner and Michael Halstead

A JOHN BOSWELL ASSOCIATES BOOK

Villard Books ◦ New York ◦ 1990

Published in the United States by Villard Books,
a division of Random House, Inc., New York,
and simultaneously in Canada by Random House of Canada Limited, Toronto.

Library of Congress Cataloging in Publication Data
Chauner, David.
The Tour de France complete book of cycling by David Chauner and Michael Halstead.
p. cm.
"A John Boswell Associates Book."
ISBN 0-679-72936-4
1. Cycling. I. Halstead, Michael. II. Title.
GV1041.C42 1990
796.6—dc20 89-48482

Design by Helen Barrow
Manufactured in the United States of America
9876532
First edition

To Greg LeMond
and the shot in the arm he has given our sport in this country,
to the future of bicycling as a major sport and recreational activity in America,
and to far-sighted companies like CoreStates Financial Corp,
which are willing to invest in making that a reality.

Acknowledgments

The authors gratefully acknowledge the invaluable contributions of the following individuals and organizations, without whom this book would not have been possible (or if so, certainly a lot more difficult). Researchers Tim Blumenthal and Jeff Fryer, photographer Seth Goltzer, illustrator George Retseck, and the hard work and magic fingers of Stacy Lytwyn and Tamra Fisher. Thanks also to our families and associates at ICP and Sports & Company, for the nagging but hopefully worthwhile diversion this project has created in our family and business lives. Thanks also to the good folks at the Société du Tour de France, chiefly Agathe Coville, Jean-Pierre Carenso, and Jean-Marie LeBlanc; to Ray Benton and his colleagues at Travent, International; to the Schwinn Bicycle Company; Specialized Bicycle Components; and Brandford Bike, as well as to the staffs of *VeloNews* and *Winning* magazines who provided us with interesting and valuable input. Finally, we would like to thank our literary agent and partner in this project, John Boswell, and his associate, Patty Brown, and above all, Helen Barrow, without whose exact eye and good taste this would not be such a handsome book. And last but certainly not least Diane Reverand of Villard Books who had the vision to see that with good writing, strong motivation, and an unbeatable brand name there is, indeed, room in the market for one more good book on cycling.

Contents

Introduction

In the early sixties, I read an article in Sports Illustrated *about the Tour de France. It was mostly photos, with brief yet poignant text that told of an incredible three-week sporting event that stopped a country in its tracks, dominated the media, and ignited the passions of people all across Europe. I was fascinated. I could not believe bike racers could go so far, so fast, and for so long, and it mystified me how they could get up and race after crashing down a mountainside.*

It was tough, it was different, and for some reason it really turned me on. Like the principal character in Breaking Away, *I became, in my adolescent fantasies, a European racer. I didn't go so far as to effect an Italian accent, but I did cut out photos of the great champions and put them on my bedroom wall. And I must admit, I did work quite hard to perfect my pronunciation of "Jacques Anquetil" (then the Mickey Mantle of the sport).*

Just as the excitement and glamour of the World Series inspires some kids to take up baseball, the Tour de France really got me hooked on cycling. I learned quickly that the Tour represents the pinnacle and the embodiment of everything it takes to be great in the sport. Unlike today, when a talented and motivated American can have a somewhat realistic shot at riding the Tour, it was unimaginable in the 1960s. (The first American to ride the Tour was a French-sounding but very American guy named Jock Boyer—and of course the only American to ever win the Tour was, interestingly enough, another all-American with a Gallic-sounding name, Greg LeMond.)

In my day, cycling in this country was miniscule by today's standards. There were at best 2,000 licensed competitors, and the scant information that did exist came via mimeographed newsletters that were passed from one zealot to another, much in the fashion of an arcane political underground. If you lived on the East coast, you could hope to ride perhaps thirteen races a year, whereas today it's possible to ride eighty or more events in this area, from February through October.

By joining the Century Road Club of America, a New York–based racing club, I rubbed shoulders with American cycling's "old timers," who spoke with passion about legendary European wheelmen like Fausto Coppi and distant American heroes, such as Frank Kramer and Bobby Walthour. I learned that my sport, in fact, had a rich tradition and history in this country. In its heyday, for example, top American cyclists earned as much or more than top baseball players. The race barrier in pro sports was broken by a cyclist decades before Jackie Robinson achieved the same in baseball.

During my early racing days, I traveled the underground circuit of weekend amateur races that were held in such out-of-the-way places as Raritan, New Jersey; Fitchburg, Massachusetts; Colt Park, in Hartford, Connecticut; and Smithtown, Long Island. Our fleeting brush with the big time was in predawn Central Park, in Manhattan, where the Sunday-morning races were completed by the time the average New Yorker had finished his first cup of coffee or made it through the first section of the Times. But I loved it. On race weekends the air was filled with French, Italian, and German, shiny racing bikes and esoteric jargon about developing "souplesse" and "coming off a wheel."

Weekday afternoons were spent in my personal dream world. The quiet back roads of Main Line, Philadelphia, became the French countryside. I wore tight-fitting black shorts, white ankle socks, and black "tap dance" cycling shoes. I even went so far as to shave my legs (a big risk when you're growing up in Philly) and to wear my cycling cap cocked at the same jaunty angle as Jacques Anquetil's. Only one other guy in my school raced bikes. He also liked snakes and wore weird clothes that rarely matched.

It was not easy to be an otherwise normal teenager in the mid-sixties in mid-America, with an unbridled passion for something few people could relate to. Those years were the "dark ages" of American cycling, but I got through them and justified my passion by striving to excel. It was easier to say I was training for the Olympic team than to reveal that my dream was to go to Europe to become a pro cyclist.

I retired from a twelve-year racing career in 1975—at age twenty-six, which is normally the beginning of a cyclist's prime. Although I had been to the Olympics twice (Mexico City, in 1968, and Munich, in 1972), and had ridden well in the Tour of Britain (my "claim to fame" is that I was the first American to win a stage in that "Milk Race"), I was an era away from having a realistic opportunity to compete as a professional in the Tour de France. It was also eight years before the Tour was given serious coverage by American television. And I had to make a living.

Since my racing days, I have had the great good fortune of being able to make my sport my career. With old racing buddies like Jack Simes and Jerry Casale, I was able to develop programs and events that were designed to move competitive bicycling back into the mainstream.

My coauthor and business partner, Mike Halstead, a lawyer, former pro skier, and experienced sports marketing and television executive, became part of the adventure in 1986. Suddenly, cycling had matured into a solid business proposi-

tion and, with events like our CoreStates USPro Championship in Philadelphia, we have been able to make the sport a viable marketing opportunity for television and sponsors and move it closer to the high standards still being set by the Tour de France.

As we hope you will discover in this book, there is much more to cycling than big events and superstar athletes. But as I learned as a teenager, it is these great events and the people who win them that create the spark for what we feel will be "the tennis of the nineties"—and (as we hope for your sake and ours) many decades to come.

DAVID M. CHAUNER

Presse Sports photo

The Tour de France Complete Book of Cycling

1 The Velocipede

The Tour de France is one of the great spectacles of modern man and certainly our grandest and most ambitious sports event. Each July, since 1903 (with breaks only during the two world wars), it has mesmerized and nearly paralyzed the country of France and ignited the passions of sports fans worldwide. Today, a global television audience numbering in the hundreds of millions watches the drama unfold as two hundred or so of the world's elite cyclists travel 2,000 miles (the distance from Chicago to Los Angeles) through France's cities, villages, vineyards, and high mountain passes in search of cycling's Holy Grail.

From a global perspective, bicycling is second in popularity only to the sport of soccer. But unlike soccer, cycling's mass popularity is not limited to foreign lands. According to the National Sporting Goods Association, bicycling is second only to swimming as America's most popular participant sport.

It is a lifetime activity and one of the few that can be experienced by the entire family. Cycling is a proven fitness activity in an age of increasing health consciousness, each day inheriting defectors from the running boom who find it produces the same benefits with less boredom and wear and tear on the ligaments and joints.

It has also become fashionable, even trendy, with the cycling look influencing fashion far beyond sportswear. Once considered the province of eccentric European mountain men, it is now coming of age and gaining respect as a serious sport in this country, helped in great measure by an all-American lad named Greg LeMond. Greg has been able to beat the world's best, on their own turf, in a sport that was once their private fiefdom. Americans love winners and things they can win at.

Bicycling is now being called "the tennis of the 1990s" and there are many parallels, including its growth as a pro sport, the proliferation of organized competitions at all levels, and its ever-increasing media exposure.

In reality, this phenomenon is not so new at all. The sport of cycling in this country is merely awakening from a state of dormancy. Let's take a look at how it all began.

Over the last century, the bicycle has wheeled in and out of favor with populations around the world, serving in many capacities, ranging from essential transportation to casual recreation to a means for serious competition. It seems logical that the bicycle (or velocipede, as it was called in its early days) must have been invented not long after the discovery of the wheel—or at least by the time the Chinese discovered gunpowder. Not so.

The first known bicycle was invented around 1816 by Baron von Drais de Sauerbrun of Germany. It consisted of two wheels and a crude steering device and was propelled by the rider pushing his feet off the ground, in the same fashion as a child's scooter. It was, however, promoted to have attained a cruising speed of ten to fourteen miles per hour. The Baron's innovation soon caught on in France, where it was known as the "*Draisienne,*" and in England, where it was referred to as the "Hobby Horse."

The next incarnation was that of English inventor Louis Gompertz who, in 1821, introduced a two-wheeled vehicle that was powered by hand, somewhat in the fashion of the modern exercycle. This was at best a curiosity, at worst a flop, and it was not until 1839 that another step in bicycle evolution took place in the shop of a Scottish blacksmith, Kirkpatrick Macmillan, who added cranks to the rear wheel of the Hobby Horse. Another curiosity.

The first successful bicycle builders were probably the brothers Michaux (Pierre and Ernest) of Paris, who created a very crude wood-rimmed, iron-tired precursor to the modern bicycle. They sold two in 1861, 142 in 1862, and 400 in 1865. An ambitious assistant, Pierre Lallement, took their creation to the United States where it became known as the "Bone Shaker" and was quite a fad in the late 1860s.

The Bone Shaker, every bit as uncomfortable as its name implies, was the vehicle of choice for many an act of derring-do. In 1869, the first bicycle trade show was held in Paris. The same year, an early cycling publication, *Le Velocipede Illustre,* sponsored the first-known road race, a 130-km (81 mile) torture test from Paris to Rouen, designed to prove that cycling was faster, more efficient, and better, in terms of endurance, than running. Two hundred thirty contestants entered the race, including six women.

The next major development came in 1870 when England's James Starley introduced the high-wheeled "Ordinary" (or "Penny Farthing," so named because the much larger front wheel looked like a British penny in relation to tiny rear wheel or "farthing"). This advancement gave rise to bigger and better feats of bravery and endurance. In 1883, Englishman J. H. Adams rode 242.42 miles in twenty-four hours on an Ordinary and, in the year following, Thomas Stevens rode an Ordinary, hard rubber tires and all, across the entire United States, traversing all forms of prairies, mountains, and deserts and passing at least one covered wagon and a few amazed Indians along the way.

In its early days, the bicycle threatened the extinction of the horse as man's chief form of individual transportation, and for a very

BICYCLING TIME LINE

1816–18
Hobby Horse invented

1869
First bicycle race: 130 km (80.78 miles), Paris to Rouen; 203 contestants

1893
First World Championship, in Chicago

1899
"Mile-a-Minute" Murphy rides 63.24 mph behind moving train

1903
First Tour de France

1919
Alf Goulet pedals 2,501 miles in a six-day race

1936
Newark Velodrome burns down

late 1950s
ten-speed bike introduced in U.S.

1969
Audrey McElmury becomes first American woman to win World Championship

1970
Annual bicycle sales top car sales in U.S.

1979
Movie *Breaking Away* released

1983
Greg LeMond wins World Championship

1984
Connie Carpenter-Phinney wins first American Olympic gold medal in cycling, at Los Angeles

1985
Eric Heiden wins first annual CoreStates USPRO Cycling Championship, in Philadelphia
John Howard paced to 152.284 mph

1986
Greg LeMond becomes first American to win Tour de France

1989
Greg LeMond wins second Tour de France

brief period in history, it ran neck and neck with the automobile as the answer to energy-efficient, nonpolluting rapid transit. In the early 1880s, this revolutionary development offered door-to-door convenience, "breathtaking" speeds of over ten miles per hour, minimal upkeep, and the promise of no more manure on the roads.

However, the "horseless carriage" eventually prevailed, despite its belching exhaust and constant breakdowns. Sadly, the technical developments arising from the bicycle sowed the seeds of its own demise as modern man's chief form of individual transportation. In fact, several inventions of important historical significance were stimulated by the search for a better bicycle. In 1888, John Boyd Dunlop, with the intent of making the bike more ridable, invented the pneumatic tire. Other great innovators, Henry Ford, and Orville and Wilbur Wright applied what they had learned in the bicycle industry to those inventions for which they have become most famous. And, ironically, the paving of America's roadways, which along with Henry Ford's "Model T" made the auto more enjoyable and accessible to the common man, grew largely out of early lobbying by the League of American Wheelmen, a group of bicycling enthusiasts, still active today, which in the 1880s had a much larger membership than any comparable auto club.

Like the horse, the bicycle, at least in the developed world, has evolved from basic transportation to a means of recreation and sport, and in this role it has flourished. Enthusiasm for cycling has created trends, influenced fashion, and mirrored social issues. Women's bloomers, for example, were created out of a need to keep skirts out of the spokes. This "scandalous" attire, worn by independent-minded women perched atop high-wheeled bicycles, in a position that doctors said risked sterility, was one of the earlier expressions of female emancipation.

It's no wonder that a century later, the bicycle is as strongly as ever entwined with the world's social fabric. In China, it has remained an

In China, parking lots fill with bicycles, not cars. *Helen Barrow photo*

essential means of daily transportation, with nearly 200 million people, or half the work force, commuting to their jobs on two wheels. It also continues its role as a barometer of female social progress, as exemplified by the fact that it has become a favorite competitive, recreational, and spectator sport for women. In the United States, for example, Connie Carpenter captured America's first-ever gold medal in cycling (L.A. in 1984), and network television coverage of the Tour de France has a 55 percent female viewership.

THE FIRST BICYCLE BOOM

The last two decades of the nineteenth century might be described as the first "golden age" of cycling, since they were a period of technological advance and tremendous enthusiasm for the bicycle. As a mechanical device this human-powered vehicle was a true marvel. Its key period of evolution—from the first pedal-driven Bone Shaker to the diamond-shaped frame, chain-driven, pneumatic-tire machine (much like today's)—lasted from roughly 1860 until 1884, the year in which John Kemp Starley (nephew of the Ordinary's inventor) introduced the "Rover Safety Cycle."

The Rover eliminated the precarious perch (biggest drawback of the high-wheeled Ordinary) and smoothed out the teeth-chattering ride. It was the first bicycle to use two wheels of nearly equal size, and its use of chain drive in combination with two different-sized sprockets, one attached to the pedals and one to the rear hub, introduced a new mechanical advantage and allowed gear ratios to be altered to suit the intended use as well as individual strength and preference. Actually, the Rover had been invented five years earlier (by H. J. Lawson) but could not find a niche in the marketplace, probably because it was ahead of its time.

Further refinements resulted in the 1896 Humber, which was manufactured in Britain and widely exported and imitated throughout the world. The Humber is considered the prototype of the modern bicycle.

By the close of the century, bicycle madness was reaching a crescendo. Cycling became increasingly well organized as a competitive and spectator sport, which in turn served to fuel a healthy and fast-growing industry. For example, in the United States, manufacture of bicycles had jumped from 200,000 per year in 1889, to an annual output of one million ten years later. Hundreds of manufacturers with well-recognized names like Pierce Arrow, Oldfield and Daimler, and Benz fed the market with sleek "wheels" costing up to one thousand dollars. Bicycle stadiums sprang up around the world

EVOLUTION OF THE BICYCLE

HOBBY HORSE
1816–18

BONE SHAKER
1861

ORDINARY
1870s

ROVER SAFETY
1884

HUMBER
1896

Drawing by George Retseck

By the turn of the century, bicycle racing had spread across the U.S. This race along the Susquehanna River was run by a local club near Harrisburg, Pennsylvania. *Pennsylvania Historical and Museum Commission*

and paved tracks were constructed to provide smooth surfaces for the most popular form of turn-of-the-century racing, the lightning-fast sprints—short-distance, highly tactical match races for up to five riders.

The greatest early champion of all was an American from New Jersey, named Arthur August Zimmerman, who almost single-handedly wrote cycling's early record books. "Zimmy," a lifetime member of the New York Athletic Club, always rode with the Club's winged foot on his chest as he humbled the greatest champions of England, France, Australia, and America in the several worldwide tours he made during his career spanning the period between 1889 and the turn of the century.

Zimmerman won the first official world championship ever held (1893, in Chicago), and during one two-year winning streak recorded no less than one hundred consecutive victories. Zimmy trained more religiously and scientifically than most, and when he retired from the sport he authored the first definitive book on training for cycling.

To put his accomplishments into perspective, one must keep in mind that during the time that Zimmerman dominated it, bicycle racing was the world's most popular sport. Hundreds of thousands of amateur racers formed the base of a pyramid with an elite corps of professionals at the apex. Pro cyclists retired rich men and were regularly feted by kings, queens, and presidents wherever they appeared.

Perhaps no cyclist was more popular or more ahead of his time than the great black champion, Marshall "Major" Taylor. In 1896, Taylor became the first black to become a professional cyclist. The

In 1894, A. A. Zimmerman of New Jersey was the world's best cyclist. *Presse Sports photo*

The popular rider "Major" Taylor is still the only black cyclist to have won a World Championship (1899). *Shurmann photo*

only other well-known black athlete during this era was the boxer Jack Johnson, subject of the play *The Great White Hope.* For fourteen amazing seasons, Taylor was one of the best in the game. His specialty was quick, come-from-behind accelerations that would gain him narrow victories at the tape. Like Johnson and other great black American athletes and performers, he was idolized in France and commanded huge appearance fees from European promoters. The world championship title he won in Montreal, in 1899, was the first and only world championship won by a black cyclist. Taylor's physical battle to stay on top and his emotional battle with turn-of-the-century racism was recorded in a fascinating autobiography, not so humbly entitled, *The Fastest Bicycle Rider in the World,* published nearly forty years before baseball player Jackie Robinson "broke the color barrier" in major league professional sports.

In those early days of cycling fever, every type of event and daring stunt imaginable on two wheels was attempted by a mixed bag of daredevils and madmen. A steady progression of technical refinements allowed the day's rough-and-tumble zealots to push back the limits of speed and endurance in a series of feats and stunts that made front-page news. It was a time reminiscent in part of the moon race of the 1960s and Evel Kneivel's outrageous motorcycle stunts of the 1970s. Remember that in the 1880s, the fastest form of transport was a galloping horse or a stoked-up locomotive. In today's world of supersonic airliners and travel through space at thousands of miles per hour, it's hard to imagine that anything traveling at a speed approaching twenty-five miles per hour could be considered fast, let alone revolutionary. The editorial pages of the day were full of derogatory comments about inconsiderate "scorchers," and the news and sports columns filled with detailed accounts of the latest exploits of the "speed merchants" who would race anything that moved, including horses, trains, and most commonly, each other.

Once it was determined that a man on a bicycle could beat a horse at almost any distance, the challenge turned to testing the limits of speed and endurance. It was soon discovered that a bicycle could go much faster if air resistance was reduced, and "pacing" became a cycling term of art. A human-paced rider, tucked in the slipstream of a special bicycle powered by as many "as ten stokers" could reach a speed of fifty miles per hour.

But the most famous pacing feat of all was achieved by Charles M. "Mile-a-Minute" Murphy on June 30, 1899. Motivated by healthy wagers and newspaper challenges, Murphy became the first man in history to crack sixty miles per hour on a bicycle. To make this feat possible, the Long Island Railroad laid "pool table smooth" planking across a three-mile stretch of railroad ties and modified a train car to act as Murphy's pacing machine. Tucked in tightly behind the car's rear platform, and nearly encased by a specially built wooden windbreak extending from the rear of the car, Murphy came perilously close to death when, at the end of the timed mile, the engineer

John Howard achieved a land speed record of 152.2 mph, in 1985, on the Bonneville Salt Flats. *Courtesy John Howard*

slowed the locomotive too abruptly. Murphy's bike slammed into the car, but fortunately he (and his "wheel") were snatched from the jaws of disaster by quick-acting officials who pulled him safely into the train.

The front-page lead story of the next day's issue of the *New York Times* proclaimed that this feat had "proved that human muscle can, for a short distance at least, excel the best power of steam and steel." Murphy's time for the timed mile was 57.45 seconds, and observers verified that he could have gone faster but for the limitations of the train. Although Murphy's record has been shattered many times (the current record is John Howard's race car paced 152.28 mph, set in 1985 on the Bonneville Salt Flats. His feat was that day's equivalent of today's attempts to break the sound barrier on land or perhaps a manned landing on Mars.

These innumerable speed and endurance tests and the beginnings of a well-organized sport characterized cycling's initial worldwide boom, and although much of its trendiness faded with the emergence of the automobile, cycling became entrenched as an international sport, with its popularity taking different forms around the world.

In America, track or velodrome racing continued to expand and

Charley Murphy on his "mile-a-minute" ride. *Courtesy Schwinn Bicycle Company*

remained a popular pastime until the eve of World War II. Over one hundred steeply banked outdoor velodromes up and down the Atlantic seaboard, in places like Providence, Newark, Philadelphia, Nutley, Coney Island, New York City, and elsewhere around the country flourished through the 1920s and '30s. A very popular mixture of vaudeville and serious sport, indoor six-day bike racing, played to packed houses in Chicago, Boston, Cleveland, and New York's Madison Square Garden every winter. The velodromes were the place to be and to be seen, and their mesmerizing nonstop entertainment and opportunities for socializing on the infield regularly drew such notables as Bing Crosby, Al Capone, Babe Ruth, Will Rogers, Jack Dempsey, and Mary Pickford.

There was much fanfare announcing the first Tour de France, originally scheduled for 1902, but actually run in July 1903. *Presse Sports photo*

While, in America, speed and flash characterized the sport of cycling, European passions ran high for endurance-oriented epic challenges of man against man in near-impossible conditions. In 1903, a French newspaper publisher, Henri Desgrange organized a publicity stunt that was designed to be the "greatest bicycle race in the world." His month-long race around France took sixty die-hard entrants over the Alps, the Pyrenees, and most of the rutted cobblestone roads in between. When it was over, the winner, Maurice Garin, was proclaimed a national hero. The Tour de France, a national obsession and now the world's largest annual sports event, was born. In the ensuing years, other great European classic stage races were established (the Tour of Italy in 1909, the Tour of Switzerland in 1933, and the Tour of Spain in 1935). Since its founding in 1903, "Le Tour" has been interrupted only by world wars. We will examine this great sports classic in more detail in Chapter 13.

Although cycling has continued to grow and prosper largely unimpeded in Europe, the Great Depression ended cycling's glory years in America. Bad management, warring, greedy promoters and their reluctance to reinvest their profits into the development of the sport resulted in dwindling talent and rundown facilities and sent the public to the ball parks. When the great velodromes either crumbled or burned down, there was not sufficient money or interest to rebuild them. Unlike Europe, no road-racing classics or sense of tradition had been established. By the time of World War II, American cycling as an organized sport was all but dead.

CYCLING RETURNS TO AMERICA

One of the interesting stories in cycling is the extent to which it reemerged as a major sport in America following World War II. The bicycle made its comeback in large numbers first as a child's toy. Who cannot remember their first Schwinn, Huffy, or Columbia? For many, the bicycle provided a first escape from our immediate

The Night Frank Kramer Retired

The year was 1922. It was the cusp of cycling's golden age in America, a four-decade era that saw a professional sport grow and fade before most others in this country even got going.

At that time, six-day bike racing was the most popular and successful annual sports attraction in New York's Madison Square Garden. In the summertime, a dozen steeply banked wooden velodromes along the Atlantic seaboard hosted high-speed sprint and motorcycle-paced races to packed houses every night of the week. Big name racers from all over the world made their big bucks here, and a handful of promoters—like "Colonel" John M. Chapman—got richer than any ball-club owner could hope to be for another two decades.

Back then, velodrome racing was the only show in town, and the hottest velodrome in the nation sat in the Vailsburg section of Newark, New Jersey, then a pleasant suburb of tree-lined streets and prosperous homeowners. From 1911 until the late twenties, nightly sellout crowds approaching fifteen thousand were not uncommon.

In 1912, the World Championship was hosted at Vailsburg. It was won by Frank Kramer, an undisputed legend of the sport. Had cycling not faded from the American sports scene, Kramer's name would be as recognized today as that of Ty Cobb and Babe Ruth. In fact, when Ruth's salary first hit the "outrageous" sum of twenty thousand dollars a year, Kramer had been making that kind of money for almost a decade. In all, Kramer won the U.S. Professional Cycling Championship eighteen times, consecutively from 1901 to 1916, and then twice more in 1918 and 1921, the latter when he was a ripe old forty-one.

Joe Neville, nephew of one of Kramer's trainers, was close to the sport throughout his youth and believed Kramer's presence was a big factor in the sport's popularity: "Kramer was an intelligent, single-minded individual," said Neville. "He set very high standards for himself. He had a grandeur, a star quality about him that gave the sport some class. He lived for the bike the way Caruso lived to sing. The same kind of people that went to the opera came to see Frank. In my opinion, when Kramer quit the bike game, it folded up."

Frank Kramer was the national professional champion 19 times. *Peter Nye photo*

Although the sport flourished for nearly a decade after Kramer took his last spin around the track, it never saw a champion like him again. Wealthy, stubborn promoters refused to adopt new ideas or develop new talent, and the public rapidly lost interest. Baseball got organized and survived the Great Depression. Cycling did not.

Perhaps Kramer's words on July 22, 1922, the night he retired at the Newark Velodrome, were prophetic: "I'm sorry," said the great champion, after sitting through choruses of "The Star-Spangled Banner" and "Auld Lang Syne," "that I'm not fifteen years younger so that I might continue to entertain you. However, I have no alternative and must bow to Father Time."

Reader Tip: Best book on cycling history—*Hearts of Lions,* by Peter Nye.

environs. It expanded our sphere of influence from a radius of one mile to ten miles or more. Whether it was a "horse," a "car," a "motorcycle," or a "rocket ship" the bike was a freedom machine which helped put kids on a more equal footing with the adult world. The child's bike of the 1950s and '60s also became a palate for the expression of individuality. Streamers, bells, saddlebags, a myriad of handlebar grips and reflectors, and yes, even playing cards pinned to the spokes with clothes pins, to create the sound of an imaginary motor, made children's bikes an extension of their personalities and a vehicle to fulfill their fantasies.

Although cycling, since its introduction, continued as both a major sport and a day-to-day means of transportation throughout most of Europe, it did not reemerge as an adult sport in North America until the late 1960s when "ten-speed" became a household term. In fact, 1970 was the first year in the United States, since the turn of the century, in which bicycle sales outstripped auto sales. It was the beginning of the fitness craze that still grips America. Adults began jogging, swimming, and cycling more than ever before.

In the 1970s, the endurance sport that really took off was running. In 1972, Frank Shorter became the first American to win an Olympic Marathon and, in so doing, proved to the country that Americans could excel in individual endurance sports. Distance running was suddenly in vogue.

During the same period, cycling was quietly attracting increasing numbers with steady sales of eight to twelve million bicycles per year. These sales were fueled in part by the energy crisis and the growing concern for the environment of the mid-seventies, but also

Bicycles of the fifties appealed more to children and, like cars, promoted the freedom of the road. This was the Schwinn "Auto-Cycle." *Courtesy of Schwinn Bicycle Company*

Connie Carpenter (head down) edged out Rebecca Twigg to win the first Olympic cycling gold medal for women, in 1984. *Presse Sports photo*

Mark Gorski (right) took the Gold and Nelson Vails the Silver, in the 1984 Olympic men's sprint. *Presse Sports photo*

Alexi Grewal won the 1984 Olympic Road Race. *Presse Sports photo*

Steve Hegg won the individual-pursuit Olympic Gold Medal, in 1984. *Presse Sports photo*

by an increasing number of runners who discovered that cycling provides all the fitness benefits of running but at a far lower cost to the body. By the end of the decade, there were an estimated sixty million bicycles in occasional use in the U.S. The impact of the bicycle on the national consciousness was reflected by its serving as the background theme for the 1979 sleeper hit movie, *Breaking Away*.

The greater numbers of Americans riding bicycles created a broader base from which better American racers might develop, but it wasn't until 1984 that these numbers really began to pay off. It was at the Los Angeles Summer Olympics that cycling suddenly became an American sport. Gold-medal winning performances proved that American cyclists were as good as any in the world. Few made note that the powerful cycling nations of Eastern Europe were not present, but perhaps that didn't matter. Americans saw other Americans winning at a sport that was previously the province of foreigners and, as a result, they suddenly developed a new interest in competitive cycling.

BACK ON THE FRONT PAGE

Two years later, Greg LeMond became the first American ever to win the Tour de France, a victory that moved cycling to the front pages and generated more publicity than any other cyclist had ever achieved in modern times in the U.S. LeMond was on the cover of major general-interest sports publications across the country, featured on television and radio talk shows, and became the first cyclist in memory to be honored by the president of the United States. It was little consolation to the French that Greg has a Gallic-sounding name. His victory, as perceived by the average European sports fan, was like Britain winning the Superbowl. Winning again in 1989 proved to the skeptics that the first time around was no fluke and that America had truly become a world cycling power.

In 1986, Greg LeMond became the first American to win the Tour de France. *Presse Sports photo*

These high-visibility international successes by Americans have done a lot to fuel other aspects of the sport. Since 1986, all forms of cycling have increased dramatically. The U.S. domestic bicycle industry has now topped $2.5 billion in annual volume. According to Ed Schwinn, president of the Schwinn Bicycle Company, sales of bicycles for use by adults outpaced children's sales in 1987 for the first time in the postwar period. During the same year, fashionable cycling wear began to appear in noncycling surroundings.

These developments, as well as the proliferation of touring groups, mountain bike riding, BMX racing, and all other forms of the sport, have been at least partially attributed to America's well-publicized racing results at the world-class level. Moreover, several new trends have been established that will encourage the sport's growth as we approach the next century.

WHERE FROM HERE?

Overall, bicycling will continue to grow dramatically, both as a sport and a form of recreation, as well as in numbers of hard core participants and variety of disciplines. This should be assured in part by the growing movement toward "wellness" and also by increasing awareness of the urgency to preserve scarce energy resources and protect the environment. Projections indicate that more people will have an increasing amount of disposable income and leisure time.

Off-road riding and racing is expected to boom in the nineties. *Photo courtesy of Specialized Bicycle Components*

Many have seen the world's great cities, monuments, and theme parks and are tired of the mass, prepackaged vacation experience. This should assure the growing popularity of the vacation bicycle tour, which itself will segment into various specialties, ranging from gourmet fun rides to rugged back country trips, more on the order of Outward Bound (see Chapter 12).

Competitive cycling will also continue to segment into specialties, with road racing continuing to dominate, but with ATB (all-terrain biking or mountain biking) and track racing growing at faster rates due to increasing difficulty in closing off busy public thoroughfares, lower implementation costs, and gate receipts as an additional incentive.

Cycling will continue to increase in importance as a key sport for women, and it will continue to gain mass spectator appeal as an increasing number of Americans achieve success in the major international events. It is unlikely, however, that cycling will dominate to the extent of its first golden age, since there is more money in circulation and many more sports, recreational, and cultural alternatives than existed at that time.

On the technical side, composite and synthetic materials, such as graphite, carbon fiber, and Kevlar will eventually replace metals as the dominant materials in bike construction, and the practical science of biomechanical analysis will be applied to make bicycles increasingly efficient and rider friendly. Cycling futurists are already designing hubless, spokeless bikes, with wheels that will be held and glide virtually friction free in a superconducting magnetic field.

Cycling wear should continue to be at the forefront of actionwear fashion and will increasingly stress function as well as form, with continuing advancements in synthetic fibers contributing to lighter materials with less wind resistance and better heating and/or cooling efficiencies.

The roadways will also become more cyclist-friendly, in recognition of the need to separate cyclists from auto traffic and other competing forms of recreation, such as jogging and roller skating. For this reason (and the reality that there will be more cycling voters), more cities and states will establish dedicated and controlled bike paths and lanes, such as those that now exist in more progressive communities such as Minneapolis, Minnesota, and Palo Alto, California.

Finally, as a result of faster equipment, more fit and competitive cyclists, and increased congestion on the roads and bike paths, it will not be long before bike riders are screened by radar and issued speeding tickets; unless, of course, they have the latest miniaturized "fuzzbuster" mounted on their handlebars.

Getting Rolling

Whether the inspiration to get on a bicycle may have come from watching the Tour de France, wanting to get fit with minimum risk to the body, or recapturing lost youth, the desire to ride is there. There are plenty of people reaping great benefits from cycling who never pinned on a racing number.

Since the decision to ride a bicycle quickly translates into an investment in a fairly sophisticated piece of equipment, it is important to have a reasonably good idea of what kind of cycling you intend to do. While Saturday morning rides with the kids, occasional commutes to the office, frequent exercise, multiday bicycle tours, and weekend citizens' racing can all be accomplished on one type of bicycle (the basic touring bike), you should be mindful that today's sophisticated bicycle industry has created several variations in quality and design, within a number of different genres.

The illustrations in this chapter depict the basic categories and subcategories of bicycles along with their relative price ranges, characteristics, recommended uses, and brands. The buyer should know that within each category of bicycle the choices are many, and sometimes confusing. And within a given price range, bicycles of the same type from well-known brands (such as Schwinn Specialized and Trek) have comparable features. In fact, they may be virtually the same bike but with different cosmetics, since most of today's brand name bikes are assembled from components produced overseas by a small number of original equipment manufacturers (OEM's). Today's wholesale and retail bicycle business has become so competitive and price sensitive that it is very difficult for a dealer to get away with charging more than the going rate for a given model. Hungry manufacturers will encourage the bike dealer to sell their brand over others by providing room for a larger markup from wholesale. Accordingly, when the salesman tells you that a $500 "brand X" is vastly superior to a $500 "brand Y," he probably has a vested interest in doing so and the only real difference will be the amount he makes on the sale.

Generally speaking, however, the old adage, "you get what you pay for," does apply when it comes to buying a bike since, in today's competitive marketplace, there is a difference between a $500 bike and a $1,500 bike, and you will usually get a much better piece of equipment if you are willing to pay the price. It is certainly possible to get a good deal by buying through a high-volume dealer in a larger market, as is the case with respect to most consumer goods in today's age of the mass merchant. There is, however, a trade off. Even though you may pay a higher price for the same bike at a smaller specialty bike shop, it may be worth the extra cost in terms of the personal service and followup maintenance the specialist might provide, and if you are interested in pursuing the sport on a serious level, the specialty shop is usually the best link to local cycling clubs and events.

Also keep in mind that when it comes to bicycles, "less *is* more." A nineteen-pound bike can cost several times more than a thirty-pound bike, but with good reason. The higher expense reflects the relatively scarce materials and increased engineering that goes into a lighter machine. In a high-end bicycle (touring, racing, or ATB), the frame itself is made out of stronger tubing, and the other components, such as sprockets, chains, handlebars, and rims, can be made extremely light and durable by using precious alloys machined to precision tolerances.

While a beginner may not be able to appreciate the subtle differences between a $500 bike and a $1,500 bike, increased riding proficiency (and time in the saddle) will bring them out. The expensive bike will tend to be more responsive and have a noticeable lack of wobble or "sponginess" when cornering or going down hills. Shifting is quicker and more precise, and the lightness makes it considerably easier to ride up hills.

It is, however, probably best not to invest the extra money in a top-of-the-line bicycle when first getting started, since the differences cannot be fully appreciated until some serious miles have been logged, and it does not make sense to spend lots of money on a bike until you are sure you will make regular use of it. No matter what you're riding, the first few times up that steep driveway will have you huffing and puffing. If after a few weeks you do get hooked, you can always trade up. Seventy-five percent of all cyclists who ride seriously (three or more times per week) purchased a new, more expensive bike, within a year of starting to ride.

THE TOURING BICYCLE

The traditional touring bicycle is the one ridden by Dorothy's schoolmarm (a.k.a. "The Wicked Witch") in *The Wizard of Oz*. Outfitted with upright handlebars, hand brakes, chainguard, fenders, kickstand, and wooden basket, this sturdy three-speed (exemplified by the black-and-white Raleigh "English bike" that was so popular before the advent of the ten-speed) was great for running around town or getting over to the park for the Sunday picnic. The internal gearing of the Sturmey Archer three-speed hub, with trigger

TOURING BIKES

$ LOW RANGE ***Price:*** $90–$150

Characteristics:
- upright handlebars
- wide saddle
- 3–5 speeds
- kickstand, chain guard, fenders
- 45–60 pounds (without load)

Recommended for:
- short rides
- short commutes
- leisurely family riding
- in-town riding

Best brands:
- Schwinn, Raleigh

$ MID-RANGE ***Price:*** $150–$600

Characteristics:
- dropped handle bars
- 10–15 speeds
- kickstand (usually optional)
- 28–38 pounds (without load)

Recommended for:
- pleasure riding
- general touring
- moderate commutes

Best Brands:
- Giant, Raleigh, Schwinn, Specialized, Trek

$ HIGH RANGE ***Price:*** $600–$5,000

Characteristics:
- dropped handle bars
- 12–18 speeds
- brazed-on mountings
- 22–30 pounds (without load)

Recommended for:
- pleasure riding
- sophisticated touring
- long rides, extended touring

Best Brands:
- Cannondale, Schwinn, Specialized, Trek, plus numerous custom-built manufacturers

Drawing by George Retseck

shifter mounted on the handlebars, required low maintenance and provided enough variable gearing to help flatten moderately rolling terrain.

Although there are still many around and it remains a staple of transportation in many of the lesser-developed countries of the world, this utilitarian vehicle has largely been replaced by bicycles that offer much wider gear selection, lighter weight, and jazzier cosmetics.

When used effectively, the modern touring bicycle can flatten the steepest hills and carry the heaviest of loads. The more expensive the touring bicycle becomes, the more specialized are its features. At the highest level, custom touring bicycles are extremely light in weight and have frames with "brazed-on" fittings that allow attachment of pannier bags, luggage racks, extra water bottles, and other accessories directly to the frame.

THE ALL-TERRAIN OR MOUNTAIN BIKE

The most recent and exciting phenomenon to ignite the worldwide bicycle industry has been a relatively heavy, fat-tire hybrid known as the all-terrain bicycle (ATB).

Since the late seventies, when the first few hundred "mountain bikes" emerged out of Marin County, in northern California, sales have reached ten million and a new version of the sport of cycling has been born. (In 1989, over half of all bicycles sold in the United States were versions of the ATB.)

The focus is off road. For touring enthusiasts, it means cycling to places previously accessible only on foot. To racers it means everything from creeping up and plunging down ski slopes on a bicycle to racing from one mountain peak to another, fording every stream, and climbing or hopping over every rock and fallen log in between. The growing popularity and institutionalization of the ATB is exemplified by the recent purchase of NORBA, its first organized sanctioning body, by the United States Cycling Federation, the official governing body of amateur cycling organizations in the United States. Starting in 1990, mountain biking will be officially recognized on the international level by the U.C.I. (the world governing body). Although there are several disciplines in all-terrain bicycling (Downhill, Uphill, Dual Slalom, Observed Trials, and Cross Country), only the latter (a blend of up-and-down-hill riding over undulating terrain, much like cross-country skiing) is counted toward the official world championship title.

Competition is only the tip of the iceberg, and off-road riding is fast becoming a very popular pastime in most corners of the U.S. The ATB has also found favor with urban cyclists, whose war with

THE ALL-TERRAIN BIKE

Price: $200–$4,600

Characteristics:
- wide, knobby tires
- 15+ speeds (triple chainrings)
- upright handlebars, heavy-duty brakes

Recommended for:
- off-road riding/racing
- city riding

Best brands:
Broad model range: Giant, Bianchi, Cannondale, Diamond Black, Peugeot, Raleigh, Schwinn, Specialized, Trek

Drawing by George Retseck

sewer grates, broken glass, and potholes can best be fought with a bicycle that has been engineered to take such abuse.

All this has been made possible through the ingenious blending of different facets of preexisting bicycle technology. Fat tires, while creating drag on smooth roads, provide high traction, stability, and shock absorption on loose surfaces, such as grass, dirt, and gravel. Superwide gear ratios and standard eighteen-speeds allow climbs up the steepest of trails. Upright handlebars with beefed-up motorcycle-type handbrakes allow positive control of the bike. And the use of lightweight frame tubing and special alloy components from racing designs makes what might ordinarily be a very heavy and cumbersome bike into a much lighter and more manageable one.

If you are pondering what kind of bicycle to buy as a first purchase, consider an ATB. They are great for all-around riding and can go where standard touring and racing bikes cannot. They are also excellent for overweight people who are trying to get in shape. They are more comfortable than a racing bike and their sturdiness makes the rider more confident. If, however, you intend to ride some longer distances (e.g., over twenty miles) and over relatively good roads, you will find the ATB slower, less responsive, and harder to pedal, all due mainly to its fatter, softer tires.

THE RACING BICYCLE

As the all-terrain bike is built primarily for bushwhacking, the racing bicycle is built primarily for speed and distance. In comparing the performance of the two, think of the difference between driving a Jeep and a Porsche.

Of all bicycles, the racing machine is the lightest, the tightest, and the stiffest. It is designed for paved roads (super skinny tires are a disaster on soft surfaces) where the objective is to cover ground with the least possible resistance, either from surface friction or wind drag. The racing bike is also engineered for great stability—much needed when soaring down mountain switchbacks at fifty-five mph or in flat-out sprints in the middle of a charging pack. The true road-racing bicycle is further distinguished from its counterparts by tighter gear ratios, generally higher gears, special wheels, and tires called tubulars or "sew-ups." A more complete discussion of these important distinctions can be found in Chapter 3.

Within the racing-bike category, there are further design specialties. The track bicycle is used exclusively for racing in steeply banked velodromes. Track bikes are very stiff, to provide for extremely quick response and handling. They have one gear and no brakes whatsoever. One cannot coast or "freewheel" on a track bike, because the one rear sprocket is screwed directly onto the hub. Slowing down is accomplished by resisting the forward motion of the pedals (as on a child's tricycle) or by applying a gloved hand to the front wheel. Obviously, track racers do not expect to stop on a dime.

The most recent racing bike developments have grown out of the study of aerodynamics. Solid disk wheels, while creating some instability in crosswinds, reduce drag. So do shortened handlebars, internally fitted gear cables and brake cables, flat spokes, and specially shaped components (seat posts, handlebar stems, brakes, etc.). Added together, the most recent aerodynamic modifications have been shown to reduce drag substantially, and that can be critical to a racing cyclist in a time trial where the objective is to go as fast as possible—unaided by any kind of pacing—over a prescribed distance. For example, according to the Shimano corporation, a front-disk wheel eliminates 180 grams of drag, saving sixty-six seconds over a twenty-five-mile time trial, while a rear-disk wheel eliminates ninety grams and saves thirty-three seconds over the same distance. Put disks on both front and back and you can theoretically knock six minutes, thirty-five seconds off a hundred-mile time trial.

While the latest in aerodynamic modification is crucial to a top level racer, such considerations are of minimal importance to a recreational cyclist or casual racer. Losing ten pounds around your middle will produce a much higher initial performance return! Cost is also a factor to consider. While a decent racing bike may cost $1,500, the latest aerodynamic fittings could add another $1,000 to the basic sticker price.

Many more people own (road) racing bikes than race. The reason is simple: the racing bike offers the ultimate in road-riding perfor-

RACING BIKES

ROAD RACING
Price: $750–$3,500

Characteristics:
- 12, 14, or 16 speeds
- tubular tires
- 19–25 pounds

Recommended for:
- serious recreational riding
- racing

TRACK RACING
Price: $750+

Characteristics:
- one gear
- fixed wheel
- no brakes

Recommended for:
- velodrome use only

TIME TRIALING
Price: $2,000+

Characteristics:
- 12 speeds or less
- small front wheel
- disk wheel(s)

Recommended for:
- time trials only

Manufacturers with most complete model ranges (offering four choices or more): Bianchi, Cannondale, Giant, Peugeot, Raleigh, Schwinn, Specialized
Higher-volume custom and top-of-the-line builders:
USA: Klein, Sachs, Serotta, Spectrum, Terry (women's)
Imports: Atala, Basso, Bottecchia, de Rosa, Gios, Guerciotti, Giordana, Miele, Cinelli, Somec, Tommasini, Tommaso, Rossin, Pinarello, Colnago

Drawing by George Retseck

mance. If having the best is important and cycling is (or may soon become) reasonably serious for you—and you can afford it—why not spring for it?

KIDS AND BIKES

The basic children's bike is a simple one-speed, with a direct chain from the front sprocket or chainwheel to a single rear sprocket. It has a simple "coaster brake," operated by reversing the pedals. However, over the past two decades, kids' bikes have become more sophisticated and specialized.

The most popular "sub cult" of children's cycling has been BMX (bicycle motocross), named and patterned after motocross or "dirt bike" motorcycle racing. BMX bikes differ from ordinary bikes in that they have a relatively small frame, knobby tires, high-rise seat post and handle bars, and motorcycle-style wheels and seats. BMX has evolved into a serious competitive sport for kids well into their teens. In fact, there are now professional BMXers who make a decent living on the circuit. The competition is a rough and tumble scramble around a dirt track and over several, often man-made, obstacles. Because of the thrills and spills inherent in their sport, BMX riders wear more protective gear than their road-racing counterparts. Recent indications show a dramatic decline in BMX fever,

WHEN BUYING A BIKE

1. Know your requirements (casual touring, off-road, long-distance road riding/racing?) and buy accordingly.
2. Read the literature (most cycling magazines review products—see Appendix for recommended publications).
3. Buy from a reputable local bicycle store (see Appendix). Remember, what you save at a discount store, you may lose in service.
4. Make sure you get a satisfactory warranty.
5. Select the proper size and appropriate components, and adjust everything to fit. When in doubt, consult your dealer (see Chapters 3 and 4).
6. Price reflects quality: You get what you pay for.
7. Once you've made the investment, understand basic maintenance requirements and learn the principles and mechanics of gear shifting (both in Chapter 6).

perhaps because of defections at an earlier age to the now trendy sport of mountain biking or ATB, as well as an increased popularity in road racing, as the result of role models such as Andy Hampsten and Greg LeMond.

A related area of kids' cycling that experienced a swell in popularity in the mid-eighties but never really got going (probably for the same reasons as the leveling off of interest in BMX) is "Formula One." Formula One is to BMX as road racing is to motocross in motorcycling. Formula One bikes are similar to BMX bikes, but with smoother tires for hard surfaces, such as paved tracks and parking lots, and a more streamlined design, for the feel and look of a road bike.

A third discipline, which continues to show remarkable popularity, is that of freestyle biking, an art practiced by those of a more individualistic and free-spirited bent. Freestyle is a dramatic spectator event, requiring relatively little space to practice. It is in some ways similar to serious skateboard competition, with some stunts performed on sharply curved ramps and others over obstacles, such as junked autos, much in the same vein as the "Observed Trials" discipline of mountain biking. See Chapter 10 for more information on kids and bikes.

3 The Fit

Everyone has a piece of clothing—a certain suit, a pair of jeans, or perhaps an old pair of tennis shoes—in which he feels comfortable and that seems to have a positive effect on how he performs. That's how your bicycle should feel. You will never do your best on an ill-fitting bicycle.

Proper positioning of your body on the bicycle is the key to comfort and performance, particularly at the higher levels of cycling where a scientifically determined position can help you achieve your full potential and give you a competitive edge. When Greg LeMond first went to Europe, as a rookie on Cyril Guimard's Renault team, he was told by the renowned team director to raise his saddle an inch and a half. LeMond objected, most respectfully, noting that he had won many races, including the Junior World Championship, with his current position. Guimard suggested that his silver medal in the Junior World Pursuit Championship might have been a gold if his position had been slightly more efficient.

As LeMond and many others have discovered, finding the proper position is a constantly evolving process. Many racers admit to spending five years or more fine-tuning their position until they feel exactly right. In fact, none of the traditional formulas—be they scientific or borne from experience—will guarantee a perfect position every time. Inseam measurements and fixed formulas do not take into account factors such as the shape and width of the saddle and the pelvic bone structure of the rider. Getting the ideal fit requires both professional advice and a lot of experimentation.

Unfortunately, there are many people out there selling bicycles who either do not know or could not care less about how your bike should fit. One of the arguments for buying a bike through a respected specialty shop is that such establishments generally have someone on staff who is knowledgeable in this area. We will assume that you do not have access to such a person and will provide a short course that, if properly followed, should contribute to your enjoyment and performance.

The root of most cycling discomfort comes from improper fit or a bad position on the bike. Proper fit does not mean that you have to spend several thousand dollars on a custom-made bicycle. In fact, most manufacturers of quality bicycles have frame options that will suit all but the most unusually proportioned cyclists. One racer we

WHY YOUR SCHWINN DOESN'T FEEL LIKE IT USED TO

	Black Phantom *Top of the line in '59*	**World Sport** *Top seller in '89*
Weight	67 lbs.	27 lbs.
Frame	Steel, one size, 26″	Chromolly® main tubes, anatomical design, 5 sizes for men, 2 for women
Brakes	Coaster foot brakes	Hand brakes with extension levers
Seat	Coil spring leather saddle	Vinyl-padded, anatomical narrow racing seat
Hubs	Bolted	Quick release
Rims	Tubular chrome	Alloy
Gears	Single speed	Twelve speeds, index shifting
Tires	26″ × 2.125″ white wall	27″ × 1.25″ black wall
Handlebars	Long horn	Dropped, racing style
Pedals	Steel/rubber	Steel quill with toe-clip attachment
Price	$89	$260
Other	Built-in, battery-operated headlight, horn tank, and taillight; chain guard, kickstand, extra wide fenders	

know has a long torso in relation to the length of his legs and was never able to find an off-the-rack racing bike that fit just right. To adjust for this, the custom frames he has used over the years required a much longer top tube than is normally provided by manufacturers of stock bicycles. This is the exception and not the rule, particularly if you do not plan to compete at the elite level.

FRAME SIZE AND SADDLE POSITION

The most important element in determining proper position is selecting the proper frame size. In order to do this, one really needs to know the basics of frame geometry. It is a good idea to study and become familiar with the illustrations on pages 28 and 29, since any discussion of frames will use these terms.

The most critical dimension of the bicycle frame is the length of the seat tube. When someone refers to a "23-inch bike," they are referring to this dimension. This, more than any other measurement, will be the key in determining proper frame size. It's analogous to waist size in selecting a pair of trousers.

The next most important measurement is the length of the top tube. It is here where individuals with longer or shorter than normal torsos may have to go into custom-frame building in order to obtain the ultimate fit.

The remaining specifications, such as seat and head tube angles, rake of the front fork, length of the rear chain stays, bottom bracket height, and overall wheel base are really determined by a combination of personal preference and the use for which the bike is intended. Frame construction and the raw materials utilized (see below) also vary with end-use requirements and personal preference.

FRAME GEOMETRY

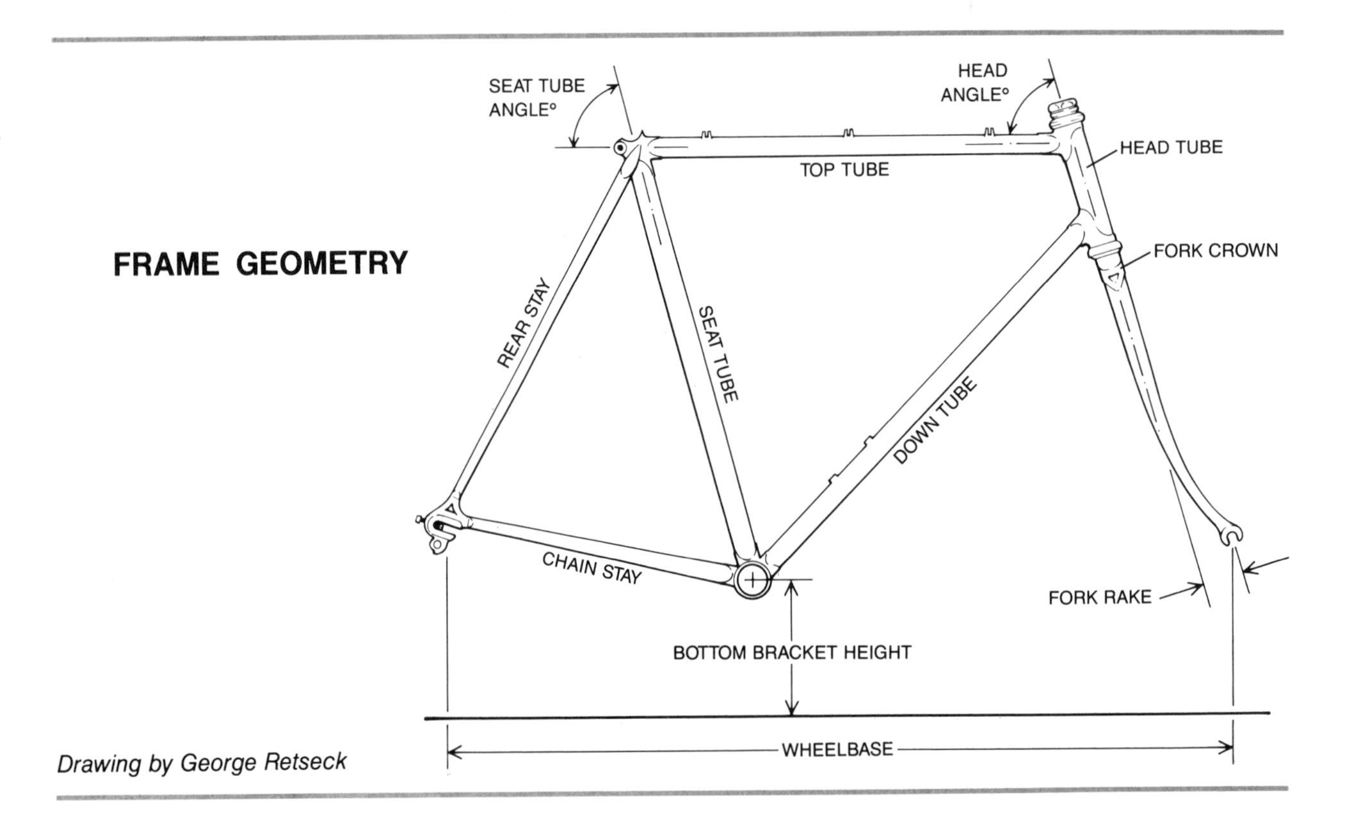

Drawing by George Retseck

SIZING COMPONENTS

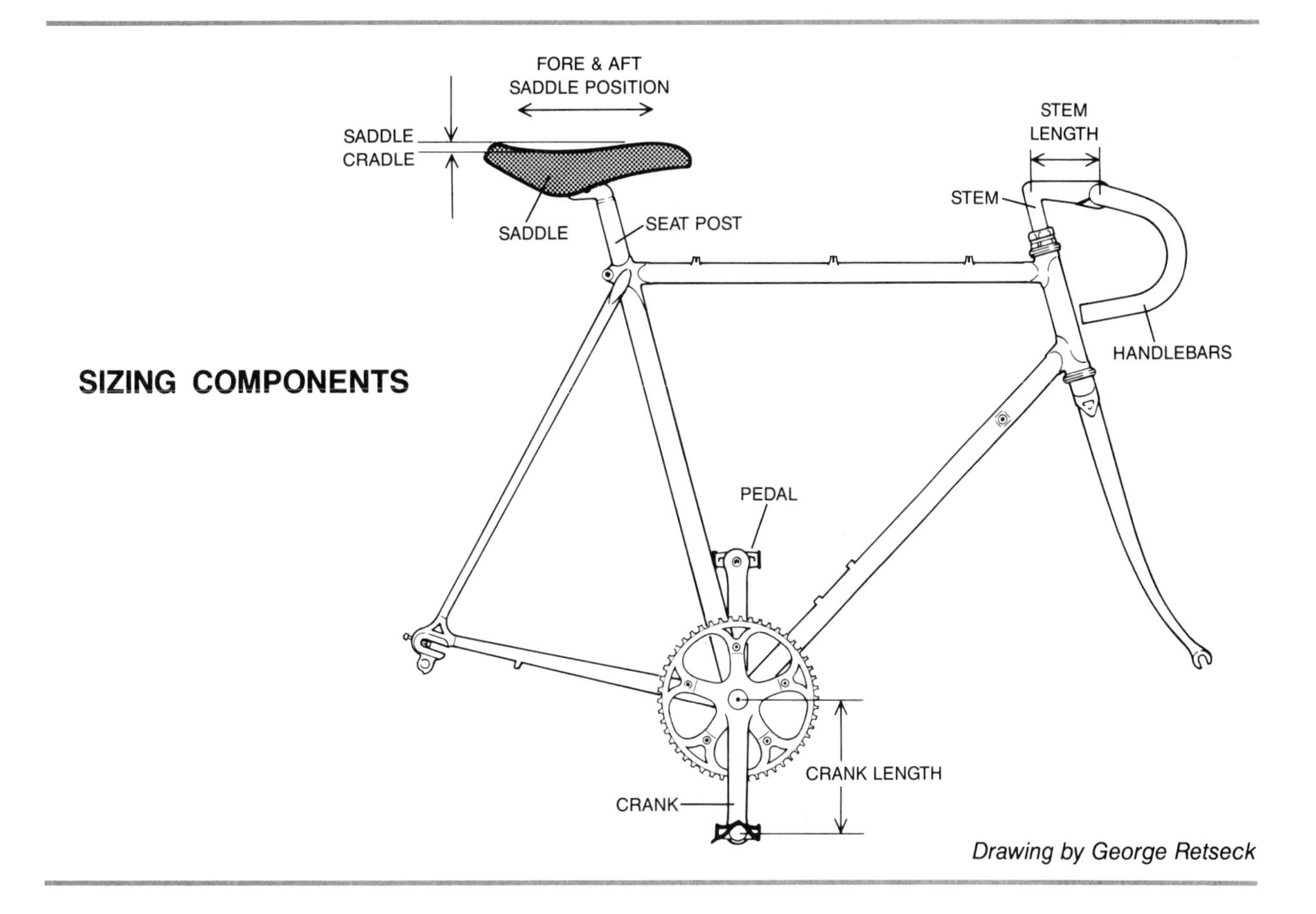

Drawing by George Retseck

For example, a bike used in short-distance, multilap criterium races calls for a higher bottom bracket, to allow more lean around the turns; a shorter wheel base, with shorter rear stays, in order to provide a tighter turning radius; and steeper (73–74 degree) head and seat tube angles, to provide a more pitched-forward "sprinter's" position. However, in a longer road race, where instant response is not so critical, a bike with a longer wheel base and more shallow (71–72 degree) head and seat tube angles will absorb more road shock and make for a more comfortable, less fatiguing ride.

Choosing these dimensions should be left to the experts. If you speak with a reputable and knowledgeable bike dealer or frame builder, all you have to do is describe how you intend to use the bike (e.g., for general recreational riding, short-distance road racing, long-distance touring or racing, etc.). The expert will translate that into the proper frame geometry and steer you to a manufacturer or frame builder that produces the style of bike you need. Chances are (particularly if you are not a serious competitor) that there will be a stock frame available that, with minor component adjustments, will reasonably meet your needs. Remember these points:

1. Virtually all adult bicycles have a standard, twenty-seven-inch wheel diameter. (Recently, however, some manufacturers have fitted a smaller, twenty-four- or twenty-six-inch front wheel to smaller-framed bicycles, to allow for better-proportioned frame dimensions and a better fit for small adults. This configuration has proven particularly well-suited to women.)

2. Most good bicycles come in several standard sizes. In inches, the readily available range is nineteen to twenty-five inches (fifty-two to sixty-two centimeters). This, of course, refers to the seat tube length, measured along the tube from the center of the bottom bracket to the midpoint of the top tube (called center-to-center measuring). Each manufacturer offers a number of different-sized options. Schwinn, for example, offers its popular, low-cost "Sprint" model in 17-, 19-, and 21-inch for women and 19-, 21-, 23-, and 25-inch for men.

3. The proper frame size for a mountain or all-terrain bike is three to four inches smaller than the normal road-riding frame.

To a certain extent, an appropriately sized stock bicycle can be "customized" to fit the rider by varying the length of the handlebar

FRAME MATERIALS

Steel Alloy:
Most widely used material in bicycle-frame tubing. Tubes are welded, generally into preformed joints or "lugs." This allows for an almost infinite range of size and geometry. Tubes for frames come in different gauges, which ultimately determines a frame's characteristic weight and rigidity.

Aluminum:
Characteristically lighter than steel alloy, but traditionalists have questioned its rigidity and durability over time. Thicker gauge, oversized aluminum tubes (as first used on Klein and Cannondale bicycles) can be made stiffer than steel. Butted (internal thickness is greater near tube ends) aluminum tubing is now being used and produces a lighter, more responsive frame than straight-gauge aluminum.

Composite:
Made from carbon or other nonmetallic fibers. Tubes are glued together, often joined under cast aluminum lugs to provide more surface area for glue bonding. The biggest problem has been in keeping frames together although they are one and one half pounds lighter than the average steel alloy frame. The French "Carbon 7" frame incorporates a layer of Kevlar and was developed from material used in bazookas and missile fuselages.

Titanium and Titanium Alloy:
With 60 percent less weight and equal to or greater in strength than steel alloy, industry experts are predicting this material could again be the wave of the future (Teledyne and Speedwell introduced titanium frames in the early 1970s). Prohibitive cost and difficulty of repair are the major drawbacks.

Kirk Precision:
Pressure die-cast magnesium alloy formed by a steel frame mold. Magnesium is the lightest structural metal and is quite abundant. The tubeless, one-piece frame design makes this frame relatively inexpensive, but very stiff.

stem and raising or lowering the seat post. However, there are limits to how much these can be altered before the general performance of the bicycle begins to suffer. The tendency for Americans is to select a frame that is much larger than necessary and to lower the saddle to make the bike "fit." This results in a frame larger and more cumbersome than necessary. The rider is out of proportion to the bike and optimum handling characteristics cannot be achieved. It's similar to choosing skis that are too long or a tennis racket with too large a grip.

Experienced racers will always choose the smallest frame possible, in order to reduce weight and provide maximum responsiveness in racing situations. There is a limit to how small you can go before you again sacrifice a proper body-to-bike proportion.

The purpose of the illustration on page 32 is to present five-time Tour de France winner Benard Hinault's theory on how to determine the optimum frame size and saddle height. Hinault has had the benefit of applying comprehensive testing results from the Renault company's physiology and biomechanics laboratory. These in-depth studies have determined the most efficient relationship between leg length and pedal stroke, in order to produce the most efficient biomechanical effort.

As a practical matter, the formula will get a rider reasonably close to his optimum position, but Hinault cautions that some slight variation is inevitable. The important thing is to use the formula as a fairly precise guideline to establish a starting point for the other adjustments referred to below, and with the realization that it can be fine-tuned later as you become more familiar with your bicycle.

At this point, it may be helpful to refer back to the illustrations on pages 28–29 to become familiar with the variable "sizing components" that must be considered in further determining the proper riding position.

Once saddle height is determined, several other adjustments need to be made in order to zero in on the optimum sitting position. The most critical of these is the fore and aft position of the saddle on the seat post.

Before determining where to position the saddle on the seat post (by sliding it back and forth), another basic step must be taken: setting the proper foot position on the pedal. The rule-of-thumb here is to make sure, no matter what kind of cycling shoes you may choose to wear, that the *ball* of your foot is positioned directly over the center of the pedal axle. In Chapter 4 we will discuss the different types of shoes and the rationale for their design. For the purpose of this discussion, just make sure your feet are neither toed-in nor toed-out when placed on the pedals and in the toe clips. You are now ready to adjust the saddle position.

BERNARD HINAULT'S THEORY FOR DETERMINING OPTIMUM FRAME SIZE AND SADDLE HEIGHT*

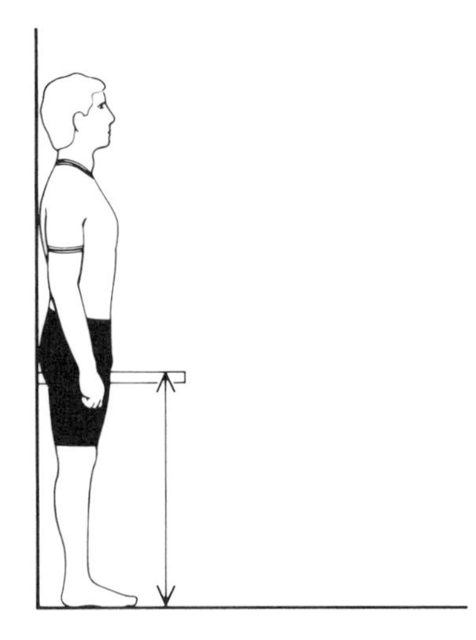

1. Measure crotch to floor in centimeters to get inseam "I." Measurement should be taken in bike shorts without shoes and with feet slightly spread. With back to wall, straddle a straightedge that is placed against the wall and extended outward parallel to the floor. Make sure the top side of the straightedge is placed firmly against the crotch.
2. Multiply "I" by .65 to get *Frame Size* (distance along seat tube from center of bottom bracket to center of top tube).
3. Multiply "I" by .885 to get *Saddle Height* (distance from center of bottom bracket to top of the saddle at midpoint of the saddle "cradle"). Note that saddle height is also affected by the thickness of the shoe sole and the length of the cranks. [Hinault's formula assumes a shoe sole width of 12 mm and a crank length of 170 mm. If, for example, your shoe sole width is 22 mm you need to raise your saddle 10 mm to compensate. Or, if your cranks are 175mm, your saddle should be lowered by 5 mm.]

* As presented in Hinault's book, *Road Racing Technology and Training* (*VeloNews*)

With your shoes and a pair of shorts on and a wall to lean against, sit on your bicycle and put your feet on the pedals, in the proper position, and rotate the pedals backward until the cranks are parallel to the ground (in other words, in the nine and three o'clock positions).

While sitting firmly on the saddle in this position, have a friend drop a plumb line (a string with a small weight, such as metal washer or nut on the end will suffice) from just behind the "hollow" of your kneecap through the pedal. Your saddle position will be within the recommended norms if the plumb line bisects the center of the pedal axle or falls somewhere within two centimeters behind.

Riders who specialize in sprinting or in short-distance criteriums will sit one to two centimeters farther forward, while road riders and long-distance specialists will sit toward the rear limit of this position. Experimentation is the key to determining optimum saddle position.

With pedals at the three- and nine-o'clock positions, a plumb line from the kneecap should fall between the center of the pedal axle and 2 cm behind.

REACH

The next most critical element in determining proper position on your bike is the extension of your body from the saddle to the handlebars. This is not easy to determine, since everyone is built differently. For the racer, the objective is to be as aerodynamic as possible without sacrificing too much comfort or creating undue strain on the shoulders or arms from leaning too far over. In the following photos of top professional riders, Fons de Wolf, Sean Kelly, and Eddy Merckx, you can see that they all appear to be well distributed over their bicycles, and even though they bend differently from the waist, or in the case of Sean Kelly, seemingly from the middle of the back, they each adopt a crouching position that is aerodynamic. (In downhill ski racing, such an aerodynamic position is referred to as "the egg position.")

Note also, that the bend of the elbow varies from rider to rider. De Wolf and Kelly appear to have arms bent at almost right angles, while Merckx' arms are reaching for the handlebars.

No matter what the body type, the relationship between torso and leg length, or the way one's back bends, there are two tried-and-true methods to help determine the proper reach. These are depicted in the illustration on page 35.

The first method is to get on the bicycle and assume the crouching position with hands on the handlebars, positioned directly be-

Presse Sports photo

Fons de Wolf (below), Sean Kelly (below right), and Eddy Merckx (right) show different riding styles at speed. Note how their backs and elbows bend differently to achieve an aerodynamic "tuck."

VeloNews photo

VeloNews photo

low the brake levers, or, as the British say, "in the hooks." In this position, with your neck and head raised enough to look forward, glance down at the front hub. (Please try this only in an empty parking lot.) If the top of the handlebars block or partially block a direct view of the hub, you should have a reasonably well-distributed position.

A second, perhaps safer, method involves standing next to the bike with the right elbow against the front tip or "nose" of your saddle. Extend the forearm and fingers forward toward the han-

In a well-distributed position, sight line to the front hub is bisected by the end of the handlebar stem. *Presse Sports photo*

With elbow butted against the tip of the saddle, extend the forearm and hand toward the handlebars. The tip of the middle finger should be roughly over the midpoint of the stem.

dlebars. If the tip of your middle finger rests near the middle of the handlebar stem, you will have at least one thing in common with the majority of the world's top riders.

Here's a tip: Most Americans ride in a more collected or bunched-up position than they should, largely because manufacturers tend to provide standard bicycles with shorter stems than are properly proportionate to the frame size. If your frame size is right but the reach is not within comfortable bounds, it is time to switch handlebar stems. Try longer or shorter ones, until that flat, aerodynamic position is achieved.

For touring enthusiasts, the rule-of-thumb is to create a forty-five degree angle between your back and the top tube on the frame. This provides a more comfortable upright position for slower riding, and it is certainly more conducive to taking in the scenery. This position would, for most people, translate into a larger frame (and shorter reach) than would be preferred by a racer.

There are evolving schools of thought on the proper size of a mountain bike or ATB. One view is that when you are standing with both feet on the ground and with your legs straddling the top tube, there should be two to three inches between the crotch of your pants and the top tube. A sensible and easy-to-accept view is expressed by Charles Coombs in his book *All-Terrain Bicycling,* in which he suggests that the same tests be applied as with respect to the ordinary road bike. Riding posture on the ATB really depends on what you are trying to accomplish. The ordinary riding position is similar to that on a regular touring bike (forty-five degree angle between torso and top tube), although a more aerodynamic position is desirable in the downhills and the mountain biker is often standing or "out of the saddle" in steep climbs and while scaling obstacles in the observed trials.

STEM HEIGHT

Virtually every properly positioned cyclist has the top of the handlebar stem positioned lower than the top of the saddle. This, again, is to create the aerodynamic position favored by the racer. Although the way one's back bends will have a lot to do in determining the relationship between the height of the stem and the height of the saddle, a general guideline is that the top of the saddle should be positioned two to three inches (five to eight centimeters) higher

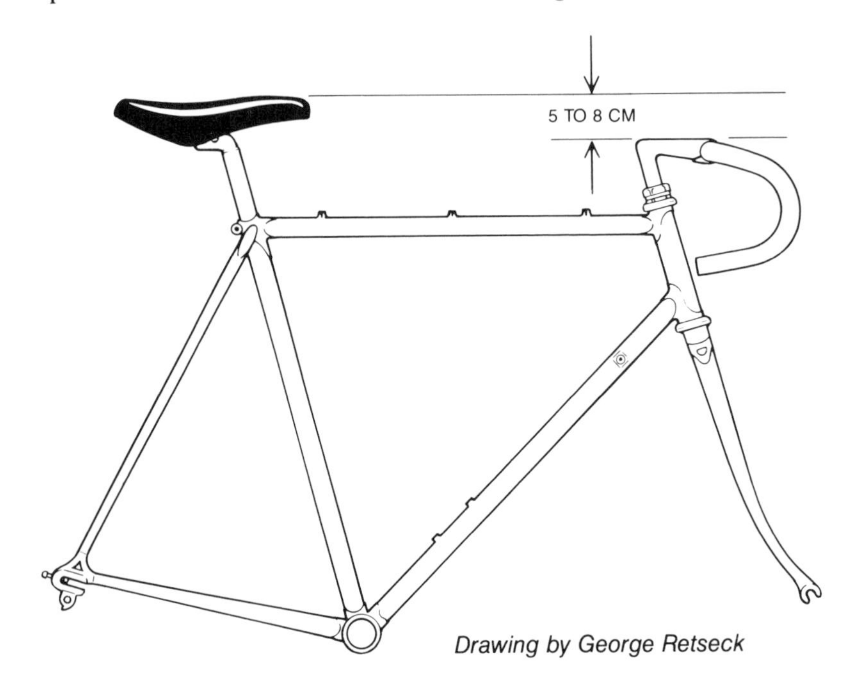

The height of handlebars should be five to eight cm lower than the saddle top.

Drawing by George Retseck

than the top of the handlebar stem (see illustration). This "pitched forward" position also allows more even distribution of body weight between hips and shoulders, whereas sitting too upright will place too much weight on the hips, leading to saddle soreness and excessive chafing. Leaning too far forward will strain the arms, neck, and shoulders. The tourist, mountain biker, or casual cyclist may want to sit more upright, and would consequently have the top of the stem just slightly lower, or even parallel with the top of the saddle. The risk of raising the stem too high is that it may break off if not enough of it is secured inside the frame.

HANDLEBARS

There are two basic types of handlebars in common use: upright and dropped. Variations of upright handlebars are used primarily on traditional three-speed bicycles, ATB or mountain bikes, and BMX bikes. The common characteristic of upright handlebars—no matter what the shape, height, or width—is that they are designed for one riding position only: hands gripped at the ends of the bars.

By contrast, dropped handlebars were designed to provide different hand-position options, on the theory that comfort, control, and aerodynamics can be significantly affected by shifting the position of the hands from place to place while riding.

For example, the tops of the bars are generally used during

Dropped handlebars allow the cyclist to change positions during a ride. *Goltzer photo*

relaxed riding or during climbing, when a more upright and less compact "lung-opening" position is desirable. Hands positioned on the brake levers (a most favored riding position) allows fingertip access to the brakes and provides for a modified aerodynamic positioning over the bike.

The most control over the bike is achieved when the hands are placed "in the hooks" or just below the brake levers. This position provides the most direct and positive access to the brakes, as well as good aerodynamic position. Negotiating tight corners, plunging downhill, and sprinting to the finish line are always done "in the hooks."

Dropped handlebars come in a variety of shapes and widths (see page 39.) The most commonly used road-racing handlebars have a straight or "square" top to allow for a comfortable, upright position and a modest drop to the hooks. A deeper-dropped handlebar may be preferred by a sprinter who needs to get as low as possible, while a lesser drop is generally preferred by the road racer. In any event, the bottom portion of the handlebar should be positioned so that it is parallel to the frame's top tube or tilted just slightly up. Too much tilt in the handlebars makes it difficult for the hands to be held firmly in the hooks, the most stable position for controlling the bicycle.

The most recent innovation in handlebars is the aerodynamic or extended handlebar that was first used by triathletes. These specially designed bars (or bolt-on extenders to conventional bars) extend the rider's arms farther forward than allowed by conventional bars. Since they draw the hands closer together and farther out from the body, the rider is put in a more aerodynamic "tear drop" shape. The resulting position is actually more comfortable than it looks and provides somewhat of a rest for the rider during those long, monotonous stretches experienced by triathletes and other endurance riders. The drawback, of course, is that the rider will not have the same control over the bike while climbing, cornering, or descending. Consequently, this type of bar is recommended only for individual endurance rides or time trials, where quick maneuvering is not generally required.

Handlebar width is also a very important dimension. This became painfully clear to Dave Chauner when he was racing in Holland some twenty years ago, as a relative newcomer to the sport. "I was riding my American-purchased Cinelli bicycle equipped with thirty-eight-centimeter, dropped bars (the distance measured at the tips of the bars from center to center) and was experiencing an extremely difficult time breathing, in the Dutch-style, super-fast criterium races." Chauner felt that somehow his chronic shortness of breath during these faster-paced events was not entirely due to a lack of ability or improper training.

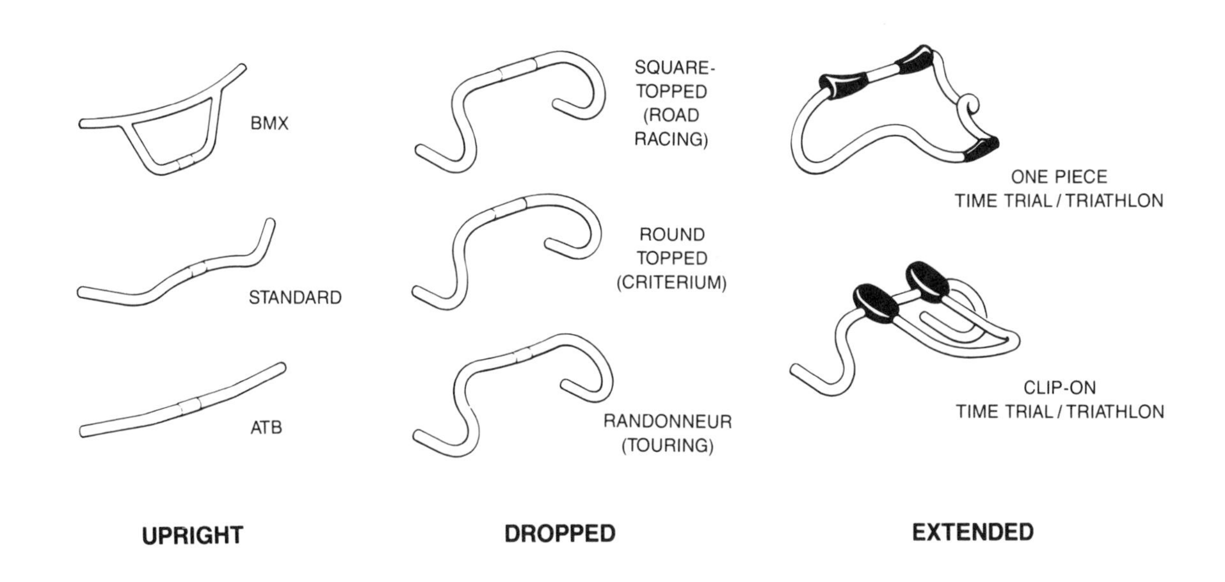

Drawing by George Retseck

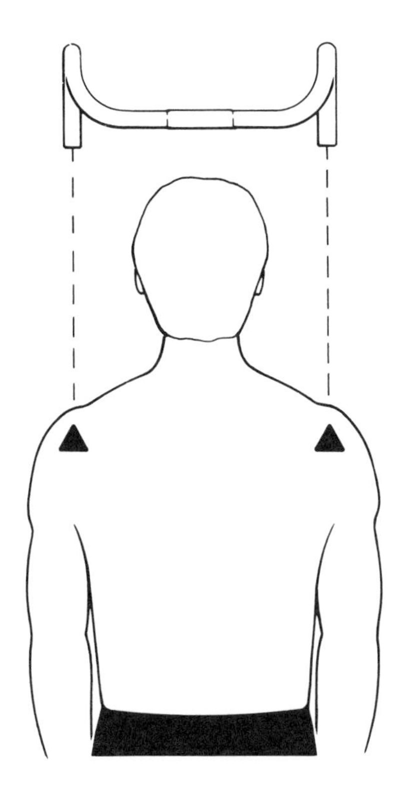

Handlebar width should be at least as wide as the shoulders.

"I went into the local bike shop, and asked the proprietor if something about my bicycle could be contributing to this problem. He pointed to my handlebars and began laughing. To overcome our language barrier, he resorted to sign language, pushing his hands together, and panting like a dog. He then reached in his cabinet and pulled out a pair of handlebars that were almost two inches wider than mine. Even though I had been racing for almost five years at the time, I had not known that handlebars came in varying widths. Through sign language, he showed me that the handlebars should be at least the width of my shoulders. We fitted the new pair to my bike and it was a revelation. It was hard to believe that such a small change made it so much easier to breathe and that the tight, constricted feeling I had frequently experienced, and the occasional sore shoulders, were due to the narrow bars that had been on my bike as original equipment."

It is important, therefore, to know that handlebars do come in different widths, particularly if one is broad-shouldered or serious about racing. The key is to select handlebars that approximate the width of your shoulders. As indicated in the illustration below, that width is determined by measuring across your shoulders from the outside edge of one shoulder blade to the other (measure from the bones that stick out beyond your collar bone—called the protruding rotators). The optimum handlebar width is within a centimeter of this measurement.

In addition to opening up the chest for better breathing, wider

THE FIT KING

In 1979, cyclist Bill Farrell started a training camp for budding competitors near his home in Danbury, New Hampshire. In keeping with the prestigious prep schools that dotted the region, he called it the New England Cycling Academy, and established a curriculum that took a scientific approach to the teaching of cycling fundamentals.

His first "students" were a ragtag mixture of novice cyclists, most of whom had little knowledge of technique, but a great desire to win races.

"I was amazed at how many people showed up with expensive but poorly fitted equipment," says Farrell. "It was purchased from shops where the dealers and staff had the best intentions but an insufficient amount of technical knowledge about frame sizing and component selection. Furthermore, most shops had no standard procedure to properly fit a bicycle to an individual."

Farrell's mission became the standardization of bicycle fitting to help bicycle shop owners and individual cyclists. The goals were to lessen the likelihood of injury from improper fit and to maximize a cyclist's biomechanical efficiency.

A decade later Farrell has turned his mission into a million-dollar venture. He has painstakingly developed the Rotational Adjustment Device, the Fit Kit, and the NECA Frame Alignment system, fitting tools now used by over one thousand bike shops in the U.S., Canada, Europe, Africa, and South America and by the United States Cycling Federation in their Olympic development programs. The New England Cycling Academy has expanded from weekly training camps to a series of technical and management cycling programs covering everything from bike shop organization to effective merchandising.

Above all, Farrell's Fit Kit is the first system to thoroughly analyze the dynamics of the body/bicycle relationship and incorporate them into a quick and accurate method of helping a cyclist find his or her proper position on the bicycle.

Farrell has compiled 4,100 profiles of recreational and elite cyclists, interviewed dealers, coaches, master frame builders, and physiologists to come up with a system to scientifically determine fit. It is the best.

For further information on dealers who use the Fit Kit, write or call:

New England Cycling Academy
P.O. Box 83
Lebanon, NH 03766
603-298-7784

bars are conducive to keeping the elbows in, which, again, contributes to that important aerodynamic position. Handlebars come in sizes from thirty-eight to forty-four centimeters. It is instructive, however, to note that most of the pros, regardless of their shoulder width, tend to choose models on the wide side.

SUMMARY

"Fit" on the bicycle is crucial to performance and enjoyment of the sport. This can be accomplished by taking advantage of the research that has been done on the subject, and then applying personal preferences through experimentation and advice from those who have been there before. If, however, the recording of body measurements and the application of the mathematical formulas illustrated above seem more trouble than it's worth, find a local bicycle dealer who uses "The Fit Kit," a reliable sizing and positioning system that puts the calculations in the hands of the dealer who can then answer questions during the fitting process.

The "optimum" cycling position is one that best accommodates three goals: comfort, energy efficiency, and an aerodynamic position. To which of these objectives you give priority depends on the kind of cycling you intend to do. For example, you might sacrifice the comfort quotient (as did Greg LeMond in his dramatic come-from-behind victory in the 1989 Tour de France) for a lower, more aerodynamic position in a time trial, while you would likely want to trade aerodynamics for a more comfortable upright position, during a long tour through the countryside.

No matter which method is used, determination of your proper position on your bike is analogous to the selection of skis and the mounting of ski bindings. If skis are too long or short or if the bindings are mounted in the wrong place, the skier will be fighting an unnecessary battle and find it more difficult to ski properly. The same is true of the proper cycling position. The reward for getting it right is well worth the effort.

SETTING THE PROPER POSITION

Must Haves:

- Bicycle shoes
- Bicycle shorts
- Tape measure
- Plumb line
- Adjustment tools for seat post and stem

Sequence:

1. Set saddle height
2. Set saddle fore and aft
3. Set reach and stem height
4. Level handlebars
5. Position brake levers on bars (top of levers parallel to ground)

4 Hardware

Despite the 1,200 or so essential parts that make up a multispeed, adult bicycle, it is still a relatively simple machine. There are no turn signals, windshield wipers, electric windows, ignition wires, or sun roof to worry about. It is an efficient mechanical device that derives its power solely from the driver (and, of course, gravity) and is intended to carry its passenger wherever and whenever they want to travel, with minimal resistance, maximum efficiency, and reasonable comfort. Keeping that in mind, and for the moment forgetting optional equipment such as rearview mirrors, foam rubber seat cushions, kickstands, and other "bells and whistles," a bicycle consists of three basic elements:

1. *The Frame* (including fork): The "chassis" of the machine and an element that determines its ultimate use (as discussed in Chapter 2).
2. *Wheels and Tires*: Don't confuse the two. A flat wheel is a lot different than a flat tire.
3. *Components*: All the nuts, bolts, sprockets, chains, and other key equipment that put the frame, wheels, and tires together and provide the mechanical advantage.

WHEELS AND TIRES

These two essential elements make an important team. The wheel consists of hub, spokes, and rim. The tire attaches to the rim and consists of two parts, the tube and the outer tire or "casing."

Wheels are defined by the type of rim. "Clinchers" and "Tubulars" are the two basic types of readily available wheel and tire combinations. A "clincher" wheel uses a clincher-style rim to be fitted with a clincher tire, and a "tubular" wheel uses a tubular-style rim to be fitted with a tubular tire (see illustration).

TIRES AND TUBES

Clinchers are by far the most widely used type, representing about 90 percent of all wheels, tires, and rims sold. Tubulars have traditionally been the exclusive choice of road and track racers, where ultimate performance is more important than price or durability.

The term "clincher" refers to a tire that clinches the rim. This is done by means of a continuous circular bead, embedded within the inside edges of the tire, that fits into a corresponding groove on the

CLINCHERS AND TUBULARS

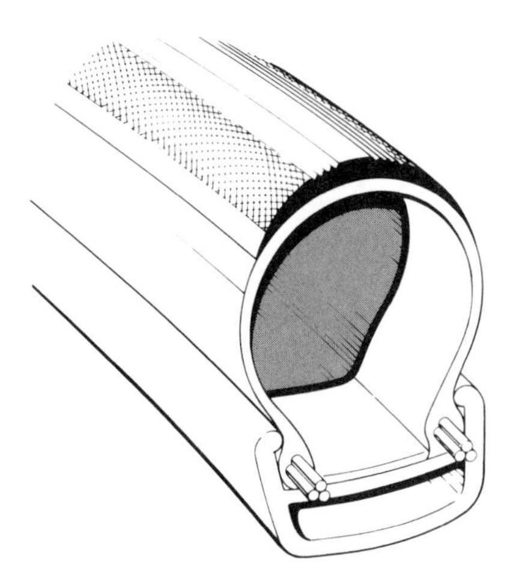

CLINCHER

Use: on 90 percent of all bikes

Characteristics:
- inner tube separate from beaded tire. "Seats" on rim with air pressure

Size Range:
- 16″ to adult (26″ & 27″), with range of widths from $^{3}/_{4}$″ to 2.2″

Weight range:
7 ounces and up (tire and tube combination). Best materials—*tires:* nylon, cotton, nylon/Kevlar; *tubes:* butyl, latex, polyurethane

Tire-tread options:
slick to knobby

Cost range:
$15–$40
(tire and tube combination)

Biggest selling points:
- high durability
- reasonable cost
- holds air well

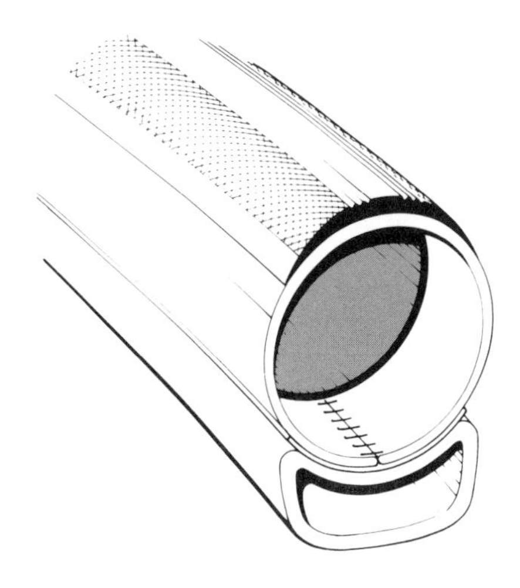

TUBULAR

Use: Road or track racing only

Characteristics:
- one-piece construction, inner tube enclosed in sewn-together casing. Glued to rim

Size Range:
- standard 27″ (roughly 70 cm). Smaller sizes for specialty uses available (smaller front wheel, etc.)

Weight range:
4 ounces to 16 ounces per tubular. Best materials—*casing:* cotton, polyamide, Kevlar, silk; *tubes:* butyl, latex, polyurethane

Tire-tread options:
slick to knobby (cyclo cross)

Cost range:
$20–$55 per tire
(record track tires more)

Biggest selling points:
- most responsive tires available
- used almost exclusively by racers
- easy to carry spares

inside of the clincher rim. When the separate inner tube is inflated, the tire bead "seats" in the rim groove to form an airtight seal. Most will recognize the clincher tire/rim combination: an inner tube that comes folded up in a box and a separate tire that holds its round shape because of the inner bead. This is the same kind of tire used on automobiles before the advent of the self-sealing "tubeless tire." The tire is removed from the rim using small tire irons that help stretch the tire bead over the rim without puncturing the inner tube. Note: Substituting a screwdriver for the tire iron is like a surgeon performing an appendectomy with a kitchen knife instead of a scalpel! Don't do it unless you want to butcher the inner tube. Before you mount a new tube and tire, you must protect the tube against the rough surface of the spoke ends, or "nipples," on the inside of the rim, by installing a protective "rim strip" (a thin, tape-like band). Follow the steps shown opposite and remember this key point: if you are doing it right, you can pry the last few inches of tire bead over the rim with just your thumbs.

Clinchers come in every standard wheel size from children's sixteen inch to adult twenty-six inch (mountain bikes) and twenty-seven inch (road bikes). Widths of rims, tires, and tubes vary from about three-fourths of an inch on the narrow end, for road racing, to about 2.2 inches on the wide end, for mountain bikes or ATBs. Rim, tire, and tube compatibility is crucial, and when selecting these items it is important to match manufacturers, or at least match sizes as labeled on the product's packaging.

Tire size is dictated largely by rim size, which in turn is dictated largely by the kind of bicycle and its intended use. For road riding only, a narrower tire is better, because it creates the least rolling resistance. (The most widely used touring tire, for example, will measure twenty-seven inches by one and one-fourth inches.) Off-road riding over loose gravel and dirt requires a wider tire with a knobby tread for better traction, stability, and durability. (Most widely used off-road tires measure twenty-six inches by one and one-half inches to twenty-six inches by two and one-eighth inches.) Your specialty bicycle dealer is probably the best one to advise you on proper size selection, but you should be aware of some of the basic principles of wheel and tire dynamics (see Chapter 6).

In recent years, lighter weight, lower profile, high-performance clinchers have made tentative inroads into road racing, but it is unlikely that serious racers will soon give up their tubulars. Here's why: The tubular combines the tube and tire in one unit. The inner tube is enclosed in an outer casing that is sewn together with special thread and then glued to the rim. Hence the name "sew-ups." Because of this one-piece construction, the tubular can be made much lighter, and it can be inflated to much higher pressures than the conventional clincher. This translates into reduced air resistance

TO REMOVE CLINCHER TIRE AND TUBE

A. Using one tire iron, pry tire bead away from rim edge. Note: this must be done on the opposite side of the wheel from the valve.

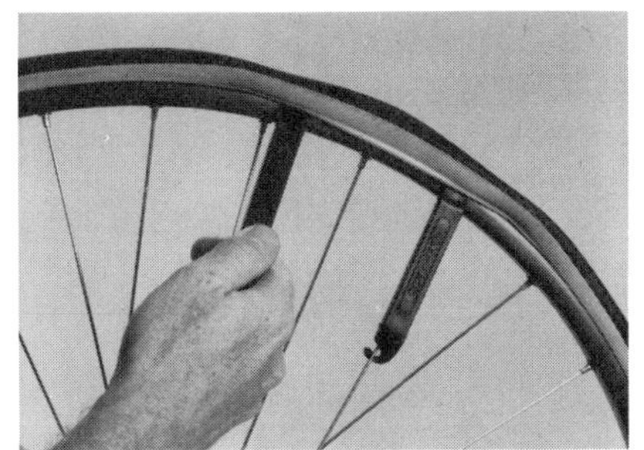

B. Hook handle of the first tire iron onto a spoke. Use second tire iron to continue prying bead away from rim.

C. If necessary, repeat the process with a third tire iron until bead is completely disengaged. Remove tire and tube from rim.

TO MOUNT CLINCHER TIRE AND TUBE

A. Make sure rim strip is affixed to rim and matched to valve opening.

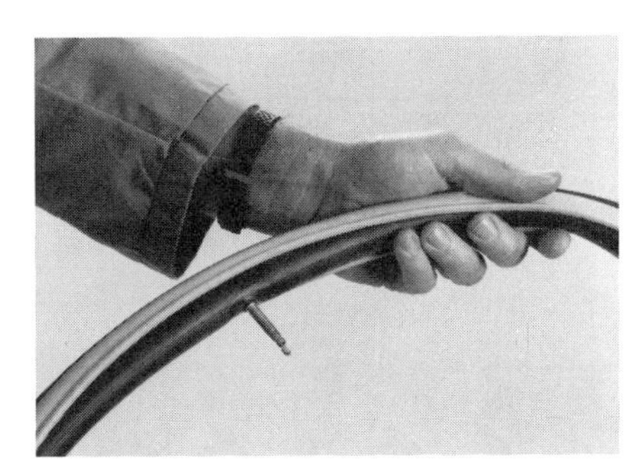

B. Slightly inflate tube and insert into tire

C. Starting at the valve stem, fit one side of beaded tire to rim all the way around.

D. To fit remaining side of tire, deflate the tube completely and push up into tire as far as possible. Working away from the valve in both directions, stretch bead over the tire.

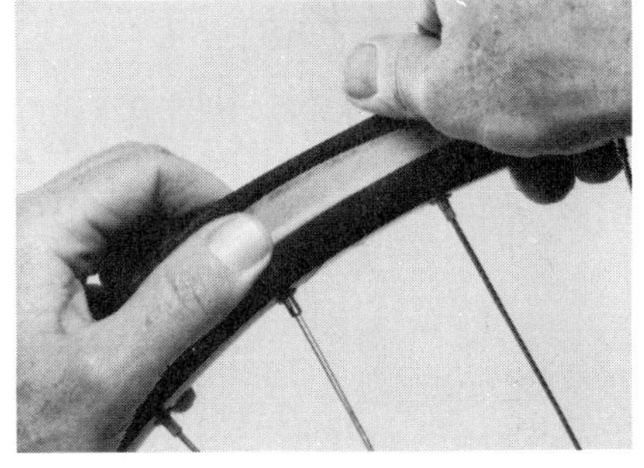

E. At the point opposite the valve, use thumbs to work the remaining few inches of bead over the rim.

Tip: If tire is too tight, apply a small amount of liquid soap to the rim to help the bead slip over.

A. Starting at the valve opening, draw a smooth bead of tire glue around the rim.

B. Using the index finger, smooth out the bead of glue. Note: using a plastic bag on the finger will make for a neater job. Allow glue to set up before mounting the tire (follow manufacturer's instructions for length of set-up time and whether or not both tire and rim should be coated with glue).

TIPS FOR MOUNTING THE TUBULAR TIRE

and surface drag—two critical obstacles for the racer (see Chapter 6).

At its extreme, a tubular tire used for the 1,000-meter time trial, an Olympic velodrome event, will weigh a mere four ounces, be inflated to 200 PSI, cost nearly $200 dollars, and be used, at most, twice—or a distance of just over one mile! The casing of these most esoteric of tires is traditionally made of silk, with a thin piece of white latex glued to the outside as "tread." The sewn-in inner tube is also of latex, similar in look and feel to that used for surgical gloves. Tubular casings come in silk, cotton, and new materials, such as polyamide and Kevlar. The new synthetic materials are generally more practical for training and everyday riding because of their lower cost, higher durability, and ability to withstand higher pressure. Silk tires have less rolling resistance than cotton tires, because the same weight tire can be obtained with a narrower profile. For this reason (and because silk deteriorates faster when wet), silk tires should not be used in the rain.

The tubular tire used to "go for the gold," on the smoothest of

C. With tire slightly inflated (just enough to give it a round shape), insert the valve into the valve opening, making sure the underside of the tire contacts the glued rim evenly.

D. With rim edge resting on a clean floor surface, use palms of both hands to stretch the tire around the rim, moving away from the valve. Make sure underside of tire is contacting the rim evenly as you go.

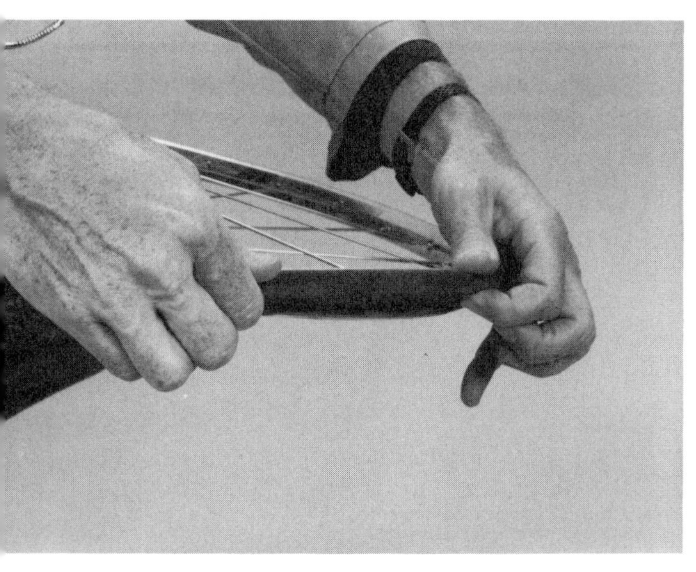

E. As you get near the end, use your fingers to lift the last few inches of the tire onto the rim. Inflate the tire immediately to near full pressure.

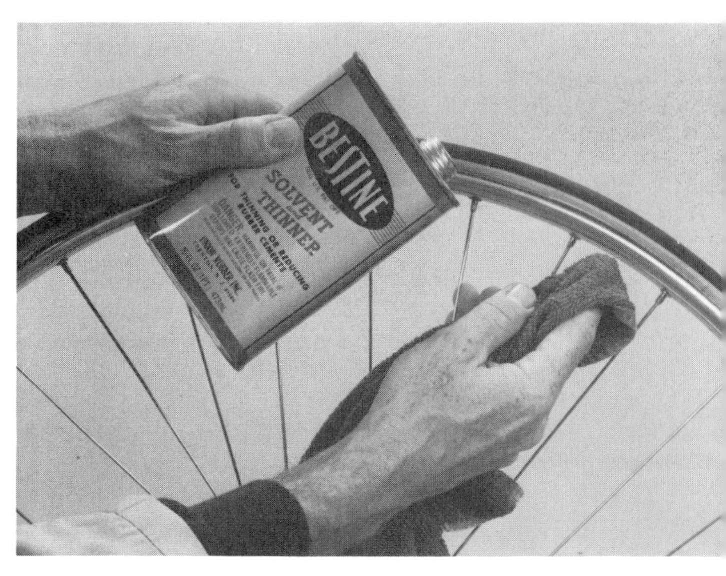

F. Soak a clean rag in glue solvent and wipe excess glue from rim and tire. Note: For most glues, Bestine is recommended (available in art supply stores). Other products can be obtained in bicycle shops.

Seth Goltzer Photos

velodrome surfaces, is a distant cousin to the more practical family of tubulars used for road racing. With dozens of weight and tread-pattern options, there is a tubular tire for every weather and road condition. The most widely available brands of quality tubulars are Clement, Continental, Vittoria, and Wolber, each with a complete range of tread patterns and weights.

The most practical weight range for tubular tires is 250 grams to 350 grams (eight and one-half to twelve and one-half ounces,) with the heavier ones used more for training than racing. The price varies from about sixteen to forty-five dollars per tire, with no mileage guarantees!

Tubulars over clinchers? If you want the ultimate in performance, if money is no object, and if you do not mind pumping up your tires nearly every time you go out for a spin, the answer is yes. But with today's lower-profile, high-pressure clinchers as an alternative, it becomes harder to recommend the more costly, more delicate tubulars for anything but top-level racing.

If you do use tubulars, it is a good idea to bring a frame air pump and an extra tire along for the ride. With a clincher, all you need is an extra inner tube or even a small patching kit and lightweight set of tire "irons." One cost advantage of the clincher is that it can usually be repaired at least once, and eventual replacement of a tube is considerably less expensive than buying a whole new tire.

Tom Schuler, winner of the 1987 CoreStates USPRO Championship and veteran 7-Eleven team rider, sums it up best: "The biggest problem with tubulars is cost. I figure I have at least 20 flats a year in training. If I had to buy my own tires, I would train on clinchers, too."

WHEELS

Your knowledge of the bicycle wheel need not be extensive, but you should be familiar with its three building blocks: the *hub, spokes,* and *rim.* (See table opposite for wheel specifications.)

As a rule, most quality adult bicycles starting at around $350 will come equipped with wheels that have:

- 36 double-butted spokes per wheel
- aluminum or alloy rims
- quick-release hubs.

Wheels that come on a new bike as original equipment from the manufacturer usually have been built by machine at the factory and tuned by hand at least twice—once at the factory, and once during final assembly at the dealer. While this provides an adequate wheel

REFERENCE TABLE: WHEELS

	Specification	*Description*
HUBS	HIGH OR LOW FLANGE	Refers to the circumference of the sides of the hub through which the spokes are inserted. High flange means a larger circumference hub, which generally makes a more rigid or "stiffer" wheel.
	WING NUTS	Axle nuts with wide flanges, to allow hand tightening.
	QUICK RELEASE	Locking skewer mechanism that fastens wheels to frame, without tools.
	AXLE	Usually made of steel (hollow to allow skewer to pass through, in the case of quick release).
	BALL BEARINGS	Made of steel and can be in conventional races or "sealed" for no maintenance. Cost range: $38 to $200.
SPOKES	DOUBLE-BUTTED	Spoke thickness is increased at either end for added strength.
	STRAIGHT GAUGE	One thickness through the entire spoke length.
	MATERIALS	Chrome, stainless steel, nickel.
	NUMBER/WHEEL	24 and 28, for track racing and time trials only; 32, for road racing; 36, most common; 40, for tandem and some off-road. Cost: $.15 to $.65 ea.

RIMS Best rims, either clincher or tubular, are heat treated for high strength and are made from anodized aluminum.
Cost range: $50 to $200 per pair.

LABOR Spokes are "laced" from hub to rim, according to a predetermined pattern, based upon how many other spokes one spoke will cross from when it leaves the hub to when it enters the rim (thus a "three-cross" wheel is one in which every spoke will cross over or under three others). Two, three, or four are possible, but three-cross is used most commonly.
Labor cost: $50 to $100 per hour.

MASTER WHEEL BUILDER

Thirty-eight-year-old Michael Hanley has a job most bicycle shop repairmen would kill for. He is a 7-Eleven team mechanic and master wheel builder.

Hanley's primary job is to create light, dependable wheels, using the best available products for use by the team all over the world—wheels that won't fall apart over Belgium's jarring cobblestones or in hair-raising descents down rutted Alpine passes.

Discovered by 7-Eleven team member Tom Schuler, at the Cyclery North bike shop, in Chicago, Hanley has been building wheels for fifteen years.

"Building a wheel is more than just lacing spokes in the right pattern," he says. "You have to select the right gauge spoke and you have to know the best combinations of spokes, hubs, and rims for every type of wheel the guys need to use."

For example, a time trial wheel may require very light rims and flattened spokes, while a wheel for a long road race may need thicker spokes and flatter cross-section rims (to seat the tire better). "Even a racer's style is taken into account when building a pair of wheels," he says.

Hanley's wheel-building secrets:

- Patience is the number-one quality of a good builder.
- The tighter the wheel, the better. Good tightness comes from knowing how to "tune" the spokes to just the right tension.
- Stress the wheel several times during building, so spokes will "seat" into nipples and hub. The wheel is stressed by placing the hub on the ground and applying pressure, with the hands, around the whole rim.
- Use "lock tight" on the spoke threads to hold nipples in place.

for most general riding, the more intense stress put on wheels in racing, long-distance touring, or serious off-road cycling is best handled by custom-built wheels, where specific materials can be selected based upon end use. Seldom will you find a serious cyclist who doesn't have at least one set of extra wheels, and it's not uncommon for racers to have at least five extra pairs hanging around (two pairs for training, and three pairs for various types of racing), all mounted with special tires and ready to go.

There are wheels and there are *wheels.* Top-of-the-line parts, such as Campagnolo record hubs, Nisi Laser hard anodized thirty-two-hole rims, and Berg stainless steel spokes, might as well stay in their boxes if they are not assembled with care and experience. Wheel building is both an art and a science (see profile of Michael Hanley), and it is important to go to a good wheel builder to ensure that this investment is a smart one.

COMPONENTS

THE DRIVE TRAIN

On a bicycle, muscle power is transmitted to the rear wheel through the drive train (see illustration on page 51). This is the combination of front sprockets (or "chainrings"), rear sprockets,

chain, derailleurs, crankset, and pedals. With experienced hands and feet in control, the drive train on a bicycle is much like the manual transmission in an automobile, except that no clutch is needed to shift from one gear to another.

In fact, learning to master pedaling and shifting on a bicycle is not unlike learning how to drive a car with a "stick shift"—once you get the hang of it (and practice *does* make perfect), the gear grinding will turn into familiar, almost automatic, fluid movements, and your concentration will shift to where and how fast you are going.

The first step in mastering a bicycle is to understand how it works. The pedals turn the cranks (opposing right and left arms that are attached to an axle that runs through the bicycle's bottom bracket). Thus, the "crankset" consists of a right crank with one or more sprockets (chainrings) attached, a left crank, and a bottom bracket axle (or "spindle") that rotates on ball bearings within the bottom bracket shell. Cranks are made to take one, two, or three chainrings, depending upon the range of gears or "speeds" desired.

The chain connects the chainring(s) with the one or more rear sprockets. Each rear sprocket is affixed to a small mechanism called the freewheel, which in turn is threaded onto the rear hub. Inside the freewheel are all the springs, ball bearings, and flywheel parts that allow the pedals and cranks to be held stationary, even though the wheels may be rolling forward. This is called "coasting," or more accurately, "freewheeling." The rear sprocket(s) when attached to

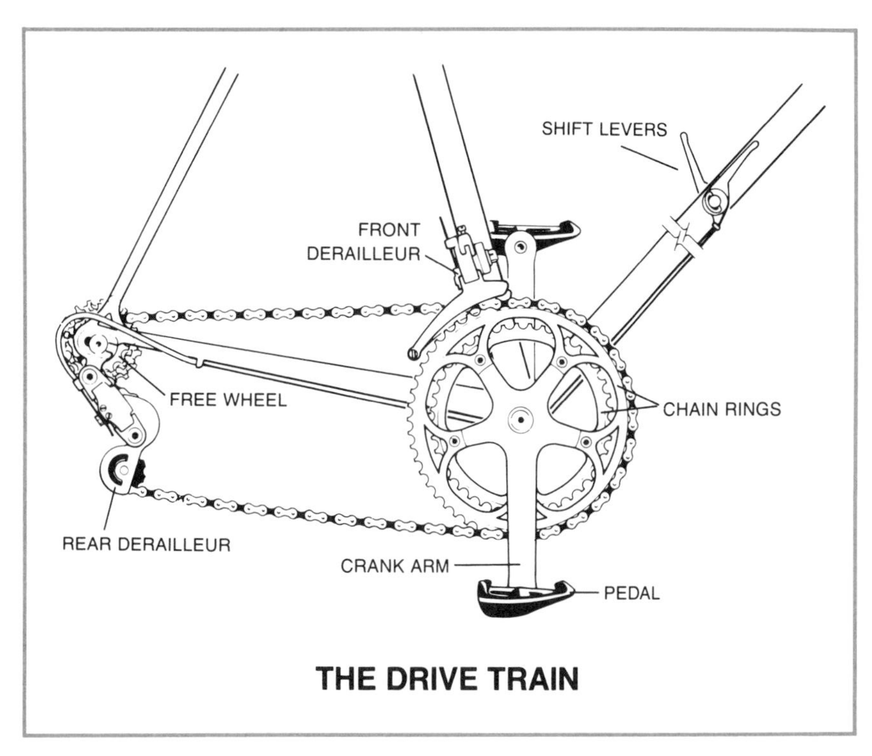

THE DRIVE TRAIN

Drawing by George Retseck

the freewheel are called the "cluster," the "block," or most frequently, the "freewheel."

Putting aside the simple children's one-speed bike and one-speeds created specifically for track racing, the number of sprockets on the freewheel will vary from five to eight, and the number of teeth on each sprocket from twelve to thirty-six. The number of gears on a bike is determined by multiplying the number of sprockets on the freewheel by the number of chainrings on the crank set. Thus, five sprockets on the back and two chainrings on front make a "ten-speed," six on the back and two on the front make a "twelve-speed," and so on.

Many off-the-rack road bikes are now twelve-speeds. ATB's or mountain bikes have three chainrings in front and six sprockets in the back, giving them eighteen speeds. The addition of a third, smaller chainring, on the inside, provides a range of six very low gears useful in climbing the steepest grades or powering through the most difficult of conditions, such as sand, stones, mud, and even streams.

The derailleur moves the chain from one sprocket to another.

Road racers avoid triple chainrings on the front, since they never need such a super-low gear, and also because the additional chainring increases both weight and drag. Standard equipment for road racing is now a seven-sprocket freewheel on the back (fourteen speeds), and, for the first time, 7-Eleven's 1989 Tour de France team used newly introduced Shimano eight-speed freewheels, giving their bikes a total of sixteen speeds. (See Chapter 6 for a discussion of gearing and gear ratios.)

Some tips to help you avoid gear grinding: To change gears, the pedals must be rotating and one of the shift levers moved forward or back. Thin steel cables connect the left-hand shift lever (with the front derailleur mounted on the seat tube) just above the front chainrings, and the right-hand shift lever (with the rear derailleur mounted on the frame's rear fork end) just below the rear hub.

The derailleurs do just what their name implies, they derail the chain from one sprocket and cause it to engage another. For example, when the left shift lever is pulled back, the cable will force the front derailleur to move to the right. Since the chain feeds through the derailleur, this will "jump" the chain from the inside sprocket to the larger outside sprocket, and a gear shift has been made!

Similarly, the right-hand shift lever manipulates the rear derailleur, so it will move the chain from one rear sprocket to another. When the rear derailleur is lined up directly below a sprocket on the freewheel, a gear is properly engaged (see illustration). If it is off center, a clanking noise will be heard, signaling that the offending shift lever needs minor adjustment. Until the recent innovation of the so-called index or click shifter, gear engagement was done more by feel and ear than by the position of the gear lever. With index

THE CHAIN COMMANDMENTS

1. Be of Proper Length.

Chains are fitted by threading the chain through front and rear derailleurs when positioned in alignment with the smallest chainring and the smallest rear sprocket, with loose ends meeting on the bottom run of the chain. Pull the ends of the chain together and overlap them until the spring tension of the rear derailleur just starts to be taken up. The chain should be riveted together at this point.

2. Cut Properly.

Chains can be taken apart with rivet extractors or rivet pliers only. When riveting the chain together, make sure that the rivet protrudes an equal distance on each side of the chain.

3. Eliminate the Stiff Link.

Chain jumping on new chains is usually caused by a stiff link where the chain has been riveted together. Find the stiff link by turning the pedals slowly backward (off the bike), until the chain binds in the rear derailleur. Place hands on either side of the offending link and flex the chain laterally (not the direction it normally rolls). Test again by backpedaling and repeat procedure until binding stops.

4. Match Chain to Freewheel.

Freewheel sprockets are closer together as their number increases. Chains come in different widths. Make sure the chain width is right for the number of sprockets on the freewheel. A chain that is too thick will get caught in between sprockets and disrupt shifting and possibly damage sprockets, chain, and derailleur.

5. Clean and Lubricate Frequently.

The dirtiest part of the bicycle is the chain and, ironically, it should be the cleanest. After every 200 miles, clean the chain with a 50-50 mixture of gasoline and diesel fuel, by passing the chain through a rag soaked in the solvent. This can be done by holding the rag around the chain, with your left hand at the chain's bottom run, as you slowly turn the pedals backward with your right hand (bike leaning against wall). Remove excess solvent with a clean cloth then oil lightly with a spray lubricant (e.g., WD 40) by spraying from above onto the chain's lower run while turning the pedals slowly backward. *Note:* Be careful not to do this around a potential spark (e.g., from a car or furnace) or open flame, and watch your fingers!

6. Retire Your Old Chains.

Even the best chains stretch and eventually wear out. Worn chains can cause gears to jump and not mesh. To check for wear, pull the chain away from the biggest front chainring at its most forward point. If the top of the chainring teeth are protruding through the links, mount a new chain. If it is really stretched, chances are that the rear sprockets are worn and should be replaced at the same time. Top racers generally replace their chains about every 2,000–2,500 miles.

shifting (and assuming the derailleur is adjusted properly), each position or click of the lever automatically lines the derailleur under the next sprocket. (If you hear a clicking, adjust the derailleur.)

Shift-lever mounting positions vary with the kind of bicycle involved. With upright handlebars, such as on mountain bikes, shift levers are usually mounted right next to the hand grips (and are operated by thumb), so that shifting can be accomplished without removing one's hands from the handlebars. The best positions for mounting shift levers on dropped handlebar bikes are at the handlebar ends (the new Grip Shift is the most innovative approach to this sensible alternative) or on the down-tube (just below the headtube), where shifters have traditionally been mounted and have proven most efficient.

A most impractical position for shift levers is clamped on the handlebar stem. It is nearly impossible to shift quickly when they are in this location, particularly while trying to achieve a low, aerodynamic profile. Also, the extra hardware and longer cables required for stem mounting add unnecessary weight, create additional wind drag, and decrease the efficiency of shifting.

The chain is the "connective tissue" of the drive train. Without it, the bike simply will not function, so it is most important that this constantly moving part be properly selected and maintained (see "The Chain Commandments"). Today's chains are becoming thinner, to handle closely spaced rear sprockets, and are made of stronger, lighter metals. The chain most widely used by racers and recreational riders is the French "Sedisport." And in the cyclist's universe of expensive little parts, it's comforting to know that this high-quality item costs less than an average bottle of good wine (about $10.00).

PEDALS

Unlike the other components in the drive train, the pedal has undergone recent radical design changes, switching from strap-in stirrups to step-in bindings in less than five years.

In 1984, five-time Tour de France winner Bernard Hinault replaced his conventional toe clips and straps with a more radical shoe/pedal binding system developed by Look, also a pioneering manufacturer of safety ski bindings.

This system involves a special hard-soled shoe, with hardware mounted under the ball of the foot, that is designed to fasten (via a clip-on, spring-loaded mechanism) to compatible hardware affixed to the pedal axle. Rather than stepping into a toe clip and strap, fastened to the pedal, one simply steps the bottom of the shoe onto the pedal-axle hardware, locking the spring-loaded mechanism in place, much like a step-in ski binding. The stiff sole of the shoe and pedal-axle hardware together serve to replace the pedal. The shoe/pedal systems are also like modern ski bindings in that they are designed to automatically release under stress. At least one manufacturer (Time) has a system that allows more lateral ankle movement than does the toe clip and strap, and this is presumably better from a biomechanical standpoint, both in terms of pedaling power and wear on the ankles.

By the time of the 1989 Tour de France, 95 percent of all teams had followed Hinault's lead and switched from conventional toe clips and straps to one of a half-dozen brands of the new, step-in shoe/pedal systems. This made sense for reasons beyond those stated above. For the first time since the turn of the century, feet could stay firmly attached to the pedals without the need for awkward straps that dug into the shoes and sometimes cut off blood circulation. Loss of the metal toe-clip meant weight reduction and

THE PEDAL REVOLUTION
In the mid-eighties, conventional toe clips and straps (left) were almost totally replaced by step-in shoe/pedal binding systems. *Seth Goltzer photos*

the safety release ensured that feet could be freed in a crash.

A common fear of the novice cyclist is the thought of falling with the feet trapped in the pedals. However, one quickly learns that quick removal of the feet from the straps or shoe pedal system is not that difficult and that the advantages of having the feet firmly attached to the pedals are many. All one needs to drive this point home is to have a foot slip off the pedal while climbing a steep hill. It is far better to keep your feet firmly on the pedals and in the same position than to risk them coming off at a bad time.

What hasn't changed in this pedal revolution is the basic principle that the pedal/shoe combination must serve to keep the foot firmly anchored to the pedal, in a position that is designed to maximize pedaling efficiency (see Chapter 6). In certain kinds of cycling, such as mountain biking, where a more conventional shoe is preferred to push off rocks and walk or lift a bike over difficult terrain, this new technology has yet to take hold, although one can be confident that an ATB version of the shoe/pedal system cannot be far away.

There is an all-terrain cycling shoe for every level of interest—from the casual rider (lower left) to the serious ATB racer (lower right).

THE SADDLE

Nothing diminishes enthusiasm for cycling more than a saddle that creates pain where you really don't want it. Cycling does *not* have to be a pain in the rear. It is now possible to get a saddle that is anatomically correct for you, without sacrificing the firmness necessary to transmit maximum leg power to the pedals. A spongy or bouncy saddle can lead to sloppy and inefficient pedaling.

The most important thing to know is that the back portion of a comfortable saddle must span the ischia, the bones at the base of the pelvic girdle, so that your weight is supported by bone rather than tissue. If you are in the proper position, 55 percent of your body weight should be supported by the saddle.

For women, who tend to have wider pelvic bones, Avocet has designed a shorter saddle with the back well flared. For both sexes, the front part, or "nose" of the saddle must be reasonably narrow to allow minimal chafing on the inside of the thighs when pedaling (see photograph below).

Twenty-five years ago, the best saddles were made of leather. An elaborate process was required to stretch and soften the new leather before it could be shaped by its owner through miles and miles of use. The old pros, very much like the cowboys of the Wild West, valued their broken-in saddles as prized possessions, and when

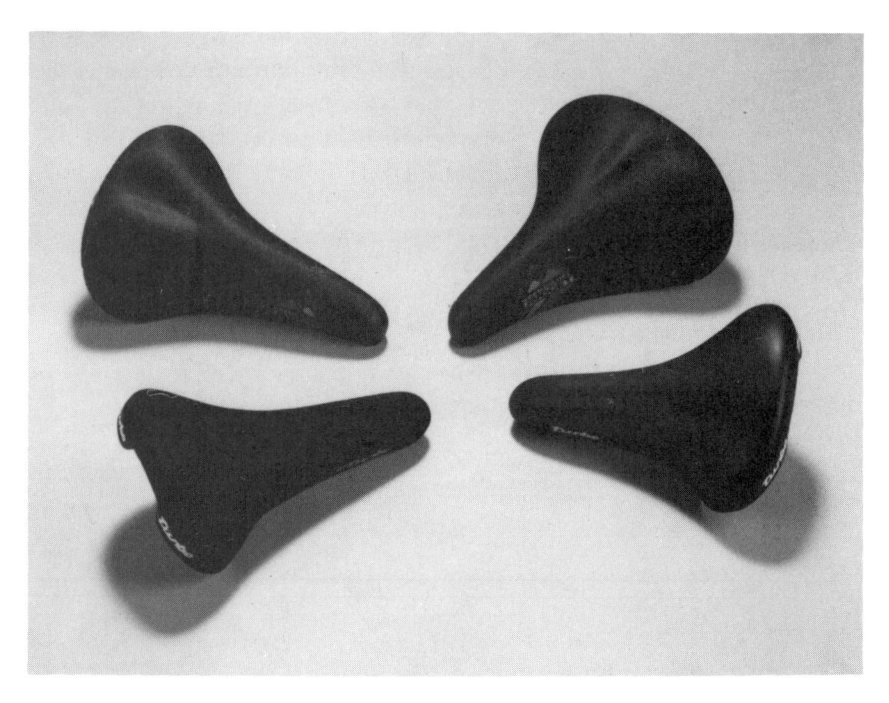

SADDLE SHAPES
Clockwise from lower left: road racing, off-road, women's off-road, women's road racing. Note differences in tip-to-tail length, amount of padding, and differences in rear widths.
Seth Goltzer photo

bikes were sold or traded the saddle often stayed with its original shaper.

Today it's different. With rare exception, the most widely used saddles are made of molded plastic covered with a thin layer of padding, such as high-density foam. The top covering is a skin of leather or suede that is just the right smoothness to provide some "hold" while not creating undue friction.

Expect to pay at least thirty-five dollars for a good saddle, such as the Avocet, Cinelli, Selle Turbo, or Selle San Marco. In saddles, you again get what you pay for. Instead of a leather coating, an inexpensive model can be covered with a synthetic, such as vinyl, lined with cheap foam rubber, and mounted on an undercarriage of soft metal that will do a nose dive when you hit a good bump. It is not uncommon for a cheap saddle to actually pop off its undercarriage, exposing two nasty looking prongs that could change your life permanently.

Avoid extra padding, springs, and other inventions that supposedly make your saddle feel softer. What they seem to provide in comfort, they lose in support. Eventually, this will contribute to soreness, chafing, and perhaps the desire to take up fishing.

There is one thing to remember. All saddles take getting used to. The initial soreness will disappear more quickly and longer-lasting comfort will be achieved with one of high quality. Better safe than saddle-sorry.

BRAKES

The two most important criteria for good brakes are: *stopping ability* and *ease of adjustment.*

The basic components of the brake are the *lever,* the *cable,* the *calipers* (which apply leveraged pressure to the wheel rims), and the *pads.* Top-of-the-line brakes like Campagnolo have a noticeably firm and strong feel when squeezed. Once the calipers and pads engage the rim, there is little give that can be felt when squeezing harder. In contrast, a cheap brake feels like the lever can be squeezed almost into the handlebar, well after the brakes have engaged the rim. A good brake not only reacts quicker to the touch, its power is also less likely to be affected by a dented rim.

Actually, the brake pads (the "shoes" that squeeze the rim) are nearly as important as the brake itself, in terms of stopping power. All brake pads lose efficiency when they are wet. Soft pads will help you stop more abruptly (not necessarily desirable), while hard pads will help you slow more gradually. When applying the brakes, the important thing to remember is to apply both at the same time, using equal amounts of pressure from each hand. You should never squeeze the front brake alone or with more pressure than the back, since it could well cause you to be thrown for an unpleasant front somersault.

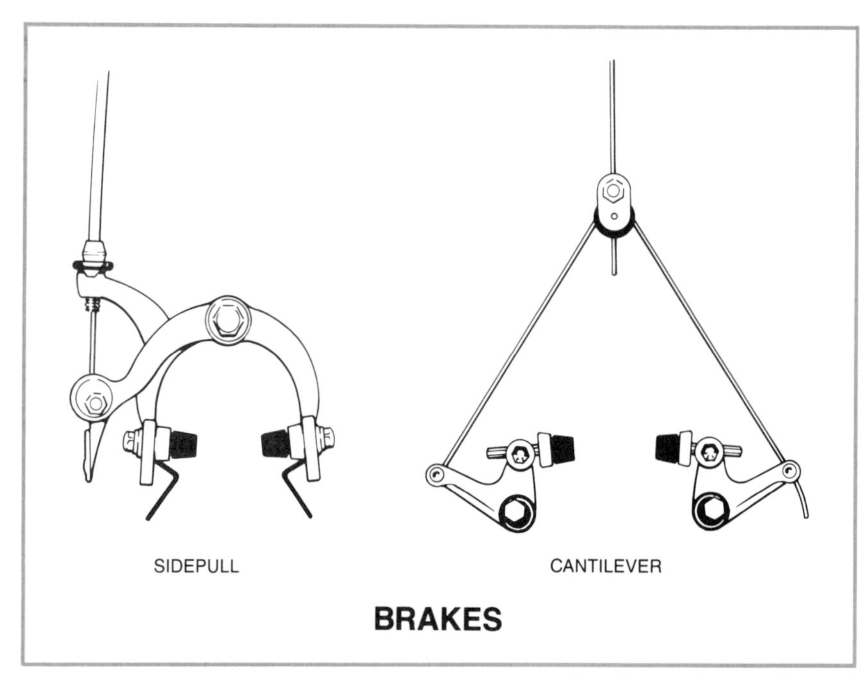

Drawing by George Retseck

In terms of adjustment, all good brakes have a quick release mechanism, usually on the caliper itself or sometimes on the brake lever. When flicked, this little mechanism spreads the brake so that a wheel can be removed easily. Also, a certain amount of cable slack or adjustment for wearing brake pads can be remedied by turning adjustment screws that are usually built into the calipers. This is a good thing to have since it allows for some caliper adjustment without the need for tools.

There are two basic styles of hand brakes: *center pull* and *side pull*, so named for the method by which the cable draws the calipers closed (see illustration above). Fifteen years ago, racers wouldn't be caught dead without center pull brakes. Then Campagnolo introduced a stronger side pull that had the advantage of eliminating the special "hangers" that had to be fitted to the frame to allow the center pulling action.

Until mountain bikes were introduced, center pulls became almost extinct. Now, virtually all mountain bikes are equipped with cantilevered center pulls (for heavy-duty stopping power and ease of cleaning) and most road-racing machines use the easier mounting, easier adjusting side pulls.

A sometimes touted feature, particularly on low-end bikes, is the so-called "safety lever," an extension of brake levers on dropped bars that allows the rider to apply the brakes with hands on the tops of the handlebars. Avoid this like the plague. The extender results in excessive "play," making proper adjustment very difficult to achieve and maintain. Positive hand-braking action should be accomplished through the most direct application of pressure possible. This is best done using the conventional single-lever design.

SEAT POSTS AND STEMS

Strong but light are the watch words for these static yet important components. The seat post fits into the frame, connecting the bike to the saddle, and plays an important role in two of the measurements that are key to proper fit: saddle height and fore and aft saddle position (see Chapter 3).

The best seat posts are made of lightweight but strong forged aluminum or other metal alloys and come in standard circumference measurements from 26.2 mm to 27.2 mm (in two mm increments). It is important to match the seat-post diameter to the inner dimension of the seat tube, since a seat post should never be forced into the frame, nor should it drop in without flush contact with the inner walls of the tube. Some manufacturers now apply aerodynamic principles to seat-post design. This is fine, if strength is not compromised. If "aero" is your interest, go with proven manufacturers like Campagnolo or Shimano.

The handlebar stem should be considered in the same way. Lengths of stems vary from seven cm to fourteen cm (measured from the center of the bolt on the stem's top surface to the center of its handlebar opening). It is a good idea to use a stem and handlebar from the same manufacturer, since handlebar diameters generally vary from one to the other, and these parts are usually engineered to be compatible.

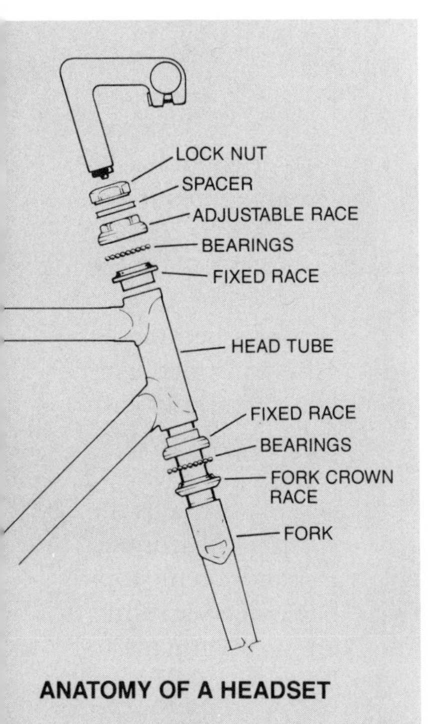

ANATOMY OF A HEADSET

Drawing by George Retseck

THE HEADSET

The bicycle's front fork (the component that holds the front wheel in place) is attached to the frame and allowed to turn by means of an ingenious component known as the headset (see illustration). The headset consists of two "cups," each enclosing a set of steel ball bearings. It takes serious abuse every time the bike is ridden. Vibration from rough roads and pressure from steering requires that it be properly lubricated and in near-perfect adjustment at all times, lest "pitting" of the cups occur, which will result in steering problems or front-end wobble (particularly when braking).

The good news is that a quality headset, adjusted properly, is made to take this kind of abuse and should not malfunction. Premium bicycles come with good headsets that are adequate for most purposes. If a custom frame is in order, have the frame builder install the headset and expect to pay about sixty-five to eighty-five dollars for a good one, like Campagnolo, Shimano, or the top-of-the-line Mavic.

For those who really want to know what brands the pros use, here's a table compiled by *VeloNews* that will tell you the real story, in the 1989 Tour de France.

WHAT THE TOUR TEAMS USE

Everyone wants to know what equipment is used by professionals racing the Tour de France, so *VeloNews* presents this full list of items used by the 22 teams at the 1989 Tour. A couple of items of note: Nearly 95 percent of the Tour pros use clipless pedals. Also, most top riders use carbon fiber tubing (TVT, Look, or Vitus) for mountain stages. These details were compiled with the assistance of Herman Seidler, assistant editor of the Austrian magazine *Pedal*.

Panasonic	Hitachi	7-Eleven	Paternina	Carrera	RMO	ADR	Fagor	Histor	Chateau d'Ax	Toshiba
Colnago	Eddy Merckx	Eddy Merckx	Orbea	Battaglin	Liberia	Bottecchia	MBK Motobecane	Diamant	Moser	Look/Gitane Delta
Columbus	Reynolds 653	Columbus SLX	Columbus SLX	Columbus SLX	Reynolds 653	Columbus TSX	Columbus SLX	Columbus TSX	Oria GMOO	Look Carbon/ Reynolds 753
Campy C-Record	Mavic	Dura-Ace	Campy C-Record	Dura-Ace	Mavic	Mavic	Campy C-Record	Campy C-Record	Dura-Ace	Dura-Ace
Campy standard	Mavic clipless	Shimano clipless	Campy SGR/ Look	Look Carbon	Mavic clipless	Mavic clipless	Time/Campy standard	Time	Shimano clipless/ Look Carbon	Look
Modolo	Mavic	Cinelli	Cinelli	Cinelli	Mavic	Mavic	Cinelli	Cinelli	Modolo	3TTT
San Marco Rolls	Italia Turbo	Cinelli	San Marco Concor	San Marco	Italia Turbo	Italia Turbo	Italia Turbo	San Marco Rolls	Vetta	San Marco Rolls
Campagnolo	Mavic	Wolber	Campagnolo	Ambrosio	Mavic	Mavic	FIR	Campagnolo	Ambrosio	Mavic
Clément	Vittoria	Wolber	Clément	Michelin clincher	Vittoria	Vittoria	Wolber	Vittoria	Michelin clincher	Vittoria
Domex	**SuperConfex**	**TVM**	**Reynolds**	**PDM**	**Kelme**	**Helvetia**	**Super U**	**Café de Colombia**	**Z-Peugeot**	**BH**
Eddy Merckx	Colnago	Zullo	Pinarello	Concorde	Eddy Merckx	Villiger	Raleigh	Vitus	Peugeot/ Vitus Carbone	BH
Columbus SLX	Columbus SLX	Columbus SLX	Columbus SLX	Columbus SLX	Columbus SLX	Oria Rauf/ TVT Carbon	Reynolds 753	Vitus Carbone	Reynolds 753/ Vitus Carbone	Columbus SLX
Weinmann/Edco	SunTour Superbe	Dura-Ace	Campy C-Record	Campy C-Record	Campy C-Record	SunTour Superbe	Campy C-Record	Mavic	Stronglight	Campy C-Record
Time	Time/SunTour	Shimano clipless	Time	Look Carbon	Look Carbon	Time	Time	Mavic clipless	Time	Look Carbon
Cinelli	3TTT	Cinelli	3TTT	Cinelli	Cinelli	Mavic	ITM	Mavic	Atax	Cinelli
San Marco Rolls	San Marco Rolls	Cinelli Volare	Italia Turbo	San Marco Rolls	Italia Turbo	San Marco Rolls	Iscaselle	Italia Turbo	Italia Turbo	Cinelli Volare
Weinmann	Ambrosio	Galli	Campagnolo	Mavic	Campagnolo	Mavic	Campagnolo	Mavic	Mavic	Campagnolo
Vittoria	Continental	Vittoria	Vittoria	Vittoria	Vittoria	Clément	Clément	Vittoria	Vittoria	Clément

Compiled by VeloNews

SUMMARY

It is important to have a basic understanding of the various moving parts that make your bicycle tick and to know how they should be adjusted and cared for. You will be surprised at the satisfaction you will derive from the "high tech" side of cycling, once you have a grasp of the basics and some experience in tuning your bike and experiencing the positive result on its feel and your performance.

It's best, however, to leave repair and maintenance of the more intricate components, such as the headset, crankset, freewheel, and derailleurs to the experts unless, of course, you have the time, patience, and desire to become an expert yourself. It is worth investing in quality, particularly with regard to key safety components, such as wheels, tires, and brakes. When it comes to weight, less is more and, unfortunately, the opposite is true when it comes to the relationship between cost and quality.

5 Software

Style is a word often associated with cycling. In fact, many of today's trendier noncycling fashions are either cycling clothing or styled specifically to achieve that cycling look. For the passionate French or Italian devotee, cycling is both a style and a lifestyle, a complete package—the relaxed yet powerful position on the bicycle, smooth-shaven bronzed legs that turn mile after mile with a certain "*souplesse*," polished bike gleaming in the sunlight, cycling cap cocked just so. . . .

When traveling through the cycling countries of Europe, this sense of style is evident even among casual recreational riders. Absent are tennis shorts and blue jeans, awkward-looking positions and high-domed helmets. Gear is functional and seldom outlandish, although the jerseys can be quite colorful. We challenge you to find a true Frenchman with a rearview mirror mounted on his helmet.

Apart from individual esthetic preferences, it is important to know what is available to the cyclist and why. *Good cycling wear begins with function and ends with style.* And today every piece of functional cycling clothing offers enough style options to meet every taste. It starts with the feet.

SHOES

The most important item of cycling clothing is a good pair of shoes. Everyone knows how important it is for the runner to choose shoes that will cushion the feet, absorb shock, and provide comfort stride after stride. No runner with even the most basic technique would consider running any distance in anything but real running shoes.

This applies to cycling as well. Cycling shoes are a very specialized piece of equipment (really a cross between hardware and software, and the link between flesh and metal). In that regard they are more similar to ski boots than to other athletic shoes. It is difficult if not impossible to walk properly or at least comfortably in cycling shoes, particularly those of the new shoe/pedal systems (see Chapter 3).

Cycling shoes are designed to transmit energy to the pedals, and since cycling is not a weight-bearing jarring sport, shock absorbing ability and cushioning are not nearly as important as a tight fit, an extremely stiff sole, and a cleat that clamps into the pedal.

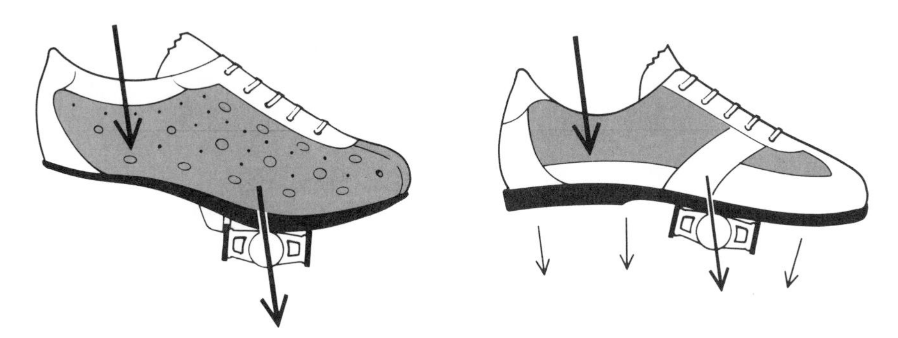

A stiff-soled shoe (left) transmits force along the entire foot when it pushes on the pedal. A soft-soled shoe (right) dissipates force when it bends around the pedal.

Drawing by George Retseck

SHOE-SIZE CONVERSIONS

Europe	U.S.
36	3.5
37	4
38	4.5
39	6
40	6.5
41	7
42	8
43	9
44	10
45	10.5
46	11
47	12
48	12.5
49	13
50	14

The sole needs to be stiff in order to transmit energy from the downward pedal stroke along the entire length of the shoe sole, not just where the foot meets the pedal (see illustration). Soft-soled shoes will curve around the pedal when riding hard, resulting in lost energy and foot cramping. Today's stiff soles are generally made of molded plastic or carbon fiber (leather and wood used to be the norm), whereas the uppers, much like running and other athletic shoes, once made exclusively of leather, are now a combination of leather (real and simulated), nylon mesh, and/or other synthetic materials.

In order to achieve the snug fit needed for maximum performance, most serious cyclists prefer shoes that are at least one size smaller than their street shoes. The best brands come from Europe, usually in European sizes (see Conversion Chart) and generally run narrower than American shoes. Cycling shoes should always be worn with one pair of thin, close-fitting cycling socks. These come in lightweight wool blends (the best) or in various blends of cotton and nylon. The design we recommend is just high enough to cover the ankles, high enough to keep out small pebbles and road dirt but not so high that they droop or add unwanted weight to the legs (particularly when wet).

Ventilation is important. Heat is reflected from the pavement to the soles, and constant pressure to the pedals creates friction and heat build-up that is transferred to the feet. Good cycling shoes have perforations both in the soles and uppers to allow heat release and reduce overall weight. The most comfortable uppers for warm weather cycling are made of 50 percent leather and 50 percent ballistic mesh, although personal preference may dictate a different choice.

The most important aspect of the cycling shoe is the cleat that is attached to the sole and locks into the pedal. There are two basic types, depending on whether you use the traditional toe clips and straps or one of the newer step-in shoe/pedal systems (see Chapter 3).

No matter which system you choose, positioning of the cleat on the shoe sole is critical. Virtually all good shoes have the cleat premounted so all that is left is to position it fore and aft and set its angle. There are two guiding principles:

- The ball of the foot should be directly over the pedal axle.
- The foot should be parallel to the crank arm (not toed in or out, which can lead to knee problems).

These two adjustments are best accomplished with the help of a friend. Wearing cycling shorts and shoes, sit on the bicycle and lock both feet into the pedals. (You'll have to lean against a wall to do this, or better yet, have your friend hold you upright.) With cleats not yet tightened and cranks parallel to the ground (at three and nine o'clock), move your feet forward and back and side to side, until you feel the proper position is reached. When your friend verifies that your feet are indeed parallel to the cranks and the balls of your feet are directly over the pedal axles, he or she should tighten the cleats while you hold the position. After a few test rides,

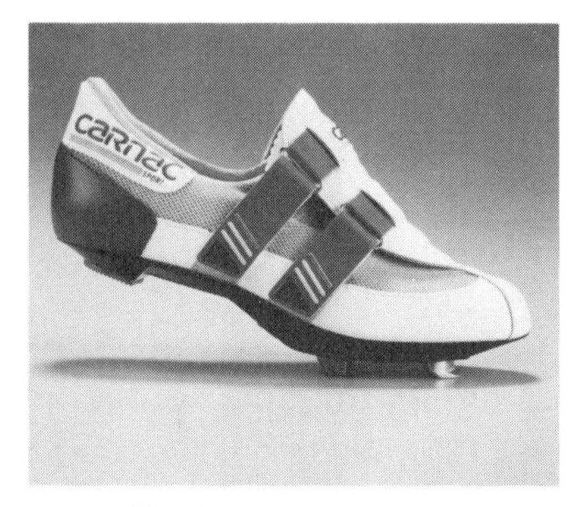

The best cycling shoes have mesh uppers, velcro closures, and a stiff molded sole, with cleat attachment.

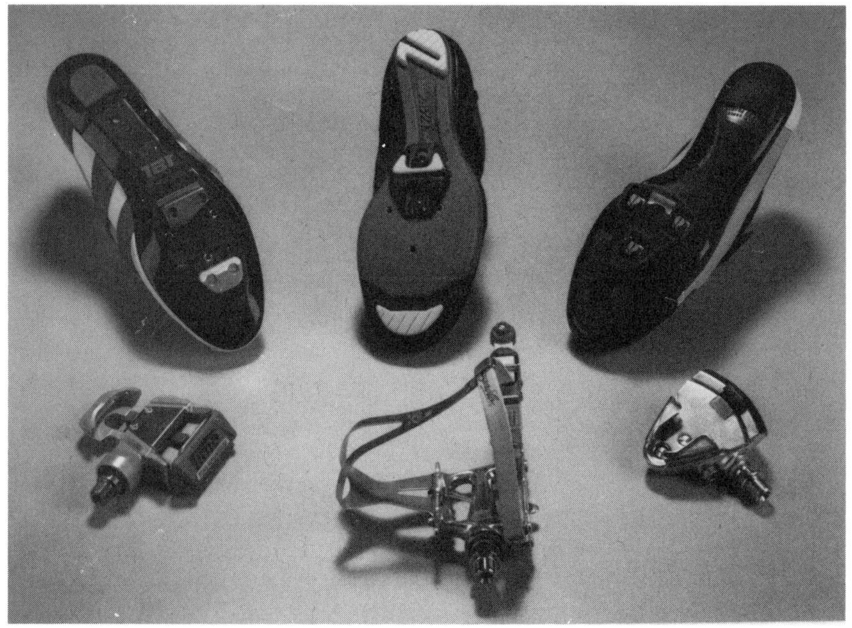

Three types of shoe cleats and pedal systems. Time's two-piece cleat and step-in pedal (left), the traditional toe clip and strap that operates with a grooved cleat (middle), and Campagnolo's step-in, featuring a step-in plate that locks into the pedal. Most good shoes can be fit with nearly every type of cleat. *Products courtesy of Brandford Bike. Goltzer photo*

Cleats can be positioned more quickly with the help of a friend.
Goltzer photo

you may want to do some fine tuning of cleat positioning on your own. (See photo above.)

Are shoes with cleats absolutely necessary? For serious cycling, *Yes.* Former Tour de France champion Bernard Hinault in his book *Road Racing,* put it this way:

> Without [the binding of shoe and pedal] it's impossible to pedal at peak efficiency. This is because, first, a moving foot doesn't stay in the position that optimizes the pedaling force, and second, the sole loses contact when the rider pulls the pedal backwards through the dead spot and when he raises his leg.

For those who expect to do a lot of walking along with their cycling or who just have an absolute fear of being locked in, there are "cheater shoes" available. These have hard soles, usually made of rubber or nylon, with a series of molded grooves that can fit into toe clips and straps, without the bulk of a cleat. Although they will never achieve the positive feel of real bike shoes, they are an acceptable alternative for the casual rider.

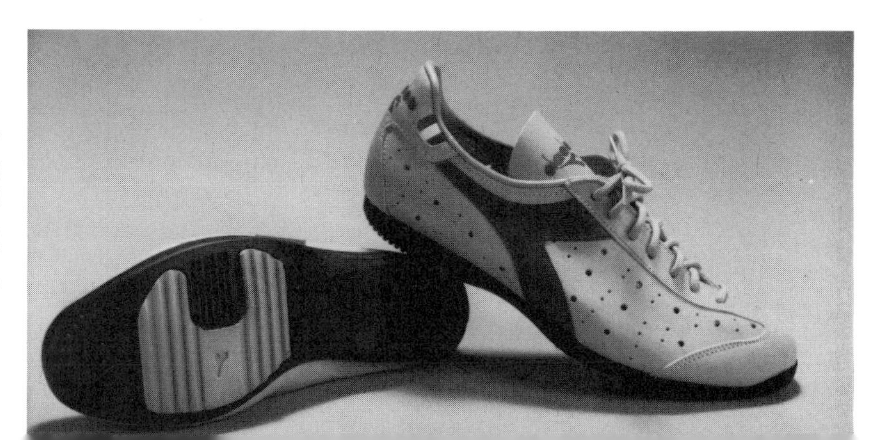

"Cheater Shoes" are practical for walking while still offering adequate stiffness and grooves to hold the pedal.
Product courtesy of Brandford Bike. Goltzer photo

SHORTS

Today, cycling shorts are in. Those thigh-hugging, stretchy (mostly black) exercise pants are nothing more than stylized versions of the cyclist's second most important item of clothing. We are hard pressed to think of a better example of function dictating fashion and life imitating sport than with bike shorts (see "Short Course," on page 67).

The traditional black color comes from the early days of cycling, when it was discovered that sitting on a bicycle saddle created embarrassing discoloration on that part of the anatomy to which it was not polite to draw attention. Nothing has changed on that end and even today's multicolored cycling shorts still usually incorporate a black panel, running between the legs from front to back.

Although they are very much in vogue in today's slick, high-tech fashion scene, cycling shorts have been tight fitting and stretchy for some time and for good reason: They cut wind drag and prevent fabric bunching under the seat. The distinguishing characteristic of the true cycling short is found on the inside. It is a piece of chamois, a soft, absorbent animal skin, not unlike the kind used to dry cars, cut into a circle large enough to cover the saddle and sewn into the inside of the pants' crotch. The chamois skin is very effective at absorbing perspiration and cutting down on sore-causing saddle friction.

Because true chamois is basically an organic animal hide, it is hard to wash and dry and thus becomes a breeding ground for bacteria. Since bacterial rashes (similar to athlete's foot) develop in dark, moist places, many cyclists have had to deal with this as a chronic problem (see Chapter 8).

Modern technology has come to the rescue, both with antirash preparations, such as Cruex, as well as with synthetic chamois made from several layers of function-specific materials. This new chamois has nearly replaced the organic kind. It can be washed and dried many times without losing its key properties, and it has shown improved durability against the friction and wear and tear of everyday cycling. Even so, serious cyclists will always have at least two pairs and will wash them after each use.

Here's an important tip: Never wear anything underneath your cycling shorts. They are designed to work alone, and the chamois must be next to the skin to perform its important functions.

A SHORT COURSE ON SHORTS

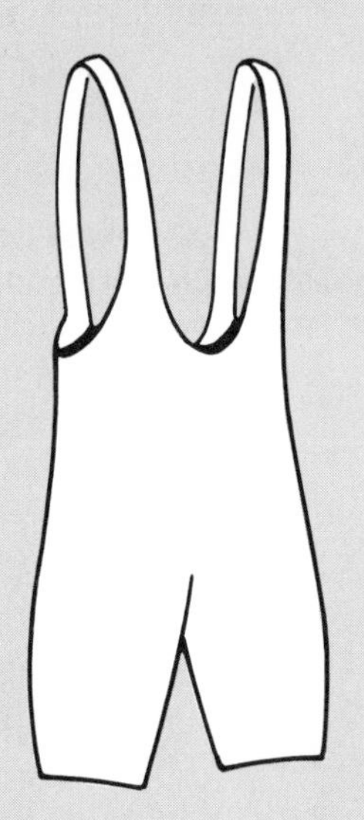

The best shorts for cycling:

- Are made out of a fabric composed of Spandex, with nylon or other polyester (brand names include Dupont's Lycra®, Coolmax®, Supplex®, and others).
- Are held up by built-in "bib" suspenders or outside elastic waist grippers (elastic bands and drawstrings hamper breathing).
- Are constructed using an eight panel anatomical design (shorts come out of the bag looking like they are in a proper cycling position).
- Are fitted with an inside crotch reinforcement made of chamois skin that is designed to control friction, absorb perspiration, and provide modest cushioning.
- Have a synthetic chamois of up to four layers:
  —A next-to-the-skin layer of ultrasuede;
  —Cotton terry cloth, to wick away moisture;
  —A thin layer of closed-cell foam for cushioning; and
  —Nylon Lycra®, treated with a heat process that closes the knit face of the fabric, to offer more protection from the elements.
- Have no seams that bulge or cross in the area of saddle contact.
- Wash easily and hold their shape.

Best bets: Assos, Descente, Gianni, Giordana, Pearl Izumi, and Tomasso.

Drawing by George Retseck

HELMETS

The purist, and of course any libertarian, will tell you that wearing a helmet should be a matter of choice. Greg LeMond, who actually wears one far more than most professional racers, comments on this issue in his *Complete Book of Bicycling:*

> I'm a professional cyclist and I depend on the sport for my living. Helmets can be very constraining and hot, especially hard-shell helmets. In many of the long, hot stage races like the Tour de France, wearing a hard-shell helmet would be unrealistic. The helmets are heavy and they're ventilated only to a certain point. In a seven- or eight-hour road race the helmet would be a significant fatigue factor. I simply can't afford to lose any time because of a helmet.

LeMond is also quick to point out that most people don't experience hard competitive conditions for six hours at a time and seven ounces or so of protective headgear is a small trade-off for added insurance

ANSI–approved helmets for racing include the lightweight styles made by Giro and Bell. Other good brands are Avenir, Brancali, Monarch, Paramount, Performance, Pro-Tec, Rhode Gear, Specialized, and Vetta. *Product courtesy of Brandford Bike. Goltzer photo*

against the most dreaded of all cycling injuries (see Chapter 8).

When Bell marketed the first hard-shell cycling helmet in the late 1970s, it was heavy, bulky, and alien looking. Not only did it disrupt the aerodynamic concept of a cyclist knifing through the air, it grated on the purist's sense of style. Racers called them "tortoise shells." The safety crusaders touted them as the be-all and end-all solution that would eliminate carnage on the roads. American cyclists became polarized over the issue, while Europeans, to this day, haven't thought much about it: They just go helmetless.

In 1986, the United States Cycling Federation (USCF), the amateur governing body of the sport, made hard-shell helmet use mandatory in all amateur races. Manufacturer's specifications now have to conform to ANSI standards for a helmet to be approved for amateur racing in this country. Since that time, approved hard-shell helmets have become lighter, more ventilated, aerodynamic, and even somewhat stylish. Acceptance is widespread even though the cost of the lightest, raciest models is approximately eighty dollars.

Here's a tip: Lighter, more compact models, like the popular Giro, are not recommended for use after one impact. Once the foam core has been compacted, it loses most of its protective qualities. Damaged helmets should be replaced or reconditioned by the manufacturer.

The final word on helmets for general cycling is that it is a matter of personal choice. State laws have not yet been passed requiring their use. In fact, in many states, motorcycle enthusiasts, through persistent lobbying, were able to "roll back" earlier helmet laws on the basis that they were a violation of basic constitutional rights—in other words, downright un-American! When faced with sharing road space with vehicles, inexperienced cyclists, and the ever-present risk of unexpected tumbles, the prudent cyclist will choose to protect his head over considerations of convenience or style. Like buckling your seat belt, donning your helmet should be second nature.

THE JERSEY

Here's where style goes wild. Thanks to today's new fabrics, one can purchase authentic cycling jerseys with a message. The message can vary from a patterned repeat of a beer can to a gaudy gaggle of European company names, logos, and colors that is an authentic replica of a real pro trade-team uniform.

Only one design is truly sacred. It is the rainbow jersey allowed to be worn only by a reigning world champion. On a solid white background, the sequence of rainbow colors around the chest, collar, and sleeves is blue, red, black, yellow, and green, the official colors of the Unione Cycliste Internationale (UCI), cycling's world governing body. To a real bike-racing fan, unauthorized wearing of this talisman is tantamount to desecrating your country's flag. Never buy one (they are sold by unscrupulous entrepreneurs, often with the colors in the wrong sequence to protect against lawsuits), and when one passes by one on the shoulders of its rightful owner, salute.

Today, there are jerseys to suit any taste. The important thing is not to confuse style with quality and to choose a product of the best materials and design.

Not long ago, the only authentic cycling jerseys were made of finely woven, 100 percent wool. Since a cyclist travels faster than, say, a runner, the rush of the passing wind acts as a fan. Wool has the unique quality (among natural fibers) of "wicking," or drawing perspiration away from the skin and to the outside of the garment, where evaporation will result in a cooling effect on hot summer

A SHORT COURSE ON JERSEYS

The best jerseys for cycling:

- Are made from tightly knit, lightweight wool or synthetics that "breathe."
- Have a half-zipper front, close-fitting tail, and sleeves.
- Reach to midgroin and have three rear pockets, with elasticized openings over the small of the back.
- Can be washed and dried, without appreciable loss of size or shape.

Best bets: Assos, Descente, Giordana, Garneau, and Pearl Izumi.

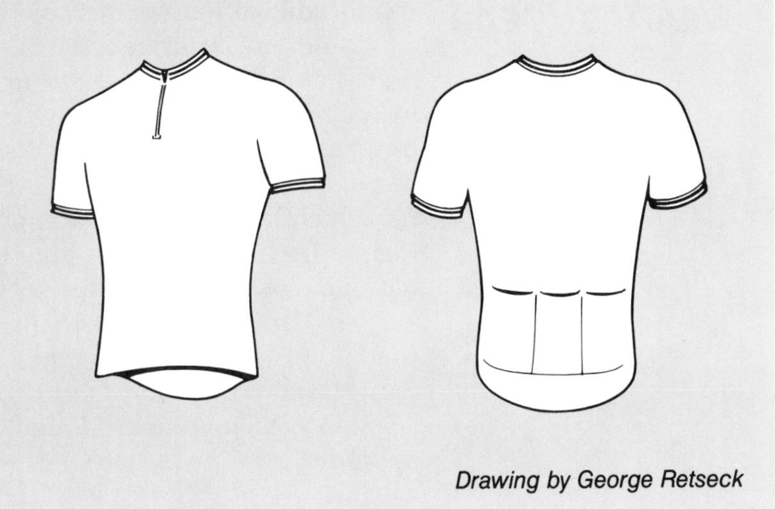

Drawing by George Retseck

days. Conversely, wool's fine insulating qualities make it warm and comfortable in far lower temperatures. Wool can absorb 30 percent of its own weight in moisture and is far more durable than cotton, silk, and even most man-made fibers. But quality wool jerseys, characterized by a thin, tight weave, seldom found in American-made garments, are very expensive—around one hundred dollars each, as manufactured by Italy's Vittorio Gianni, considered the premier designer of fine woolens for cycling.

A synthetic breakthrough was inevitable, and it first hit the public at the 1977 World Championships in Venezuela, when the East Germans showed up in one-piece Lycra "skinsuits." In addition to the ability to "breathe" and "wick," this new fabric had the added capability of easy sublimation, an imprinting technique used to reproduce sponsor's logos and colors on professional uniforms. The material also lent itself to the bright, irridescent (and more recently, fluorescent) textures and hues so popular in today's sportswear. By the 1980s, the new fabric and design process were standard. The rest of the industry followed suit, and the trickle-down effect, coupled with aggressive promotion and distribution, saw even the most casual cyclists buying designs inspired by Tour de France teams.

Today's better jerseys utilize the best properties of natural and synthetic fibers, with infinite style options, while still incorporating the functional elements so important for cycling: trim, aerodynamic cut in the tucked position, half-zipper at the collar, gathered tail and sleeve ends and, for the road jersey, the obligatory three rear pockets for taking food on the fly.

WET- AND COLD-WEATHER GEAR

Thanks also to the fabric revolution, it is now possible to cycle comfortably in wet weather and temperatures well below freezing.

A major breakthrough, during the last decade, was the introduction of Gore-Tex®, a synthetic material, much in look and feel like nylon, but with tiny breathing holes, small enough to keep out rain droplets, yet large enough to allow the escape of water vapor caused by perspiration. This fabric serves as an excellent windbreaker and rain shield, but at the same time can "breathe," thus keeping the wearer dry from the water-vapor buildup that had been an unfortunate characteristic of most water-repellent garments.

Apart from keeping dry, the key to keeping warm in colder conditions is adequate insulation for hands, feet, and head. Since these are also the areas most prone to frostbite, it makes sense to invest in special products designed to protect them (see illustration opposite).

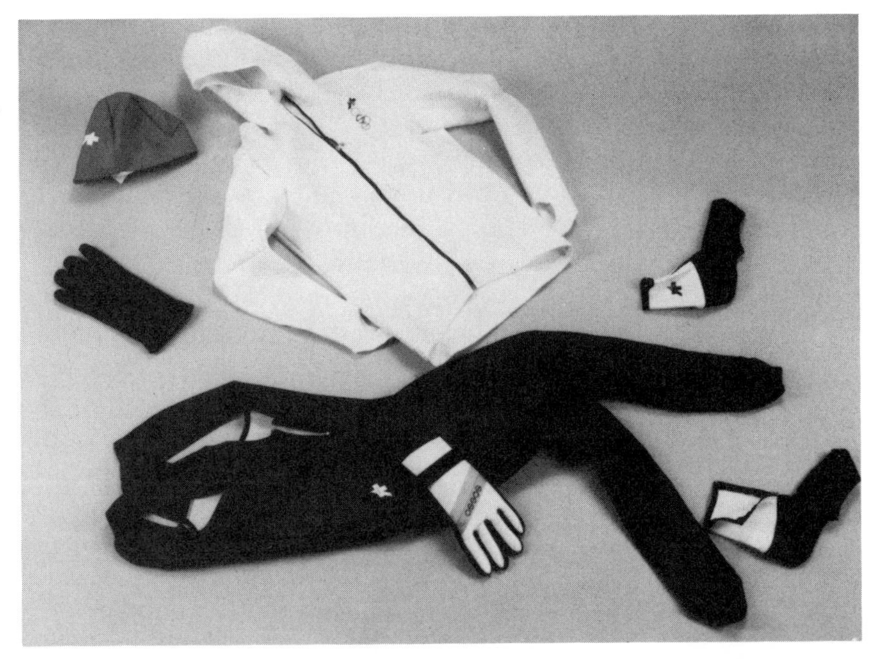

Assos of Switzerland makes high quality, formfitting winter wear, from cap to booties.
Product courtesy of Brandford Bike. Goltzer photo

The most debilitating cold comes from the feet. The only thing that really works is a good pair of insulated shoe "bootees," available from any good bicycle dealer for less than $30 a pair. These come with a hole cut in the bottom so the entire bootee can fit over the shoe while allowing the cleat to come through and properly engage the pedal. (Most can be cut larger to accommodate a bigger cleat without sacrificing warmth.) Underneath the bootee, wear your normal cycling shoes and only one or two pairs of thin socks between foot and shoe. Even with one thin sock, good insulated bootees will have your feet sweating in no time, no matter what the temperature.

Hands should be covered with well-insulated gloves or mittens and, although there are specially designed ones for cold-weather cycling (with a piece of fabric sewn on the back to wipe your nose!), good cross-country ski gloves made of materials like Gore-Tex® and Thinsulate® will do just fine.

When dressing for winter cycling, always don your bike shorts first. Over them should go a pair of long "tights" made of finely woven wool or one of the new breathable synthetics. The best cold-weather protection for the legs is from bib-style tights that come in various materials, each suited to a different temperature range. The built-in shoulder straps and high waist on the bib-style tights ensure that your lower back is always warm and covered, even when leaning over. The best cold-weather tights will have a stretchy, almost rubberized feel (not unlike a skin diver's wetsuit), with a thin inner lining of a more breathable polypropylene or cottonlike polyester. Following the theory that breathability is important even in cold weather, several manufacturers offer garments with wool on the backs of the legs and a less porous synthetic "windbreaker" material (preferably Gore-Tex® or its equivalent) on the front, where there is more exposure to chilling winds.

Winter cycling caps can be worn a dozen different ways, e.g., flaps up, flaps down, frontward or backward, and so on. Quality, knitted, wool ski caps also do the trick, since they do a good job of covering the ears. On the coldest of days, a face mask will protect the nose and cheeks from frostbite.

The brunt of the cold winter wind will be taken by the chest. Several layers of thin shirts, starting with a wool or polypropylene t-shirt and including a good, snug-fitting turtleneck are a must. Old pullovers and long-sleeved cycling jerseys work well, so long as they are formfitting and not too bulky. *Here's a tip:* As any good hobo can testify, a layer of newspaper is probably the best chest insulation you can use, and it can easily be discarded if the weather warms up.

Over it all should be a good cycling top, complete with zippered front, high ribbed collar, and rear zipper pockets. The best manufacturers of quality winter cycling wear are Assos (Swiss), Descente (Japanese), and Giordana (Italian).

EVERYTHING ELSE

Key accessories for the smart, well-equipped cyclist are gloves, cap, headband, and eyewear.

The best gloves are fingerless, made of leather, with ample padding in the palm area, and a webbed or fabric upper or back surface, fitted with an adjustable snap or velcro closure (and, of course, displaying a manufacturer or team logo). Many serious cyclists wear gloves every time they ride, as is evidenced by the deeply tanned circle on the back of the otherwise white hands of many a top pro.

Beyond advertising a sponsor or providing a weird tan that marks you as a dedicated cyclist, cycling gloves perform important functions that make them well worth the investment of ten to twenty dollars:

- They absorb hand moisture that can cause slippage on handlebars.
- They provide padding for the hands (great when riding on bumpy roads).
- They come in handy for brushing off tires when they pick up puncture-causing tar particles and other objects from dirty roads.
- They protect the hands (particularly the vulnerable palms) in case of a fall.

Caps and headbands provide another exposure opportunity for sponsors.
Presse Sports photo

Caps and headbands are designed to keep the sweat from running into the eyes, while, of course, providing the sponsor with another billboard opportunity that is hard to eliminate from photos. Cycling caps resemble painter's caps. The best ones are made of 100 percent cotton and have a small brim that can be worn up or down, in the front or back. Cheap imitations are skull-grabbing "beanies," while the real thing is comfortably large. A small elastic piece sewn on the back holds the cap in place with a thin, flat, inner cotton band covering the seams. When soaked with water, the cap is a great coolant on hot days, and its turned-down brim offers a certain amount of shading for the eyes or back of the neck (see above). The best cycling caps are made in Italy.

The item of equipment that has most recently become "standard issue" for serious cyclists is specially designed eyewear. Made in the "wraparound" style, they are lightweight and safe, with important standard features like shatterproof plastic, interchangeable lenses, and a thin foam lining across the inside top edge to act as a sweat barrier and keep them from slipping off. Today's most popular models, such as those distributed by Bollé or Oakley, run about $75 and offer frames in various flashy colors, several lens tints, and lightweight carrying cases.

SUMMARY

Like skiing, cycling is very much a style-conscious sport, offering many design and fabric options.

Also like skiing, the best cycling clothing is technically and functionally specific to the sport. The following proven design characteristics are important:

- *Cycling attire is formfitting.* The best designs take aerodynamic and anatomical characteristics into consideration.
- *Particular care must be taken in choosing attire for the contact points on the bicycle.* Thus, shoes must fit snugly and be positioned properly and shorts must be lined with chamois, with no cross seams, and worn next to the skin.
- *Materials must blend cooling and wicking ability with wind breaking.* Good cycling clothing is designed to "breathe," as well as block.

6 The Principles of Cycling

Remember this name: Francesco Moser.

On January 19, 1984, in the rarefied air of Mexico City, he pedaled a bicycle 50.808 km (31.57 miles), in exactly one hour. When he got off he said, "It's not quite as demanding as the last stretch of Paris–Roubaix. . . . I'll be ready to do it again in four days."

Moser's words were heard round the world. By January 23, the spectators' galleries of the Mexico City C.D.O.M. Velodrome, which had been only half-filled four days earlier, had standing room only. An international press link-up to over fifty countries was hastily installed. Three chartered planes from Italy, each filled with Moser's countrymen, flew halfway across the world just to see him pedal round and round.

The packed house watched breathlessly as Moser, perched on an outlandish-looking bicycle, circled smoothly around the track, lap after lap. Back in Italy, thousands sat transfixed, glued to their television sets, praying for Francesco.

Moser was in his 154th lap when the greatest hour of his life was over. He had pedaled 51.151 km (31.78 miles), breaking his own three-day-old world record, for the farthest distance ever pedaled unaided in one hour, by 343 meters.

The cycling world was stunned. Francesco Moser, a 34-year-old aging champion, had shattered the hour-distance record held by the great Belgian, Eddy Merckx.

Twelve years earlier, Merckx had agreed to tackle the record, one of the most difficult and prestigious in cycling, only because he was at the peak of his brilliant, seemingly superhuman career. His 49.23 km (30.6 miles), also set in Mexico City, was, in his words, "The hardest effort I have ever made in cycling."

That comment, coupled with Merckx' unsurpassed record in the sport (winner of five Tours de France, three World Championships, and at least one victory in every major classic), suggested that his record would stand as the ultimate human performance on a bicycle. It would take a future superstar of Merckx' stature to break it.

Moser's feat was highly controversial. He was a champion, but certainly no legend. He had bested brute force and athletic prowess with high technology. He was a harbinger of the future, and the cycling world both loved and hated him for it.

Moser, you see, was the first real champion to take an almost zero-based look at the principles of cycling. All the latest knowledge on aerodynamics, human physiology, kinesiology, and psychology were funneled through Moser into his bicycle during that one magic hour, and tradition went out the window.

Moser's quest took over a year. In addition to a scientific physical-training program that put him in the best shape of his life, he and his technicians spent weeks in secret laboratories, testing everything from tire profiles to jersey materials. The goal was to leave no stone unturned in pursuit of pushing back the barriers to absolute human-powered speed. The result was that by traditional measures, Moser looked like he had come from outer space. His bicycle flowed from an undersized front wheel to an oversized back wheel. Solid wheel disks and his pitched-forward and tightly crouched

Eddy Merckx (left) rode 49.3 km (30.6 miles) in one hour in 1972 on state-of-the-art equipment. Francesco Moser (right) broke Merckx' record twelve years later, by applying the principles of aerodynamics to radical new equipment designs. *Presse Sports photo*

position furthered the illusion of a flying wedge. Even his spinning feet were encased in aerodynamic bootees.

To say the least, Moser's appearance was radical. While the traditionalists scoffed, coaches, managers, athletes, and manufacturers scurried between the lab and the workbench. Machines had to be redesigned, bodies tested, and rules clarified: Just what *is* a bicycle, anyway?

What had started as a tentative exploration of aerodynamic principles, several years before Moser's records, suddenly opened the floodgates of innovation in the cycle sport. At the 1984 Olympics, radical differences became apparent in the equipment rooms of the various countries, and security became the watchword. Doors were locked, and guards posted.

In this chapter, we look at the basic elements and principles of cycling that Moser so successfully reexamined and turned to his advantage, bringing about the most radical changes in cycling technology since the turn of the century:

RESISTANCE, MECHANICAL EFFICIENCY, TECHNIQUE, PHYSIOLOGY, AND PSYCHOLOGY.

RESISTANCE

At speeds of over twenty mph, a cyclist on a level road with no headwind or tailwind will use 90 percent of energy expended overcoming *air resistance* (drag). It's no wonder that the challenge of reducing drag, by streamlining clothing and cycle, has been attacked with gusto.

Some interesting facts from research on the subject are:

1. Seventy percent of air resistance is caused by the rider's profile; 30 percent by the bicycle.

2. A normal road-racing bicycle, modified with aerodynamic components and a rider wearing aerodynamic clothing, can result in a saving of at least three minutes, thirty seconds over a twenty-five-mile course, with no increase in rider effort.

3. A cyclist "tucked" behind another can maintain the same speed as the leader while exerting 15–20 percent less energy. It becomes easier to go faster as the size of the pacer increases, be it a cyclist, motorcyclist, automobile, or, as in the case of Mile-a-Minute Murphy, a speeding locomotive!

Particularly in time trials, where one is racing only the clock, the effort to reduce wind drag has reached monumental proportions. In addition to aerodynamic equipment, clothing and body positions that help the cyclist "knife" through the air, wind drag can be reduced by another 5–10 percent by moving the venue to higher altitudes. That, along with slightly reduced gravity, is the reason Merckx, Moser, and other cyclists and athletes from other sports

DRAFTING. The lead rider "breaks the wind" for the following rider whose energy saving can be as much as 20 percent.

choose Mexico City (elevation 7,800 feet) for their world-record attempts.

The average cyclist who may be concerned with shaving off minutes rather than seconds must keep these basics in mind:

1. *Losing a few extra pounds* of body weight is far more effective in reducing wind drag than a big investment in aerodynamic equipment.

2. Assuming the proper *aerodynamic position on the bike* will result in the greatest energy savings (see Chapter 2). A rider can theoretically shave as much as four and one-half minutes off a twenty-five-mile time trial, just by riding with hands in the "drops," as opposed to on top of the brake levers. This point is further illustrated by comparing Greg LeMond and Laurent Fignon's body positions, in the final time trial of the 1989 Tour de France. LeMond beat Fignon in the 24.5-km test by a whopping fifty-eight seconds, to take the overall Tour win from Fignon by only eight seconds, the smallest victory margin in the race's history.

What if Fignon had also mounted a pair of Scott handlebar extenders like those LeMond used? Would he have been able to save those precious eight seconds?

To answer that question, *VeloNews* did a scientific experiment. Here are the findings as reported on August 18, 1989: "The results of wind-tunnel testing indicated that LeMond was 15 percent more

HOW THE PROS REDUCE WIND DRAG

Presse Sports photo

BODY
- Sleek, aerodynamic position (back flat, arms extended, head lowered)
- Shaved legs (and sometimes arms)

CLOTHING
- One-piece Lycra skin suit (no wrinkles, folds, or flapping)
- "Teardrop" aerodynamic helmet (pointed tail, sometimes in a blade shape, to cut through wind when head is lowered)
- Skintight fingerless gloves
- Laceless shoes, skintight ankle-socks (sometimes covered with aerodynamic booties)

BICYCLE
- Smaller front wheel (24 to 26 inches in diameter)
- Disk coverings fitted over spokes (reduces stability in crosswinds, particularly on front wheel)
- Aerodynamic spoke pattern on wheels (particularly if disks aren't used); flattened front spokes in radial pattern
- Components in aerodynamic shapes (brakes, cranks, hubs, pedals, derailleurs, stem, handlebars, seat post, rims, water bottle)
- Handlebar extenders to create an air-piercing point. Hands, elbows, and face close together, as opposed to an open-armed "scoop" with conventional bars

THE FANATIC'S FINISHING TOUCH:
Coat entire body with silicon spray

streamlined than Fignon. Translated into total drag forces (aerodynamic and rolling resistance), LeMond had a 3.5 percent advantage. LeMond completed the 24.5-km course in 26:57, compared to the 27:55 of Fignon—the American went 1.889 kph faster, or 3.587 percent! The imponderables of road time trials make it impossible to fully confirm these wind-tunnel results, but they certainly indicate that the power output of LeMond and Fignon was about the same—and that the aerodynamic superiority of LeMond's bar and helmet set-up did make the difference."

3. *Formfitting clothing* should always be worn. A skintight Lycra bodysuit can reduce drag by 6 percent over traditional cotton or wool clothing.

Rolling resistance is the next most significant form of resistance. It comes into play "where the rubber meets the road." The more tire surface area to make contact with the road, the more resistance you'll encounter, and the slower you'll go.

That's why racers choose narrow tubular tires (approximately 18 mm in width) and "dynamite" them to extremely high pressures

IDEAL INFLATION BASED ON LOAD AND TIRE SIZE

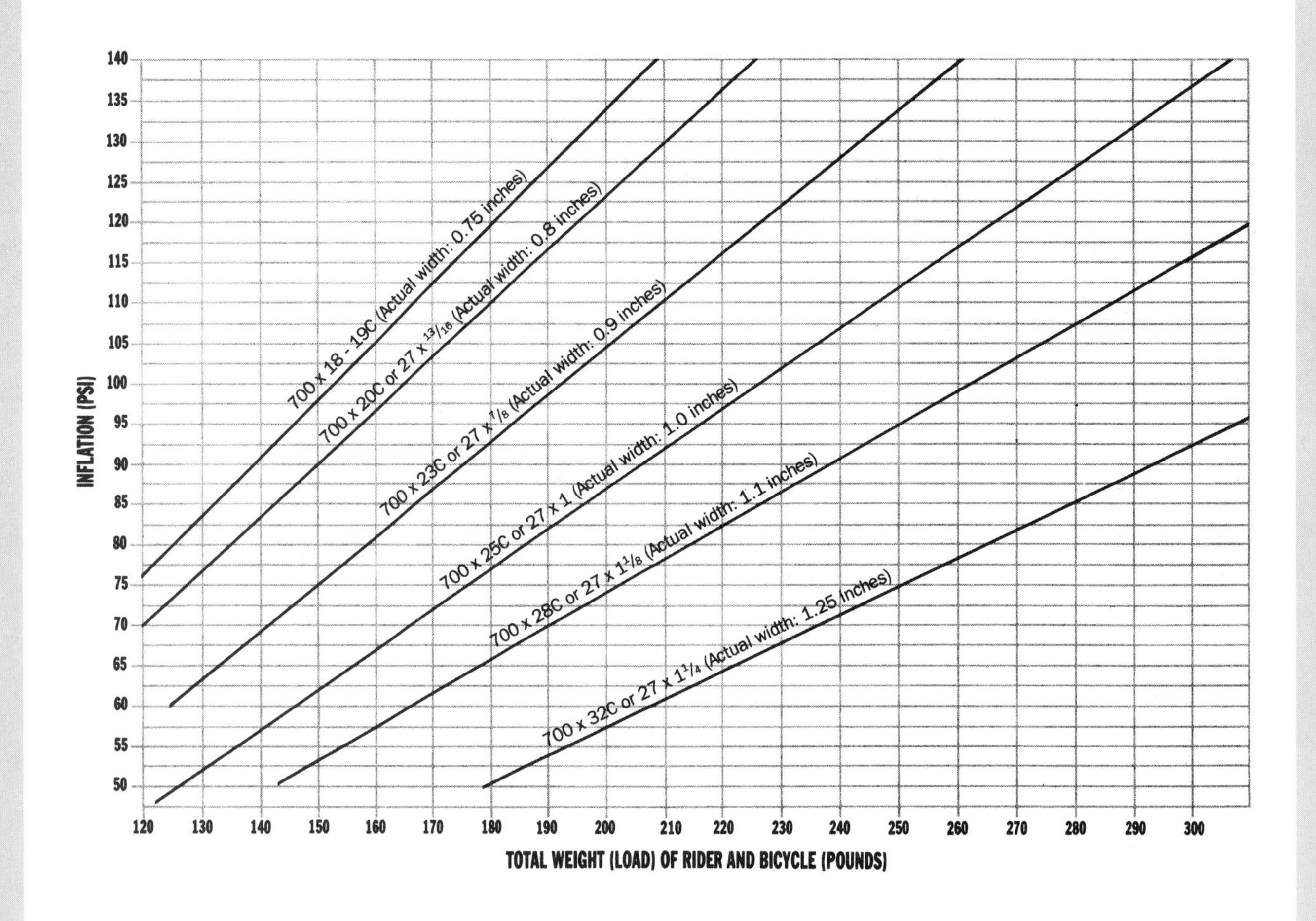

USING THE GRAPH

To determine the ideal inflation level for your tires, follow these steps:

1. Weigh yourself and your bike together (in pounds) by standing on a scale.

2. Measure the actual width of one of your inflated tires with a caliper or ruler.

3. Find the diagonal line on the graph that corresponds to this width (or is closest to it).

4. Find your load on the horizontal axis.

5. Locate the point where your load intersects the line representing your tire width.

6. Using this point, find your ideal inflation level on the vertical axis.

For example, the graph says that our 175-pound rider and 25-pound bike should use the following inflation levels for the different tire widths:

- 0.75 inch (700x18–19C): 134 psi
- 0.8 inch (700x20C or 27x$^{13}/_{16}$ inch): 123 psi
- 0.9 inch (700x23C or 27x$^{7}/_{8}$ inch): 104 psi
- 1 inch (700x25C or 27x1 inch): 87 psi
- 1.1 inch (700x28C or 27x$1^{1}/_{8}$ inch): 74 psi
- 1.25 inch (700x32C or 27x$1^{1}/_{4}$ inch): 57 psi

Interestingly, few riders intentionally use pressures as high as 123 psi (for the 700x20C or 27x$^{13}/_{16}$-inch tire in our example) or as low as 57 psi (for the 700x32C or 27x$1^{1}/_{4}$-inch tire).

From Bicycling Magazine, *June 1989*

WHEN MORE RUBBER MEETS THE ROAD

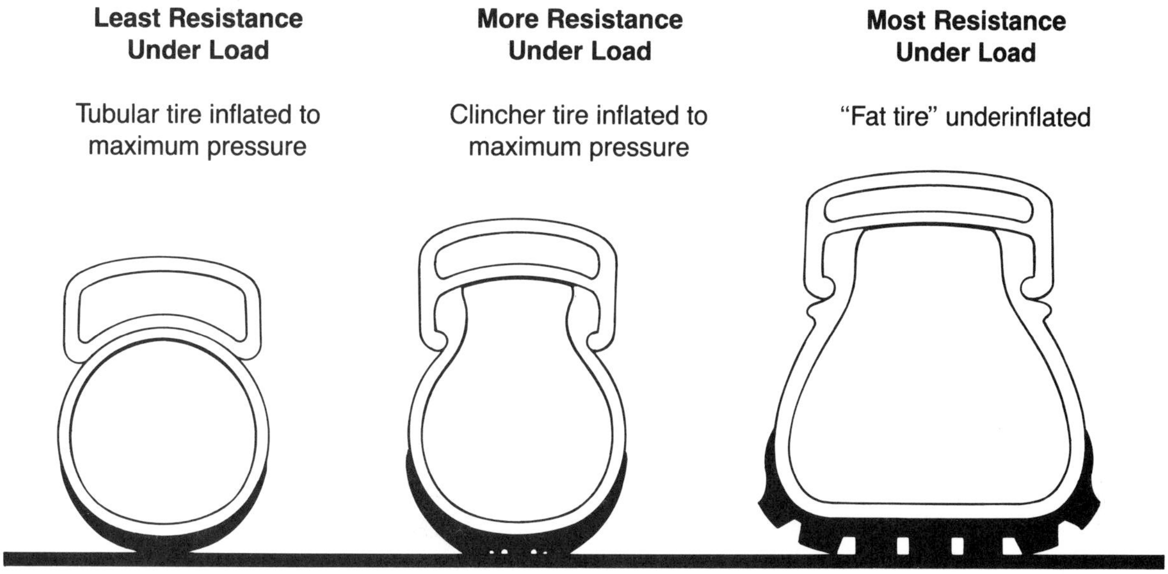

Least Resistance Under Load	More Resistance Under Load	Most Resistance Under Load
Tubular tire inflated to maximum pressure	Clincher tire inflated to maximum pressure	"Fat tire" underinflated

More surface contact increases rolling resistance

(over 120 pounds per square inch is not uncommon). It is also why fat-tire bicycles are so sluggish on smooth roads.

On the other hand, take care not to over-inflate tires in the zeal to go faster. This will result in increased possibility of blowout, higher road shock, and loss of traction, particularly around turns. Optimum pressures for the most popular sized clincher tires under load (supporting total weight of bicycle, rider, and gear) are presented in the following graph. Properly inflated tires will minimize resistance, be safer, and improve handling.

A second source of rolling resistance is the friction of moving parts, such as chain over sprockets and ball bearings in the hubs, bottom bracket, and rear derailleur (see section on mechanical efficiency, later in this chapter).

The most common form of resistance known to the cyclist (and mankind in general) is gravity. Anyone who has struggled up a steep hill can attest to this. As the road turns upward, gravity begins to replace air resistance as the dominant force in slowing a cyclist. Aerodynamic helmets and disk wheels are useless at slow-climbing speeds.

The two factors that determine climbing ability are:

- *Physical:* high power-to-weight ratio (light weight, low body fat, strong muscles) and finely tuned cardiovascular system (fitness always shows when going uphill).

- *Mechanical:* low bike weight and low rolling resistance, particularly from wheels and tires.

MECHANICAL EFFICIENCY

Any discussion of mechanical efficiency (or "mechanical advantage") begins with gearing. It is the mechanical advantage and efficiency produced by special gear ratios that allow the off-road cyclist to pedal up a rock-strewn, 20 percent incline, at less than a walking pace and, at the other end of the spectrum, helped John Howard set his 152.28 mph bicycle speed record on the salt flats at Bonneville.

The principle behind multiple gearing on a bicycle is that gears allow a cyclist to maintain the same energy-efficient pedaling cadence, regardless of terrain, speed, and atmospheric conditions.

Cadence refers to pedaling speed and is expressed in revolutions per minute ("rpm"). One complete turn of the pedals is a revolution. Physiologists have determined that the most efficient pedaling cadence is between eighty-five and ninety-five revolutions per minute (that's a fairly rapid one and one-half turns per second). At this rate, heart, lungs, and muscles are working together like all the parts of a well-tuned engine.

Speed is another matter. Maintaining a cadence of ninety rpm uphill, as opposed to maintaining the same tempo down the other side, could mean a difference in speed of forty miles per hour! The same cadence is possible on both the up-and-down slopes of the mountain, because of variable gearing: Low gears going up, high gears coming down, ninety rpm the whole time.

In cycling, gearing is expressed in somewhat confusing *ratios.* A bicycle gear ratio is computed as follows:

$$\text{Gear Ratio} = \frac{\text{Number of Chainwheel Teeth}}{\text{Number of Rear Sprocket Teeth}} \times \text{Wheel Size}$$

Thus, the ratio for your highest gear (when your chain is on the biggest chainring on the front, usually fifty to fifty-three teeth, and the smallest sprocket on the back, usually twelve to fourteen teeth) would be computed as follows:

$$\frac{52 \text{ (Chainring)}}{13 \text{ (Sprocket)}} \times 27 \text{ (wheel size)} = 108 \text{ (gear ratio)}$$

Just so you know, if you multiply the gear ratio (here 108) by Pi (3.14) you will get the actual *roll-out* of that gear (the distance, in inches, that your bike will travel during one complete revolution of the pedals).

If you want to be precise as to how far your bicycle will travel during one pedal revolution, in each of your gears, use the actual circumference of your wheel (measuring around the outside of the fully inflated tire, not twenty-seven inches as the wheel size) and multiply that number by the ratio of chainring teeth to sprocket teeth (you don't need Pi for this one).

It is unlikely, however, that you will ever need this esoteric information, unless you want to talk shop with the technical editor of a cycling magazine. The important thing is to understand that gear ratios are computed in order to establish a useful *range* of gears for your specific riding needs. It is possible to have twelve combinations on your bike that yield only a half-dozen ratios. In that case, your twelve-speed is really only a six-speed. The best way to check to see how many gears your bike *really* has is to determine your own ratios using a precalculated gear table for twenty-seven-inch wheels (twenty-six inch, in the case of off-road bikes). See table below.

GEAR-RATIOS CHART

Number of Teeth in Freewheel Sprocket	*Number of Teeth in Chainwheel*																		
	38	**39**	**40**	**41**	**42**	**43**	**44**	**45**	**46**	**47**	**48**	**49**	**50**	**51**	**52**	**53**	**54**	**55**	**56**
12	85.5	87.8	90	92.2	94.5	96.7	99	101.3	103.5	105.7	108	110.2	112.5	114.8	117	119.2	121.5	123.7	126
13	78.9	81	83.1	85.2	87.2	89.3	91.4	93.5	95.5	97.6	99.7	101.8	103.8	105.9	108	110.1	112.2	114.2	116.3
14	73.3	75.2	77.1	79.1	81	82.9	84.9	86.8	88.7	90.6	92.6	94.5	96.4	98.4	100.3	102.2	104.1	106.1	108
15	68.4	70.2	72	73.8	75.6	77.4	79.2	81	82.8	84.6	86.4	88.2	90	91.8	93.6	95.4	97.2	99	100.8
16	64.1	65.8	67.5	69.2	70.9	72.6	74.3	75.9	77.6	79.3	81	82.7	84.4	86.1	87.8	89.4	91.1	92.8	94.5
17	60.4	61.9	63.5	65.1	66.7	68.3	69.9	71.5	73.1	74.6	76.2	77.8	79.4	81	82.6	84.2	85.8	87.4	88.9
18	57	58.5	60	61.5	63	64.5	66.0	67.5	69	70.5	72	73.5	75	76.5	78	79.5	81	82.5	84
19	54	55.4	56.8	58.3	59.7	61.1	62.5	63.9	65.4	66.8	68.2	69.6	71.1	72.5	73.9	75.3	76.7	78.2	79.6
20	51.3	52.7	54	55.4	56.7	58.1	59.4	60.8	62.1	63.5	64.8	66.2	67.5	68.9	70.2	71.6	72.9	74.3	75.6
21	48.9	50.1	51.4	52.7	54	55.3	56.6	57.9	59.1	60.4	61.7	63	64.3	65.6	66.9	68.1	69.4	70.7	72
22	46.6	47.9	49.1	50.3	51.5	52.8	54	55.2	56.5	57.7	58.9	60.1	61.4	62.6	63.8	65	66.3	67.5	68.7
23	44.6	45.8	47	48.1	49.3	50.5	51.7	52.8	54	55.2	56.3	57.5	58.7	59.9	61	62.2	63.4	64.6	65.7
24	42.8	43.9	45	46.1	47.3	48.4	49.5	50.6	51.8	52.9	54	55.1	56.3	57.4	58.5	59.6	60.8	61.9	63
25	41	42.1	43.2	44.3	45.4	46.4	47.5	48.6	49.7	50.8	51.8	52.9	54	55.1	56.2	57.2	58.3	59.4	60.5
26	39.5	40.5	41.5	42.6	43.6	44.7	45.7	46.7	47.8	48.8	49.8	50.9	51.9	53	54	55	56.1	57.1	58.2
27	38	39	40	41	42	43	44	45	46	47	48	49	50	51	52	53	54	55	56
28	36.6	37.6	38.6	39.5	40.5	41.5	42.4	43.4	44.4	45.3	46.3	47.3	48.2	49.2	50.1	51.1	52.1	53	54
29	35.4	36.3	37.2	38.2	39.1	40	41	41.9	42.8	43.8	44.7	45.6	46.6	47.5	48.4	49.3	50.3	51.2	52.1
30	34.2	35.1	36	36.9	37.8	38.7	39.6	40.5	41.4	42.3	43.2	44.1	45	45.9	46.8	47.7	48.6	49.5	50.4
31	33.1	34	34.8	35.7	36.6	37.5	39.3	39.2	40.1	40.9	41.8	42.7	43.5	44.4	45.3	46.2	47	47.9	48.8
32	32.1	32.9	33.8	34.6	35.4	36.3	37.1	38	38.8	39.7	40.5	41.3	42.2	43	43.9	44.7	45.6	46.4	47.3
33	31.1	31.9	32.7	33.5	34.4	35.2	36	36.8	37.6	38.5	39.3	40.1	40.9	41.7	42.5	43.4	44.2	45	45.8
34	30.2	31	31.8	32.6	33.4	34.1	34.9	35.7	36.5	37.3	38.1	38.9	39.7	40.5	41.3	42.1	42.9	43.7	44.5

True cyclists never describe bicycle gears in automotive terms. There is no "first," "second," or "third gear" on a bicycle—and most certainly no reverse! Cycling gearing is expressed in terms of *ratios* and *ranges,* such as "a low of 36," "a range between 56 and 102," or a "top gear of 108," and the gear *range* is a good indication of the kind of riding one intends to do. Generally:

- *Racers will prefer a higher range of gears with close spacing between each gear* (e.g., a range between 50 and 110, with twelve or fourteen speeds. Gear ratios will vary from three to five points apart).
- *Tourists will want a wider range of gears to give them lower lows,* the "alpine" gearing they prefer for climbing (e.g., a range between 35 and 100, with twelve speeds).
- *The off-road or ATB rider will want a wide, low range,* since they need extremely low alpine gearing to get them up steep hills on loose surfaces (e.g., a range between 25 and 90, with eighteen speeds).

The accepted vernacular when talking about gearing is to refer to a gear ratio by the chainring/sprocket combination. Thus, a low gear of "forty-two/twenty-one" refers to an inside chainring with forty-two teeth, in combination with the largest sprocket on the freewheel, having twenty-one teeth. Once you've developed an understanding of ratios and how they relate to pedaling and sprocket sizes, it is far easier and simpler to discuss gearing by sprocket combinations, rather than by ratios.

Bike-shop buzzwords aside, it is important and useful to develop your own gear chart. Until gear selection and shifting become second nature, cyclists will often mount their personal gear chart on the handlebar stem, for easy reference while riding. Examples of such gear charts, as selected by serious pros, tourists, and off-road riders are on page 85.

Chain alignment is a key factor in optimal mechanical efficiency of the drive train (see photos on page 86).

As the chain is shifted from sprocket to sprocket, the front-to-rear angle of the chain changes. The drive train operates most efficiently when the "chainline" is straightest. At the most extreme angles, known as "maximum deflection" (e.g., from outside chainring to inside rear sprocket and from inside chainring to smallest outside rear sprocket) the chain and gears don't work well, even on the most expensive bikes.

Use of these extreme gear settings will hasten wear on sprocket teeth and chain. Furthermore, the chain will often rub and clank, both on the adjacent sprockets and the inside of the front derailleur cage. For these reasons, the two most extreme sprocket combina-

PROFESSIONAL (FOURTEEN-SPEED)

Sprocket Teeth	Chainring Teeth 42	53
	Gear Ratios	
13	87.2	110.1
14	81	102.2
15	75.6	95.4
16	70.9	89.4
17	66.7	84.2
19	59.7	75.3
21	54	68.1

TOURIST (TWELVE-SPEED)

Sprocket Teeth	Chainring Teeth 42	52
	Gear Ratios	
14	81	100.3
16	70.9	87.8
18	63	78
21	54	66.9
24	47.3	58.5
28	40.5	50.1

OFF ROAD (EIGHTEEN-SPEED–TWENTY-SIX-INCH WHEELS)

Sprocket Teeth	Chainring Teeth 28	38	48
		Gear Ratios	
14	52	70.6	89.1
15	48.5	65.9	83.2
17	42.8	58.1	73.4
20	36.4	49.4	62.4
23	31.6	43	54.3
28	26	35.3	44.6

tions (outside to inside, inside to outside) are rarely used on ten-, twelve-, and fourteen-speed bikes.

Also, depending upon sprocket sizes, extreme deflection may be present on more than the two outermost gears. For example, on a mountain bike with triple chainrings, using the inside chainring with the *three* outermost rear sprockets is not recommended.

CHAIN ALIGNMENT AND DEFLECTION

EXTREME DEFLECTION
(smallest to smallest)

DIRECT ALIGNMENT

EXTREME DEFLECTION
(biggest to biggest)

MASTERING THE GEARING MYSTIQUE

1. Each front-to-back sprocket combination gives a different speed, gear, or gear *ratio:* Thus, two chainrings × six sprockets makes a twelve-speed (twelve possible combinations).
2. Lowest gear: smallest chainring on front, with largest sprocket on rear. Easiest pedaling for up hills.
3. Highest gear: biggest chainring on front, with smallest sprocket on rear. Hardest pedaling for down hills.
4. Middle gears: everything in between.
5. Fifth gear: overdrive on an automobile; meaningless on a bike.
6. Gear ratio: a number that is determined by this formula:

$$\frac{\text{Number of Teeth on Chainring (front)}}{\text{Number of Teeth on Sprocket (rear)}} \times \text{Wheel Size (inches)}$$

Gear ratios are used to compare sprocket combinations.

7. Gear Table or Gear Chart: Work-saving device that makes it unnecessary to do your own gear-ratio calculations.
8. Overlap: When one gear ratio comes out the same or nearly the same as another, by using a different combination of chainring and sprocket. For example, a 52 × 20 yields a gear ratio of 70.2 and a 42 × 16 yields a gear ratio of 70.9. These gears are essentially the same or "overlap."

THE ANGELS

It stands to reason that the best climbers are generally small and always lean. Luis Herrera of Colombia weighs scarcely 130 pounds and, with a height of under five and one-half feet, easily gets lost in the pack. Until the mountains that is.

Like the other diminutive climbing machines that battle for the prestigious Polka Dot jersey of the "king of the mountains" in the Tour de France, Herrera is referred to as an "Angel" because he can pedal so furiously toward the heavens.

A few times in the history of the Tour an angel has won the race. But this has always been when the route has been particularly mountainous or when the riders with great overall talent have been absent or off form.

The high-speed, flatland racing and the horsepower demands of time trialing usually leaves the climbing specialists far behind. No, an angel's glory must come in the clouds.

Cor Vos Photo

SHIFTING TECHNIQUE

After you understand the mystique of gearing (see above table), it is time to master the technique of shifting. This can only be achieved through practice on the bike. However, here are some tips that will speed the learning process:

1. *Study the action.* Clamp your bike in a repair stand. With your left hand, turn the pedals, and with your right hand, work the gear levers. Note what happens when you pull the right lever back. (The chain is "jumped up" the freewheel sprockets and into lower gears.) Push the lever forward and the chain "jumps down" the sprockets, into higher gears. The left-hand lever controls the front chainrings. Pull it back and the chain will "jump" to the biggest chainring, push it forward and it will "drop" to the smallest.

2. *Start riding in the middle gear.* At first, ride with the chain on the inside front chainring (or middle, on a bike with triple chainrings) and a middle freewheel sprocket. Count your cadence to get a feel for the optimal ninety rpm.

3. *Practice shifting with the right gear lever first.* It controls more ratios (six rear sprockets, as opposed to two or three front chainrings). You will get a better feel for the difference in gears this way.

4. *Practice with the left lever next.* Because there is more variation between front chainring teeth, this shift will take longer. (Note:

many cyclists prefer gear ratios that run through the sprockets on the back with the inside chainring before shifting to the outer chainring, for a progressively higher second range of ratios.)

5. *Simulate malfunction.* Purposely shift into the gears where chain deflection is greatest (one lever all the way forward, the other all the way back). Note the clicking and rubbing sounds. This is what you want to avoid.

6. *Trim your gears.* If you don't have index or "click" shifting, it is often necessary to fine-tune your shift. With subtle moves of one or both of the shift levers, you can stay in the chosen gear and eliminate rubbing or clicking noises caused by the variations in chain deflection.

7. *Shift before you strain.* Size up the terrain and *anticipate* the need to shift into a lower gear before the hill really gets to you. Even the best bikes won't shift properly, if you are applying full pressure to the pedals.

8. *Practice makes perfect.* Basic shifting can often be mastered during just a few sessions. If not, be patient. Your learning curve should be similar to your mastery of shifting a manual car transmission.

Mechanical efficiency—fully realizing the mechanical advantages of your bicycle—is dependent upon the smooth working of all

PERFORMANCE CHECKLIST

1. *Keep those bearings rolling.* Ball bearings are found in hubs, bottom bracket, headset, rear derailleur wheels, and freewheel. They run best when "packed" in light grease, and they should be repacked every 10,000 miles—sooner if riding in wet weather or if any binding is noticed by spinning the part in the hands.
2. *Follow the "Chain Commandments"* (Chapter 3).
3. *To your wheels be true.* Wheels that wobble slow you down. Make sure wheels run true and rims are free from dents and dings.
4. *Keep your brakes in line.* Brake shoes rub on the rim if a side caliper is not springing into the open position when the lever is released. Use a thin "cone wrench" to reach the adjustment nut on the brake, where it is attached to the frame. The entire brake can be centered by rotating the cone wrench in one direction or the other.

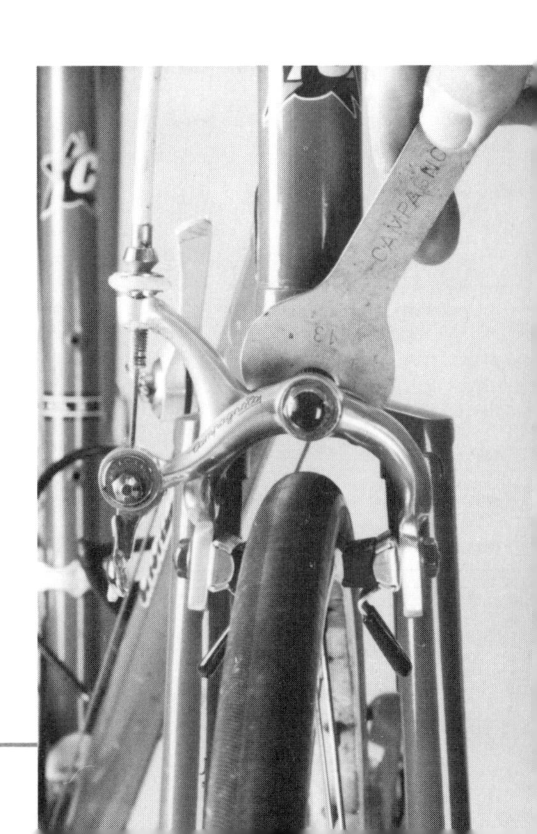

Most brakes can be centered over the rim by using a narrow "cone" wrench to rotate the entire brake caliper assembly to one side or the other. *Seth Goltzer photo*

its moving components. Facing is a brief checklist to help ensure that your bike is in top form.

PEDALING TECHNIQUE

The principles of proper cycling encompass everything from bicycle adjustment to physical conditioning to racing tactics. However, the most basic and important element of all is *pedaling technique.* As Greg LeMond put it in his *Complete Book of Bicycling:* "Anybody can get onto a bike and turn the crankarms, but that's as close to good pedaling technique as taking a tennis racket and swinging it wildly. Good pedaling technique is the heart of the cycling exercise, and is as important for the part-time fitness enthusiast as for a professional racer."

The way you pedal has more to do with defining your cycling style and stature than the equipment you ride or the clothes you wear. It's not unlike the perfect swing of a great golf pro, the fluid launch of a World Series fastball or the clean, efficient carved turns of a World Cup skier. Some seem born with the talent, while others may strive for a lifetime and never quite get it. But there is no doubt that everyone can improve their basic pedaling technique.

The artistry of pedaling is the ability to "stay ahead" of (actually on top of) the pedals with the feet, applying direct and near-perpendicular force to them at practically every point of the revolution.

Most people's concept of riding a bike is pushing down on the pedals, first one side, then the other. But proper pedaling is a rotary, not an up-and-down motion, and when the feet are attached to the pedals via a toe clip or shoe/pedal system, it becomes possible to pull up and around with one leg and simultaneously down and around with the other. Even near the top of the stroke, when the cranks are perpendicular to the ground (the "dead spot"), a degree of lateral force can be applied before the next down (or more properly "down-and-around") stroke. Although this lateral force is far less than that applied on the full downstroke, when the leg's total power is utilized, it enables the technically proficient pedaler to power through the upper and lower dead spots, with no exaggerated effort or perceptible loss of rhythm.

Are you a good pedaler? Here's how to find out:

1. Make sure you have the proper position on your bike (Chapter 2).
2. Make sure you are wearing bike shoes that hold your feet firmly on the pedals and in the correct position (Chapter 3).
3. Put your bike in a middle-range gear (e.g., 42 × 15) and head

BIOMECHANICS OF PEDALING

(Force indicated by direction of arrows)

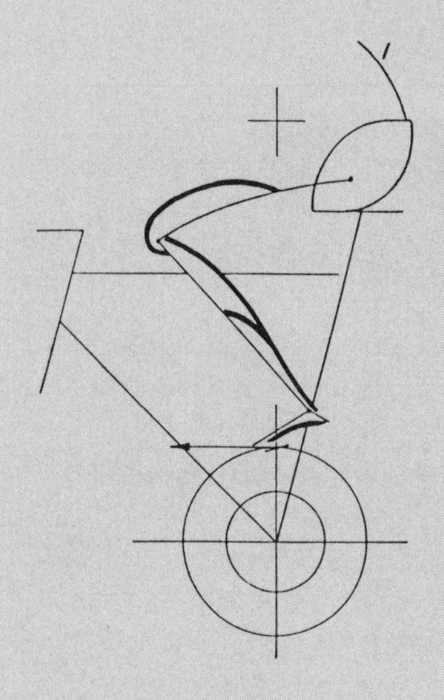

Fig. 1 Dead spot at top of stroke, minimal forward force applied

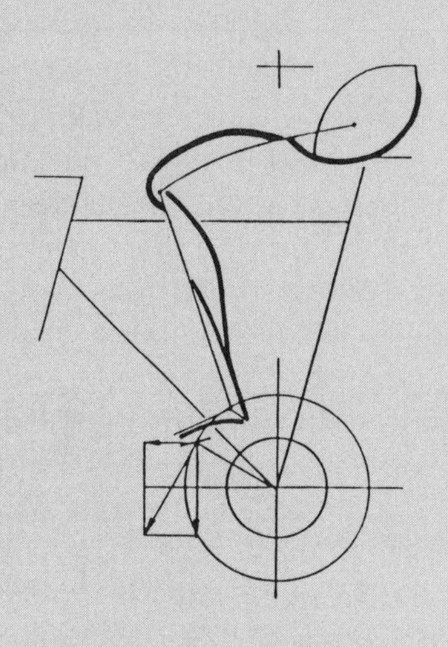

Fig. 2 Power portion of downstroke, strong force applied forward and down

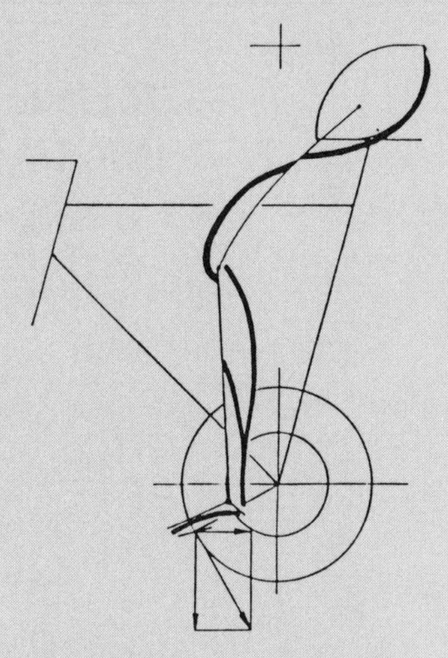

Fig. 3 Lower portion of power downstroke, strong force applied down and pulling back

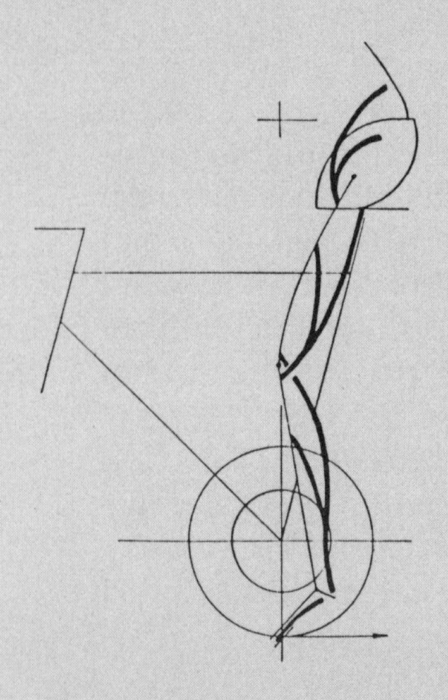

Fig. 4 Dead spot at bottom of stroke, minimal rearward force applied

Fig. 5 Upstroke using pulling force as leg comes up

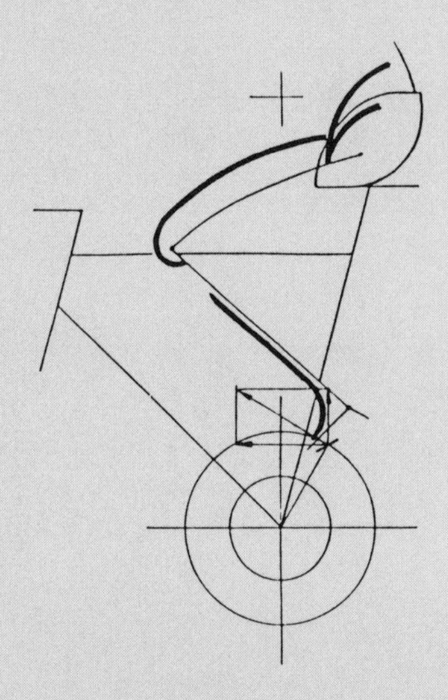

Fig. 6 Forward-pulling force near the top of the upstroke helps power through the upper dead spot

Drawings adapted from C.O.N.I. Central Sports School of the U.C.I.

down a slope that will have your legs spinning like crazy (over 130 rpm) to keep up with the pedals. What happens just before you get "spun out" (cannot spin the pedals any faster)?

Are you bouncing on the saddle?
Are you feeling "gaps" in your pedaling as you turn faster and faster?
Most beginners will have to answer yes to at least one of these questions. Imperfections in the pedal stroke are magnified as rpm increase.

Bouncing in the saddle is symptomatic of an inability to smoothly apply pressure to the pedals *through the entire rotation.* The pedals are driving the legs, not the other way around, as it should be. Hesitation at the upper and lower dead spots are creating pauses or gaps that exaggerate the bouncing.

Here's how to smooth out your "pedal action":

1. *Concentrate.* Use mental imaging to picture your legs and feet turning the pedals in perfect circles while you are seated firmly in the saddle.

2. *Pedal around,* not up and down. Pedals are best driven by an alternating pushing forward and pulling back as they complete a revolution. There should be no pause at the top or bottom of the stroke.

3. *Let your feet help.* The power of pedaling comes primarily from the thighs, but the ankles and feet can be used to extend the power at the end of the stroke. Think of the feet as helping the thighs exert force in a circle. Alternately and almost automatically, toes will be pointed, ankles flexed, and heels dropped at the proper stages of each revolution. However, exaggerated attempts to drop the ankles just before reaching the top of the pedal stroke won't help if it's not part of your natural flow of movement.

4. *Keep a quiet upper body.* A good pedaler doesn't get his whole body into the act. A bobbing head, rolling shoulders, rocking torso, and wiggling hips are great on the dance floor, but they are a waste of energy on the bicycle. Concentrate on sitting rock steady with the power coming from the muscles of the hips and thighs.

5. *Practice "spinning."* Developing smooth pedaling can be helped by regular spinning exercises. During each training session, practice riding for one mile on a flat road in a low enough gear to maintain 120+ rpm. During this mile, concentrate on pedaling *around,* using the techniques suggested above, with no bouncing on the saddle or gaps in the pedal stroke. Some top cyclists like to begin the season with several weeks of "spinning," on lower than normal gears, over slightly rolling terrain. This helps smooth out the pedal

FAUSTO COPPI: MASTER PEDALER

Presse Sports photo

The greatest Italian champion to ever live was two-time Tour de France winner Fausto Coppi. As a poor youth growing up in a small village in Italy, Coppi was thin, awkward, and unhealthy, but he had powerful legs and when he got on a bicycle Coppi was somehow transformed into a picture of power and grace.

French commentator Roger Bastide, was lyrical in his description of the "Championissimo": "With his firm, stiff and awkward feet which were somehow too big for him he was like an albatross with wings folded back perched on the bridge of a ship. He was himself only when he was on his bike. His long limbs would then turn into an unbelievable harmony of lines. More than that, there was a sort of lightness or smoothness of a divine being in his pedaling."

Even Jacques Goddet, codirector of the Tour de France, couldn't help but comment with awe on the Italian's special style. In the 1950 pages of *L'Equipe* Goddet wrote: "Coppi has appeared, a supernatural rider on these frightful roads used only by ancient horse-drawn carts. He wiped out these hateful roads as if invisible shock absorbers isolated him from them. Here, where for 20 years I have watched the greatest champions falter like ships on a reef and the most courageous riders lose their form and look like scissor grinders, Fausto became sublime. With a favorable wind along the last 40 kilometers, his pedal stroke seemed so airy that his wheels seemed literally to fly above the chaos of the cobbles."

stroke and develop the proper rotary-power pattern, before moving up to the higher gears demanded for racing.

Pedaling is also affected by the length of the cranks fitted to the bicycle. Crank lengths for road racing come in standard millimeter sizes ranging from 170 mm to 180 mm in 2.5 mm increments. Crank length should be chosen according to leg length, as follows:

INSEAM (CROTCH TO FLOOR)	CRANK LENGTH
74–80 cm (29–31½ inches)	170 mm (6¾ inches)
81–86 cm (32–34 inches)	172.5 mm (6⅞ inches)
87–93 cm (34¼–36½ inches)	175 mm (7 inches)
Above 93 cm (36½ inches)	177.5 (7⅛ inches) to 180 mm (8 inches)

Although these are the sizes recommended to achieve optimum biomechanical efficiency, many racers and almost all mountain bike riders will select cranks that are a size or two longer than recommended. The reason is simple: greater mechanical advantage. Longer cranks provide increased leverage and decrease the muscular force needed to turn the pedals in the same gear. This is particularly useful in time trials and in climbing, where power is at a premium. The downside of longer cranks is that they are more difficult to "spin" rapidly, thereby decreasing the ability to accelerate quickly.

Some of the greatest champions, starting with master pedaler Jacques Anquetil, frequently fitted longer cranks, to maximize performance under different conditions. Eddy Merckx went from 175 mm cranks, in most conditions, to 177.5 mm cranks, in time trials and in mountain stages of major tours.

No discussion of pedaling would be complete without mention of the one time when it needs to be modified—during climbing. Climbing technique is highly individualized and has much to do with cardiovascular capacity, power-to-weight ratio, body type, and level of fitness. See the sidebar for pointers on good climbing technique.

Hinault (left) and Moser (right) show two types of good climbing technique on the same ascent, in the 1985 Giro d'Italia. *Presse Sports photo*

CLIMBING TECHNIQUE

Technique	Long Climbs	Short Climbs
POSITION	• Sit toward back of saddle • Hands on top of bars • Out of saddle to relieve pressure when road is steeper	• Out of saddle, upper body vertical, arms move bike back and forth • Arms wide to help breathing
PEDALING	• Arms wide to help breathing • Drop ankles at top of stroke • Relax more on upstroke	• Legs alternate between driving and resting
GEARING	• Choose what's comfortable, generally lower rpm than on flat	• Same
PACE	• Steady, avoid accelerations • Climb at own pace	• Same • Same

PHYSIOLOGY

The beauty of cycling is that it does not exclude participation by body type. In the Tour de France, for example, the smallest rider is hardly bigger than a jockey and the largest is usually tall enough to be a guard on a basketball team.

Here are some of the physiological characteristics common to cyclists:

1. *Lean and mean.* Body types are on the sinewy side, although track sprinters can look like boxers. Muscles, particularly those of the inner thigh (quadriceps), will show overdevelopment.

2. *Fast twitch/Slow twitch.* Muscle fiber makeup is inherited and is usually an equal balance between white fibers (fast twitch) and red fibers (slow twitch). Fast twitch fibers are needed for explosive efforts, slow twitch for repetitive effort. Both forms can be improved somewhat but the proportion won't change. Speed, an important element in racing, comes more naturally to those with a high proportion of fast-twitch fibers.

3. *Lever legs.* There have been great cyclists with long legs and with short legs, in proportion to their bodies. In theory, long thighs and big feet create more powerful leg levers.

4. *Old enough, strong enough.* The fully mature body responds better to the power demands of cycling. Racing cyclists reach their peak in their mid-twenties. Raymond Poulidor of France placed third in the 1976 Tour, when he was forty.

Cycling talent has been characterized as coming 75 percent from heredity and 25 percent from training. While muscle strength, cardiovascular efficiency, and body-fat ratios can be improved dramatically by training, it helps to come equipped with the basics. But cycling is not without its share of stories of how sheer determination and hard work have overcome the odds.

PSYCHOLOGY

It is no secret that among athletes trained to perfection, there must still be winners and losers. A champion at the highest level of the sport must have the rare combination of physical ability and the psyche to exploit it.

Bernard Hinault, a five-time Tour de France winner and a man who should know what it takes, says that the key psychological qualities required to become a great cycling champion are *willpower, courage,* and the *ability to withstand pain.*

It was willpower that enabled Francesco Moser to focus on the goal of breaking Eddy Merckx' world hour-distance record. As is the case with most winners, Moser knew deep inside that he could accomplish this feat. But willpower was the essential element that

turned him into a student of his own performance and made him determined to reach his goal.

Greg LeMond has emerged as a master of courage. After nearly being killed in a 1987 hunting accident, LeMond faced a long, hard trail to regain the form he had been in when he became the first American to win the Tour de France the season before. Accidents and operations, over a two-year period, kept knocking him back. In 1989, his return to health was marred by substandard performances and an increasingly loud chorus saying he could never again win the Tour de France. Despite all this negative feedback, LeMond's courage never faltered, and his 1989 victory over Fignon in the Tour and a who's who of cycling greats in the subsequent World Pro Road Championship, in Chambery, France, bore this out.

Eddy Merckx, arguably the greatest cyclist of all time, was believed to be immune to pain. It never seemed to touch him like it did the others. In 1975, Merckx, already a five-time Tour de France winner, was in form and expected to be the first to win six.

Before the start of the seventeenth stage, in the Alps, Merckx landed on his face in an awkward fall. The broken cheekbone he suffered put him in so much pain that his lead was overtaken by the Frenchman Bernard Thevenet, on a very tough stage to the top of one of the Tour's legendary climbs, the Puy de Dome.

For the remaining week of racing, Merckx struggled on, dealing with the most pain he had ever experienced in the Tour or elsewhere, but he never gave up. He ended up second in Paris but never used the pain he was in as an excuse for not winning his last Tour.

SUMMARY

Cycling at its top level is a highly technical sport. As Francesco Moser proved in shattering the world hour-distance record, a thorough understanding and application of cycling's most basic physical principles will lead to the best possible performance.

Overcoming resistance, understanding the mechanical efficiencies and advantages of proper gearing and well-maintained equipment, developing proper pedaling technique, and maximizing one's physiological and psychological potential are the ingredients of a champion.

7 Basic Conditioning

SETTING THE GOAL

Few people will purchase a bicycle if they don't have some kind of goal in mind, however vague it may be. The gamut runs from "I want to shed a few pounds and ride with my kids once in a while," to, "I want to win the Tour de France."

Setting a realistic goal, outlining a plan for reaching it through a series of manageable steps and moving from one to the next as each is accomplished, is the way most people get things done. Slowly but surely they achieve their objectives, however grandiose.

SETTING GOALS

- Aim high
- Be realistic
- Commit
- Reassess
- Recommit
- Be satisfied

Greg LeMond, the first American to do what many thought was impossible for an American—win the Tour de France—had not even imagined such a feat was possible until he had a couple of racing seasons under his belt. However, in 1977, when he was just sixteen and being hailed as a hotshot junior racer out of Nevada, Greg wrote his goals on three pieces of paper: By 1981, he wanted to be a professional, and by age twenty-five (1987) he wanted to win the World Championships and the Tour de France, a "double" that only a few great European cyclists had accomplished.

Pretty ambitious for a young kid. But obviously LeMond had something special. How many of us can say we achieve our loftiest goals—and ahead of schedule at that? But LeMond was able to turn his dreams to reality and that puts him in the company of history's great achievers, a select few who through a combination of high focus, energy, persistence, and talent have reached the ultimate in sport, art, music, science, or industry.

The first step in achieving a goal is setting one that is realistic and achievable in light of your capabilities and circumstances. If you do not truly believe you can succeed, you never will. So set goals accordingly. If you are forty years old, have four kids and a nine-to-five job, you will never win the Tour de France, but you can do this: *Ride ten miles on a bicycle in less than forty minutes.*

FITNESS THROUGH CYCLING

This chapter is about basic conditioning for the cyclist. Riding ten miles in forty minutes means you can pedal at fifteen mph for a respectable length of time. It's enough to work up a good sweat and you will be burning calories at the rate of between 400 and 500 per

Greg LeMond won his first World Championship in 1983 (top) and took his first Tour de France in 1986. He did both a year ahead of his goal. *Presse Sports photo*

hour. This is the stepping-off point for basic cycling conditioning.

A strong healthy kid with an athletic background might be able to meet this challenge the first time out. A sixty-five-year-old grandfather may have to train day in and day out for two years, but he can do it too. Riding ten miles in forty minutes is impossible only for those who physically cannot ride a bike (or believe they can't).

If you want to give cycling a serious try and have a reasonable interest in learning how to improve, but do not have a specific goal in mind, take the ten miles in forty minutes challenge as your first step. It can be accomplished through a few sessions, each less than an hour in time. But here's what you should do before you break out the stopwatch:

1. *Make sure your bike is in good working order.* Clean it, inflate the tires, and oil the chain. Make sure the gears and derailleur are adjusted, and check the brakes. Also, make sure the bike is properly fitted to allow a correct riding position (see Chapter 3). Proper shorts and shoes will also help.

2. *Select a user-friendly course.* Do your early rides on flat, smooth roads, with a minimum of intersections. Options might include ten times around a one-mile circuit of blocks in your neighborhood to a drive within a nearby park to a round-trip to a point five miles away. With the out-and-back approach, you've committed yourself to go the distance, and that obviously has its pros and cons.

3. *Warm up before you push hard.* This is true at any level of training in any sport. Cold, stiff muscles are the easiest to injure.

4. *"Walk before you run."* Work into it. If you are hopelessly out of shape, try five miles first and don't look at your watch. (If you must take a peek, don't let a slow time discourage you.) Whatever you do, don't try to go as fast as you can until you've logged a few miles over several sessions and feel comfortable on the bike, both in terms of fitness and balance.

Working toward this simple goal of ten miles in forty minutes will put you on the road to fitness. Here's what you can expect to have experienced when you finally crack that forty-minute barrier:

- Increased lung power (taking in more air with less effort) and efficiency (higher oxygen consumption)
- Increased heart efficiency (larger, stronger, and fewer beats per minute)
- Increased number and size of blood vessels
- Increased blood volume
- Reduced blood pressure
- A firmer, leaner body
- A sense of accomplishment and a better outlook on life: improved self-image, easier and more restful sleep, reduced fatigue, better stress tolerance

- You will also learn to cycle more efficiently, fine-tune your equipment, and you will start setting new goals.

How much riding is needed to get fit and stay fit depends, of course, on such factors as an individual's age, athletic background, body type, and genetic endowment.

Dr. Kenneth Cooper in his bestseller, *Aerobics,* developed a point system based upon extensive physiological studies on the benefits of strenuous exercise and the amount needed each week to achieve and maintain a satisfactory level of fitness.

Cooper says to be at a good fitness level, one must score at least thirty points per week through one or more forms of exercise (running, swimming, cycling, etc). For cycling, a ten-mile time trial looks like this:

TIME	SCORE
1 hour or longer	2 points*
59:59–40:00 min.	5 points
39:59–30:00 min.	10 points
under 30:00 min.	15 points

* Exercise of minimal duration to be of cardiovascular benefit. Ordinarily at this speed, no training effect would occur. However, the duration is of such extent that a training effect does begin to occur.

Thus, achieving the goal of ten miles in less than forty minutes three times a week will, by Cooper's method, score the desired thirty points. This indicates that a moderate amount of cycling will allow most people to achieve and maintain a basic and reasonable level of fitness. Below, we outline the sixteen-week program Cooper suggests a beginner should use to reach this level. See page 100.

As a general yardstick, cycling proficiency has traditionally been measured in terms of total miles ridden during a minimum of four sessions per week. The following table depicts the mileage levels most often associated with various performance categories:

MILES PER WEEK	PERFORMANCE
30–50	• Basic fitness
50–150	• Short-distance novice racing • 25–75-mile day tours
150–250	• Serious amateur racing over shorter distances • Extended touring (100+ mi./day)
250–400	• Serious amateur racing over longer distances • Extended touring
350–800	• Professional road racing • Ultra marathons

16-WEEK CYCLING EXERCISE PROGRAM FOR BEGINNERS

WEEK	DISTANCE (miles)	CYCLE	TIME GOAL (minutes)	FREQ/WK	POINTS/WK
1	2.0	Cycle	10:00	5	5
2	2.0	Cycle	9:00	5	5
3	2.0	Cycle	7:45	5	10
4	3.0	Cycle	11:50	5	15
5	3.0	Cycle	11:00	5	15
6	3.0	Cycle	10:30	5	15
7	4.0	Cycle	15:45	5	20
8	4.0	Cycle	15:30	5	20
9	4.0	Cycle	14:30	5	20
10	4.0	Cycle	14:00	4	
	and				21
	5.0	Cycle	18:30	1	
11	4.0	Cycle	14:00	3	
	and				22
	5.0	Cycle	18:00	2	
12	4.0	Cycle	13:45	3	
	and				24
	6.0	Cycle	23:30	2	
13	4.0	Cycle	13:30	3	
	and				24
	6.0	Cycle	23:00	2	
14	5.0	Cycle	17:00	3	
	and				27
	6.0	Cycle	22:00	2	
15	6.0	Cycle	21:00	5	30
16	8.0	Cycle	28:30	4	32

From Aerobics *by Kenneth H. Cooper, M.D., M.P.H.*

TRAINING TO IMPROVE

Once you get into the swing of things and experience the good feedback of fitness, it is unlikely that you will be satisfied with achieving a merely satisfactory fitness level, particularly if it comes quickly. You will find that there are new mountains to climb and pounds to shed, and it will be fun to see how much faster you can go and how much more ground you can cover, with seemingly the same effort.

A great thing about improvement is that it comes quickly at the beginning. A good example is a New York lawyer we know who decided to take up cycling in his late forties. His athletic career had ended when he hung up his college track shoes some twenty-five years earlier and he had become overweight, overwrought, and unfit. The first spin he took around the six-mile loop in Central Park took him forty-five minutes with two rest stops. But he persevered. Within a year, he had cut his time to sixteen minutes per lap, and he could do three of them back-to-back in about the time it had taken him to crawl around the park that very first time.

Such improvement is within everyone's capability. Our attorney friend seldom rode over a hundred miles a week throughout that entire year, but he was committed and *consistent.* Although he is a very busy man, he made cycling a priority and created the time to get out as often as possible. One way to rationalize this reordering of priorities is to enter times for cycling into your appointment book, as you would a business meeting or dentist appointment. Consider it "an appointment with your future." You should also be aware that improvement comes even faster when you take time to learn the fundamentals.

FUNDAMENTALS OF TRAINING

When it comes to basic training, there are three important things to know about your body:

How does it work?
Where should I start?
What can it handle?

The body adapts quite nicely to exercise. Before we had machines to do most of our work, exercise was a fact of daily life.

Studies on athletes reveal that, on a daily basis, hard work followed by recuperation, followed by slightly more intense work, and so on, will enable the body to improve at repeated functions. As Bernard Hinault, in his book *Road Racing Technique & Training,* puts it:

> The athlete voluntarily submits his body to a given workload, selected with a particular goal in mind, and persists beyond the initial fatigue which would ordinarily cause someone to quit. He recuperates between two sessions—or else between two successive exercises if it's repeat training—and begins again, with the idea of increasing the workload even if only slightly. "More than yesterday, less than tomorrow." This old saying of lovers everywhere has become the athlete's motto as well. Love of sport is not

> an idle phrase. The most curious thing is that it all happens as if the body in some way understands the message it's receiving. For during the recuperation phase it prepares itself to bear a heavier workload than before. This has the effect of raising the pain threshold, which acts as a safety valve. The athlete's body seems to be thinking: "You got me that time, but you won't next time around. I'll be ready for you!" But the next training session is even more challenging. And patiently, enthusiastically, or just resignedly, the body obeys—within its own physiological limits, of course.

THE QUICK PULSE CALCULATION

1. Place your index and middle finger over your heart, or on your wrist artery or neck artery.
2. Count the number of beats you feel during a ten-second period using a stopwatch or second hand on your wristwatch for accurate timing.
3. Multiply the number of beats by six. This will give you your current pulse rate.

A good place to start your quest to get into shape is to first take an "audit" of your physical condition. We recommend that you begin by having a physical exam to determine whether there are any hidden health problems to be aware of as you enter increasingly intense levels of exercise. This should include a stress test that will tell you the safe level at which to begin your training program. This is particularly the case if you are over forty years old, out of condition, or have a history of medical problems (particularly involving the heart). Your doctor will probably give you the green light, but as we say many times in this book, better safe than sorry.

The next step in your fitness audit is to determine your endurance quotient or Anaerobic Threshold ("AT"). The AT is the body's breaking point during exercise, in other words, when you "run out of steam." The less fit you are, the lower your AT. You will improve as an athlete and a cyclist by gradually increasing your Anaerobic Threshold until you can pedal farther, ride faster, or win races before you "hit the wall," as they say in running.

Your AT is related to your pulse rate. To see how to quickly and easily calculate your pulse rate, see left margin. Subtract your age from 220 to get your maximum recommended pulse rate during exercise (see table on page 103).

The recommended exercise "zone" in which you can safely build endurance while not exceeding your AT is between 65 percent and 85 percent of your maximum pulse rate. We will call these the minimum and maximum thresholds. Refer to the following table for the recommended pulse rate exercise thresholds, by age.

Some may find it hard to exercise within this zone, while for others it will be considerably easier. Your body will tell you if you are exercising too hard. Although it may be uncomfortable, it does no harm to huff and puff, but you should back off it if you grow weak or your breathing becomes very labored or painful.

Gasping for air and feeling suddenly rubber-legged, as a result of pushing too hard (pedaling fast for a long stretch or climbing a tough hill), is usually a sign that you are crossing your Anaerobic

EXERCISE THRESHOLDS BY PULSE RATE (BEATS PER MINUTE—65 TO 85 PERCENT OF MAXIMUM)

Age Group	Minimum Threshold (65 percent of Maximum)	Maximum Threshold (85 percent of Maximum)
16–20	133	170
21–25	129	166
26–30	126	162
31–35	123	157
36–40	120	153
41–45	116	149
46–50	113	145
51–55	110	140
56–60	107	136
61–65	103	132
66–70	100	128
71–75	97	123

Threshold. This means you are going from an aerobic exercise state (processing sufficient oxygen to allow the muscles to function efficiently) to an anaerobic state (not processing enough oxygen to meet your body's needs and therefore creating an "oxygen debt"). Muscles, heart, lungs, and finally the brain will not work very long in an anaerobic state where the body's ability to process sufficient oxygen is being overcome by the production of lactic acid by the straining muscles.

In this state, your body tells you to slow down or get off and walk until the oxygenation process catches up. The fitter you are, the more quickly your body will repay this oxygen debt.

BUILDING THE FOUNDATION

Whether your goal is to lose weight or win the Tour de France, the foundation for your training is miles in the saddle.

For the previously sedentary person, five to ten miles every other day at a pace that will keep the pulse rate at least at 65 percent of maximum, for the duration of the ride, will bring noticeable improvement within a month.

For an athletic person (say a fifteen- to twenty-mile-per-week runner), it will be much easier to ride at least ten miles at a time, right off the bat.

Each beginner will have a level where he or she suddenly feels like they've "become a cyclist" or passed the "break-in" period. You will know the break-in period is behind you when:

- The bike feels comfortable to ride
- You develop smooth, consistent pedal cadence
- Gear shifting is easy and smooth
- Hills can be ridden to the top
- Breathing is easier
- You can maintain a steady pace throughout the ride
- Muscles feel tighter
- Weight seems redistributed
- Fatigue quickly diminishes after each ride
- You begin to look forward to the next ride

When this level is achieved, you will probably have logged at least 1,000 miles within three months, and you should easily be able to ride that ten miles in forty minutes. The door is now open to the true pleasures of cycling.

CYCLING AND WEIGHT LOSS

Will I lose weight if I ride a bicycle?

Most newcomers to the sport eagerly await the metamorphosis that will occur when they buy that first bike.

Weight loss is definitely in store, but it will only happen along with a life-style change. Here's how it works:

1. *Muscle weighs more than fat.* As you get into a cycling program, muscle tissue builds up and fat tissue starts to burn off. In the early stages of riding, weight may actually increase for some people while this process occurs. The first sign of a fitness payoff is usually a "redistribution" of weight as opposed to actual loss.

2. *Fitter body, better burner.* With strength comes the ability to go longer and faster. Going longer and faster is better for burning calories. When you can consistently handle hard two-hour rides, weight will really start to come off.

3. *Eat fuel, not fat.* Eat a nutritionally balanced diet emphasizing foods high in carbohydrates, like whole wheat breads, potatoes, fresh fruits, and vegetables. Cut back on (but not necessarily eliminate) foods that are higher in fats, like butter and red meat.

4. *Give it time.* Losing weight through regular, strenuous exercise and developing good nutritional habits may take longer than a crash diet, but it will make a better final product.

THE WORKOUT

It's no longer good enough just to pedal along at a relaxed, leisurely pace. The true cyclist wants more. There is a desire to break your course record. Suddenly it's important to catch that guy ahead of you. Maybe this time you can make it up "Heartbreak Hill" in a higher gear.

If travel is in your blood, you will soon start thinking about doing your first hundred mile ride or "Century." If you're more competitive, you will look for a race to enter.

EVEN THE BEST HAVE LIMITS

Take Greg LeMond's ride in the 17th stage of the 1989 Tour de France. The race was 100 miles from Briancon to L'Alpe d'Huez. Three major passes had to be climbed during the day: the 8,661 ft. Col du Galibier, the Croix de Fer, and finally L'Alpe d'Huez, 21 switchbacks on a narrow road that rose to 6,002 ft. in 14 unrelenting miles. LeMond, wearing the overall race leader's "Maillot Jaune" (yellow jersey), had ridden shoulder-to-shoulder with arch rival Laurent Fignon of France all day. But with only three kilometers to the summit, Fignon attacked.

LeMond's reserves were depleted. His heart was no doubt beating at its maximum threshold. Although he knew he had to stay with Fignon, he also knew that to try to match the Frenchman's violent attack would finish him. LeMond's response was to push on as steadily as he could—not so hard as to risk collapse, but enough to keep Fignon's time advantage to a minimum.

On that day, LeMond lost 1:19 and the yellow jersey to Fignon. But he kept the Frenchman's overall lead to twenty-six seconds. And because LeMond had not "blown-up," he recovered quickly. Within minutes after the finish, he was calm and composed, and three days later, he was strong enough and fast enough to take back Fignon's advantage and win his second Tour de France.

Three hard mountain passes in one day took their toll on LeMond, near the top of L'Alpe d'Huez.
Map courtesy of VeloNews; *Presse Sports photo*

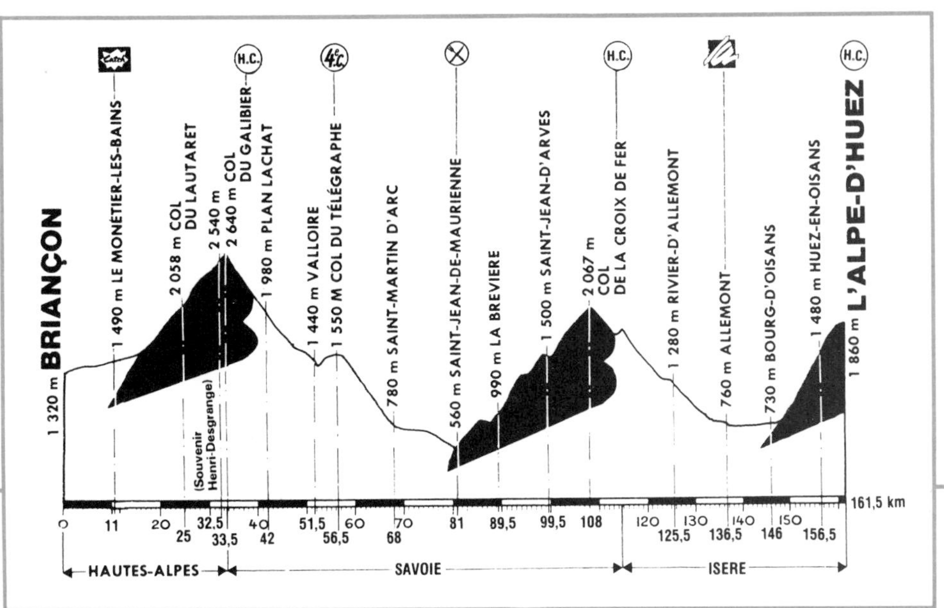

Whatever challenges you choose, your thinking will begin to make the subtle change from "ride" to "workout."

Taking training seriously does not mean giving up job and family. A respectable level of fitness for recreational racing and touring can be accomplished through one to two hours of cycling per day, five times a week. For the motivated, there is always a way to find the time, be it during early morning, incorporated into the commute to work, or even after dark on lighted streets. You may well find that making this time will actually improve your performance and concentration on the job and make for a happier home life.

The key to good cycling on a tight schedule is to follow the basic principles of training for the sport. (See Principles of Basic Training below.)

The crux of training, particularly at the beginning level, is to vary one's routine from day to day between the two broad categories of workout: *Tempo riding* and *Intervals.*

Tempo riding is maintaining a "threshold pace" for at least 80 percent of the total workout. (Threshold pace is defined as the speed achieved when your pulse is at a constant 75 percent or more of maximum.) For one cyclist, this could be fourteen mph, for another twenty-two mph, for Greg LeMond probably around thirty! A fifteen-mile "tempo" workout would look like this:

- Two-mile warm-up (low gears, ninety revolutions per min.)
- Twelve-mile tempo (threshold pace)
- One-mile cool-down (low gears, ninety rpm)

You will be amazed at how your threshold pace increases after just a few weeks.

Intervals are bursts of relatively short, intense effort, interspersed

---

PRINCIPLES OF BASIC TRAINING

1. *Vary tempo days with interval days.* Steady speed workouts alternating with days of interval sessions are the best for building stamina.
2. *Always train at between 65% and 80% of maximum pulse rate.* Lower than this is not real exercise; higher can be dangerous.
3. *Pedal at a cadence between 85 and 95 rpm.* The human engine has been proven to be most efficient at this rate.
4. *Get good rest.* A good night's sleep helps the body recover and makes a tough workout easier.
5. *Maintain a nutritious diet.* A high-performance car needs high-octane fuel.
6. *Take longer rides on weekends.* Forget intervals and tempo riding. Group riding will help chart progress.

---

with periods of easier riding (rest). Entire books have been written on interval theory and how various kinds of intervals should be used to develop speed, power, anaerobic, and aerobic capacities. Interval training is discussed in more detail in Chapter 8.

For beginning and novice cyclists who wish to improve their overall stamina and endurance, the best type of interval is called the "long interval." This is a period of hard effort (between 75 and 85 percent of maximum pulse rate) for two to four minutes, followed by a rest period that is three to four times the length of the effort.

For interval workouts, in fact for any workout, warm-up and cool-down are very important. The warm-up serves to make the muscles more elastic and less subject to injury from sudden strain, while the cool-down allows the lactic acid formed during rigorous exercise to dissipate before a more sedentary position is assumed. Lactic acid in the muscles will cause the uncomfortable after-the-fact stiffness so common to new athletes.

Here's a good one-hour interval workout for basic conditioning:

1. Fifteen-minute warm-up (low gear, ninety rpm)
2. Thirty minutes of intervals:
   - Two minutes hard (75–80 percent max. pulse rate)
   - Six minutes rest (low gear, ninety rpm)
   - Repeat the above sequence four times
3. Ten minute cool-down (low gear, ninety rpm)

It is best to do intervals (at least the intense part) on flat roads, although the same effect can be achieved by "attacking" a one-half to three-quarter mile hill every six or seven minutes during the interval portion of the workout.

The two- to three-month "break-in" period, followed by a month or two of more serious workouts, which alternate tempo riding with intervals, will provide a foundation for more specialized training for specific cycling challenges, such as your first race or century ride (see page 108).

THE BASIC TRAINING WEEK

Monday
Rest

Tuesday
One-hour tempo workout

Wednesday
One-hour-long intervals

Thursday
One-hour tempo workout

Friday
One-hour-long intervals

Saturday
Two-hour group ride

Sunday
Two- to three-hour group ride

SUPPLEMENTAL ACTIVITY

Although terms like "total fitness" and "cross training" have found their way into the lexicon of the modern athlete, the majority of those who exercise regularly do so primarily in their one favorite sport. We all know what they say about "too much of a good thing" and it is therefore good to participate in other enjoyable activities that complement and will contribute to our performance in our favorite one.

FOUR WEEKS TO THE FIRST CENTURY (100-Mile Ride)

Prerequisites:
- Break-in period
- Six weeks of basic training

The Weekly Program
- Ride six days per week, rest on Mondays
- *Tuesday:* Long ride, increasing mileage each week: 30, 35, 40, 45
- *Wednesday:* One-hour tempo ride
- *Thursday:* Same as Tuesday
- *Friday:* One-hour-long intervals
- *Saturday, Sunday:* Two long rides back-to-back (at least 50 miles on Saturday; two-thirds that distance on Sunday)
- During final week:
  Thursday: Replace long ride with long intervals.
  Increase carbohydrates beginning Thursday
  Friday: 20 miles easy
  Saturday: 20 miles easy
  Sunday: Century ride

FOUR WEEKS TO THE FIRST RACE (25-Mile Time Trial)

Prerequisites:
- Break-in period
- Six weeks of basic training

The Weekly Program
- Ride six days per week, rest on Monday
- *Tuesday:* Increase tempo workout from 1 hour to 1½ hours
- *Wednesday:* Add one long interval each week (4, 5, 6, 7)
- *Thursday:* same as Tuesday
- *Friday:* 12.5-mile time trial, flat out (10-minute warm-up and 10-minute cool-down).
- *Saturday:* Longer or group ride (minimum of 30 miles)
- *Sunday:* Fast group ride (up to 50 miles)
- During Final Week:
  Thursday: Replace tempo workout with 10-mile TT flat out.
  Increase carbohydrates beginning Thursday
  Friday: 20 miles easy
  Saturday: 10 miles easy
  Sunday: 25-mile time trial

Cycling is part of the endurance sport family, hence other sports that build stamina and exercise the same muscle groups can provide a break in the routine or perhaps serve as a substitute when traveling or during inclement weather, when cycling is not that convenient.

Cyclists commonly use the following as a complement, or off-

season alternative, to road cycling: running, swimming, cross-country skiing, speed skating, team sports (for fast reactions and dexterity), cyclocross, and track riding. Aerobic dancing is also an excellent off-season conditioner. For the hard core, training on a stationary bike or exercycle is an excellent way to maintain cycling form.

Regular stretching (see pages 110–111) and weight training will help round out the complete cyclist's training program. Since cycling requires a limited range of motion, stretching should become part of the daily routine. This is particularly important in case of falls, when the cyclist can be quickly forced into unusual positions.

Paul Kochli, the famous Swiss coach who has helped both Greg LeMond and Bernard Hinault, suggests stretching at least once a day, preferably before and after each workout.

Cycling also requires a strong back, shoulders, neck, and arms and does not provide much of the needed strength in the abdomen. A routine of circuit weight training can help keep those muscles performing well, both for cycling and all-around fitness. Most cyclists do little (apart from cycling) to strengthen the legs, but will head for the weight room up to five times per week in the winter.

SUMMARY

Basic conditioning for cycling involves these basic steps:

GOAL SETTING

Think about what you want out of your investment. If you are starting from ground zero or aren't sure, shoot for ten miles in forty minutes.

FITNESS THROUGH CYCLING

Achieving basic proficiency will pay quick dividends, in terms of increased fitness and the desire to set higher goals. Improvement can come rapidly, particularly at first.

MASTERING THE FUNDAMENTALS

It is important to know how the body reacts to exercise. The basic indicator of fitness is the Anaerobic Threshold, the point at which we "run out of gas." Regular training helps increase the AT.

There is no substitute for "miles in the saddle." Every conscientious beginner reaches a time when cycling becomes more comfortable and enjoyable.

After the initial "break-in" (usually around 1,000 miles of riding in three months or less), it's possible to start Basic Training, which

SEVEN STRETCHES FOR CYCLISTS

1. **Side Stretch:** Stand with feet 12 inches apart and arms at sides. Raise one arm above and over head while sliding the opposing hand down the outside of the leg. Don't bend forward and keep the head up. Repeat on the other side. Stretch is felt on the sides.

2. **Shoulder Stretch:** Stand with feet 12 inches apart. Clasp fingers of both hands and extend arms in front. With chin tucked in, roll palms outward while lifting arms over the head to reach as far up and behind as possible (see **A** and **B**). Stretch is felt in shoulders and sides.

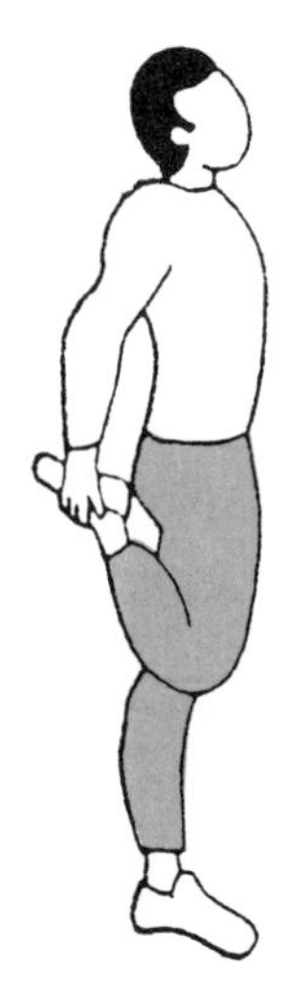

3. **Quads Stretch:** Stand next to a wall using right arm for support. Bend right foot toward the buttocks and grasp ankle with the right hand. Arch the back while pulling the ankle gently toward the buttocks. Repeat with left side. Stretch is felt on the front of the thigh.

4. **Hamstring Stretch.** With feet spread slightly more than shoulder width and legs straight, bend forward and with both hands clasp one leg below the knee. Gradually slide hands toward the ankle to feel the hamstrings stretch. Repeat on other leg.

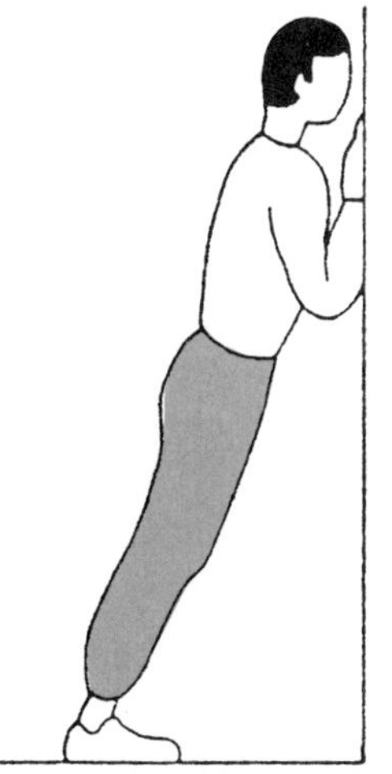

5. **Calf Stretch:** Stand facing the wall approximately three feet away and lean forward to rest the forearms on the wall, palms down. Keep heels on the floor, buttocks tucked in and body in a straight line. Hold for thirty seconds to feel stretch on calf muscles.

6. **Inner-Thigh Stretch:** Assume a crouching position with knees bent and back as straight as possible. With hands on knees, extend one leg to the side. Lean toward the bent knee to feel stretch on inside of the thigh. Repeat on the other side.

7. **Hip and Back Stretch:** While lying on back, bring both knees up to chest. Grasp both knees with hands and simultaneously bend face down to touch knees. Stretch is felt in hips and lower back.

consists of daily workouts alternating tempo riding and interval training. After a couple of months of basic training, you can train toward specific goals, such as a century ride or twenty-five-mile time trial.

CROSS TRAINING

Complementary sports, such as cross-country skiing, speed skating, and running help cyclists build strength and endurance. Stretching, weightlifting, and aerobic dancing are excellent conditioners as well.

8 Advanced Conditioning

If you can ride ten miles in forty minutes or less, you have to be in pretty good physical shape. If you could ride the same distance ten minutes faster, there is no question that your body would be leaner. You would be at least a few pounds lighter and your weight would be distributed differently. Your thighs, in particular, would feel stronger and tighter, and your doctor would probably tell you that you are a fine physical specimen. You would also be able to eat nearly everything you want, without showing it.

So what more needs to be done? If your goal is simply to look good and feel great, nothing.

There are people who can ride ten miles on a bike in twenty minutes. One in particular, Greg LeMond, covered that distance in

Greg LeMond's aggressive time trialing won him two crucial stages of the 1989 Tour de France. *Presse Sports photo*

just over seventeen minutes on his way to winning the final time trial of the 1989 Tour de France. LeMond's average speed in the sixteen-mile stage was thirty-four mph, a Tour de France record.

Going from being physically fit by riding a bicycle to the super fitness required to compete at the Tour de France level obviously requires the setting of loftier goals and a tremendous sense of commitment. When racing success becomes the goal, conditioning becomes a means to an end, rather than an end in itself, and training becomes a full-time proposition.

Here is some consolation for the up-and-comer: The biggest performance gains are in the early stages of training. Jim Ochowicz, director of the successful 7-Eleven pro team, has this to say about the relationship between conditioning and performance: "It's like the law of diminishing returns. Conditioning improves rapidly at first, but as a rider approaches his absolute best, it requires more and more specialized work and training time to shave off that last few seconds. I would estimate that it takes 50% more work to get to that final 100% of upper level performance."

There are no trade secrets to advanced conditioning for cycling. Tour de France riders must follow the same basic training principles as the beginner. The differences are ones of:

- time commitment
- degree of intensity
- greater specialization

This chapter will explain advanced conditioning for cycling and describe the programs of some athletes who have clearly achieved it. With modification, the champion's program can greatly help the aspiring one or even the weekend racer, much as high-performance race car development inspires the production of better mass-marketed sports models.

WHAT IS ADVANCED CONDITIONING?

Advanced conditioning allows you to go further, faster, and harder than you ever thought possible. The body has been transformed from a merely smooth-functioning organism to a highly specialized, fine-tuned machine.

The biggest differences between the fit and the superconditioned are in *body-fat* levels (fat tissue as a percentage of total body weight) and *cardiovascular efficiency* (the ability of the lungs, heart, and circulatory system to process oxygen). (See accompanying comparison of pro cyclist and average healthy person.)

The harder and longer one exercises, the more body fat is burned away. A pro cyclist in a five-hour stage in the Tour de France,

COMPARISON OF PROFESSIONAL CYCLIST AND AVERAGE HEALTHY AMERICAN

	NORMAL	CYCLIST
Body Fat		
Male	over 15%	3–5%
Female	over 20%	6–10%
Resting Pulse	72 beats per minute	32–45 bpm
Heart-Pump Volume (near AT or 88% of max. pulse rate)	12.5 liters per minute	22.5 liters per min.
Heart Size	normal	6–10% enlargement
Walls of Heart	normal	3–5% thicker

averaging twenty-five mph, will burn about 6,000 calories. Under these conditions, it takes a phenomenal amount of high-calorie food just to maintain body weight, and that's why bicycle racers must frequently eat on the go. It is no wonder that body-fat levels of pro cyclists are extremely low (3–5 percent of total weight, as opposed to 15 percent and above for the normal person).

The advantages of low body fat for the cyclist include:

- *Better heat tolerance.* Fat insulates the body. On a hot day, less fat means less energy is needed to cool the body and more can go to power muscles.
- *Superior power-to-weight ratio.* Fat is like dead weight. Dropping the weight means it's easier to go faster, particularly uphill.
- *Improved cardiovascular performance.* Studies show that the body processes oxygen more efficiently as weight is lost, thus increasing aerobic performance.

Three methods for determining one's body-fat level are depicted in the accompanying illustration.

The heart is a muscle, and when muscles are exercised they get larger and stronger. It follows, then, that cyclists develop large hearts with strong beats. This is certainly healthy within reasonable limits, particularly if cardiovascular exercise is maintained regularly throughout one's life. However, some top-endurance athletes can experience risk from developing an enlarged heart. (See profile on Lucien Gillen.)

Advanced conditioning also results in a slowing of the heart and

DETERMINING BODY FAT

Method One: UNDERWATER WEIGHING

Subject is weighed while fully submerged in a special tank. Submerged weight is compared with normal weight, according to a scientific formula. Since fat is more buoyant than everything else, its percentage of total is easily calculated.

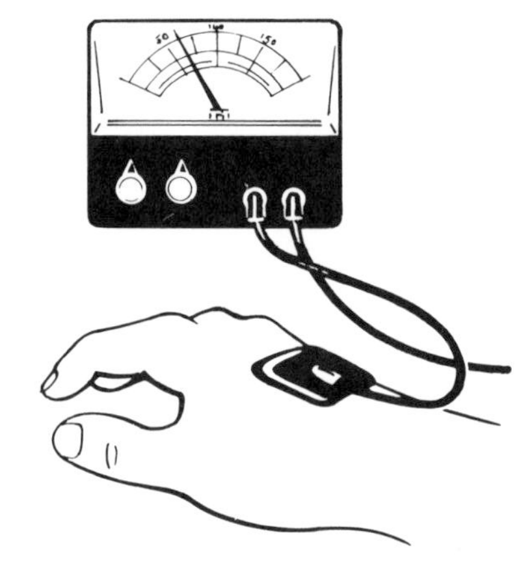

Method Two: ELECTRICAL IMPEDANCE

A mild current is passed through the body between electrodes attached at hands and feet. Electrical resistance is different with fat than muscle. Thus, body-fat percentage can be readily calculated.

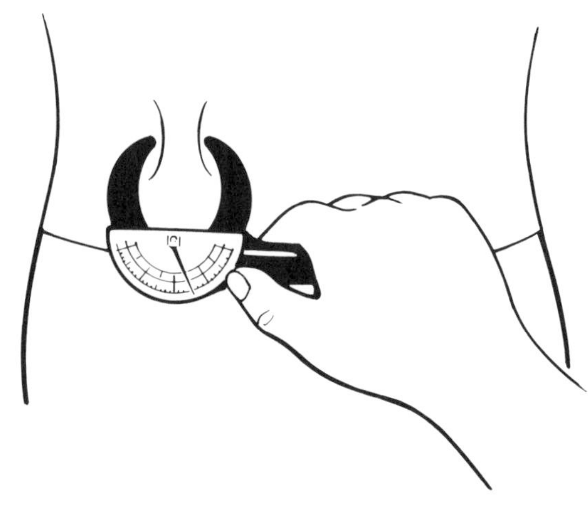

Method Three: PINCH TEST

Folded skin in several areas of the body is measured using specially designed calipers. Measurements are plugged into a data base to get body-fat reading. This method is the quickest, easiest, and most readily available (most health clubs and fitness centers offer this method).

Drawing by George Retseck

PRESCRIPTION FOR AN ENLARGED HEART

Pro cyclists who have spent a good part of their adult years racing and training day-in and day-out can experience a negative effect from an enlarged heart, when they retire. If physical activity abruptly ceases, the risk of excess muscle tissue atrophying too quickly can be dangerous to the heart.

LUCIEN GILLEN, from Luxembourg, a great all-around pro cyclist in the fifties and early sixties, had developed a heart nearly 20% larger than normal for his size. He rode six-day races indoors all winter and road races all summer, for a dozen years. As soon as his racing career ended, Gillen started a new career as an international banker. In order for Gillen to make the adjustment from super-endurance athlete to sedentary executive, without endangering his heart, Gillen's doctor gave him an unusual prescription: "Ride your bike 20 miles every day for the rest of your life."

pulse rate. The resting pulse of Jacques Anquetil, France's great champion and five-time Tour de France winner, was once measured at thirty-two beats per minute. An average, healthy adult's heart, at rest, will beat more than twice that rate.

However, an extremely low resting pulse rate is not an absolute indicator of fitness, since heredity also plays a role. A more important indicator of top conditioning is heart-stroke volume. A well-conditioned heart can pump considerably more blood per beat than an unconditioned one. The unfit heart may respond to strenuous exercise by rocketing up to a dangerously high 200 beats per minute, while the same exercise by a fit person may push the pulse rate to 180 beats per minute. The fit heart accomplishes the same work by pumping more blood per stroke, not by beating faster. Also, the highly conditioned athlete can maintain a high pulse rate for considerably longer.

The ability to recover quickly and completely from monumental efforts is perhaps the most remarkable characteristic of advanced conditioning. Physiologically, this means pulse rates drop quickly, as soon as exercise stops, and resting pulse rates will stay at the same low level, day after day, no matter what effort the body has been asked to make.

Laurent Fignon, who lost his fifty-three second lead to Greg LeMond in the final sixteen-mile time trial in the 1989 Tour de

France, mentioned that on the morning of the race his resting pulse was up to a very high (for him) sixty beats per minute, a factor that indicated he had not fully recovered from strenuous earlier days in the Alps. Whether Fignon's higher pulse meant incomplete recovery or just a case of nerves going into the final day is uncertain, but clearly, top performance is less likely if the body is not fully recovered from previous efforts. The fact that Tour de France riders can push themselves to the maximum every day for three weeks says much about the correlation between advanced conditioning and the recovery rate.

TRAINING PROGRAMS OF CHAMPIONS

The most common element of the training programs for top cycling champions is the approach. Virtually every top cyclist:

1. Starts by setting performance goals for the next season at the end of the current one.
2. Divides the year into distinct periods during which certain types of work must be done.
3. Makes sure that weaknesses or deficiencies receive specific emphasis in the program.
4. Plans time for rest, diversion, and medical attention.
5. Keeps a daily training diary.

Secondly, every top cyclist adheres more or less to this adage:

"The best form of training is racing."

Unlike top marathon runners, who can race only a few times a year and spend the rest of the time training, cyclists will enter as many races as are available. It is not uncommon for a pro, based in Europe, to compete 150 days per year. Cycling is less traumatic to the muscles and joints than distance running. Since it is impossible to achieve peak performance in every race entered, pros set priorities for their events and use the less important ones as quality training sessions.

Most pros, like Tour de France stage winner Davis Phinney, believe that it is impossible for a cyclist to reach top condition, without competing nearly every day during the season: "At the highest level, training is a matter of adapting your body to real hard racing and racing really hard. If you can stay healthy through that kind of racing, it's really the only way you can be ready for a big event like the Tour."

There are, of course, thousands of serious cyclists below the pro level who are not able to race so frequently and others who believe that training is a relief from the constant pressure of competition.

In the U.S. in particular, most races are on weekends. For this reason, several training sessions per week that approximate race conditions are essential to achieve the best possible fitness.

Since the goal of advanced conditioning is peak performance in competition, most top racers design a year-round training program, timed to put them at peak condition for key events during the March-through-October racing season. Accordingly, they will divide the year into three or four periods:

1. *Off-season maintenance and preparation* (November to early January)
2. *Preseason training* (January and February)
3. *Early racing season* (March and April)
4. *Peak racing season* (mid-April through October)

Paul Kochli, perhaps the most influential cycling coach today, who has guided the careers of many top pros, including Bernard Hinault and Greg LeMond, further divides the key periods of the year into what he calls "macrocycles": three- to seven-week blocks of time that take a rider through a cycle of preparation for a specific event. During the peak racing season, for example, a rider may want to prepare specifically for the World Championship, held annually at the end of August. The World Championship macrocycle may then consist of the four-week period from the finish of the Tour de France, in late July, to the day of the World Championship road race. The goal of this macrocycle would be to bring the rider "down" from the Tour and "up" for the World.

Kochli further breaks down each macrocycle into "microcycles," three- to seven-day periods that build and taper according to the ultimate goal of the macrocycle. Training sessions, races, and rest days are the daily building blocks that make up each microcycle.

Thus, the business of training for top-level cycling events has become a science, with numerous variables and performance yardsticks, such as pulse rate, body weight, and AT data telling a coach like Kochli what the rider needs to do on a day-to-day and week-by-week basis, in order to complete a macrocycle and achieve the targeted goal successfully.

Putting individual needs and goals aside, Greg LeMond, in his *Complete Book of Bicycling,* lays out a basic "training program for the pro racer" that gives a good idea of what kind of time and mileage a pro must log in order to be competitive (see p. 120). This program also indicates how amateur racers at various age levels can adjust the pro regimen to suit their needs.

As you can see, LeMond's rigorous pro program seems to leave little time for anything else. Despite this, he and most other top pros do find the time to raise families and engage in complementary,

GREG LEMOND'S TRAINING PROGRAM FOR PRO RACERS*

From Greg LeMond's *Complete Book of Cycling*

	Nov.–Dec.	*January*		*February*		*In Season*	
	HOURS†	HOURS	KM	HOURS	KM	HOURS	KM
Monday	Rest	Rest		Rest		Rest	
Tuesday	1½–2½	1½–2½	45/60	1½–2½	45/75	1½–2½	45/60
Wednesday	Rest	2 –3½	60/105	3 –4½	90/135	3½–4½	105/135
Thursday	3½–6	3½–7	90/210	4½–8	135/240	6 –7	180/210
Friday	Rest	1½–2½	45/60	1½–2½	45/75	1½–2	45/60
Saturday	1½–2½	2 –3½	60/105	3 –4½	75/135	3½–4	105/120
Sunday	3½–6	3½–7	90/210	4½–8	120/240	6 –6½	180/195
Totals	10–17	14–26	390/750	18–30	510/900	22–26	660/780

LeMond also recommends a modification of this program for other categories of competitors. Note that exact tables have not been reproduced for each category. The percentage reduction of LeMond's Pro Program, for the various categories listed, are an approximation, to provide a comparative sense of training effort required as a top cyclist moves up the ladder toward the demands required of professionalism.

AGE/SEX CATEGORY	REDUCE PRO'S PROGRAM BY	MAXIMUM DURATION/ DISTANCE FOR LONGEST RIDE
1. 15-year-old racer	50–55 percent	4 hours—120 km
2. 16-year-old racer and young female racer	40–45 percent	4½ hours—135 km
3. 17-year-old racer	30–35 percent	6 hours—180 km
4. 18-year-old racer or top female racer	15–25 percent	7 hours—210 km
5. 19-year-old racer	10–20 percent	7 hours—210 km
6. 20-year-old racer (or any top amateur)	5–10 percent	7 hours—210 km

* This program presumes that the rider has been "seasoned" through at least several years of training and racing as a top-level amateur. Note that duration or "time in the saddle" is more important than actual distance ridden. The dash separating the two values in the hours and duration columns represents the suggested starting point and ending point within this phase of training (macro cycle).

† During the November to December period, "time in the saddle" is more important than the actual number of kilometers ridden.

supplemental, and diversionary activities to round out their intense cycling programs.

Clearly, once the racing season gets underway, the demands of competition, training, and travel leave little time for additional training. If the foundation has been properly built during the off-season, such supplemental training (apart from daily stretching) is not needed.

SPECIALIZED TRAINING

Most seasoned competitors know enough about training, preparation, and themselves to plan and execute their personal year-round programs. The primary advantage of coaches and team directors is to provide management, consultation, and support. In cycling, you will not find a sweat-suited coaching staff, with clipboards in hand and whistles around their necks, barking out moves and drills.

Special drills and custom training techniques are highly individualized and brought into play for a specific purpose, usually to strengthen or improve a particular ability (see below).

SUMMARY OF SPECIAL TRAINING TECHNIQUES FOR ADVANCED CYCLISTS

TYPE	DESCRIPTION	PURPOSE
Long Intervals	2–4 minute effort at near maximum pulse rate, followed by rest period 3–4 times length of effort. Goal is partial recuperation (65–70 percent of max. pulse rate) before beginning next interval.	Increase anaerobic capacity. Increase anaerobic threshold. Help build sustained high end-speed (for short time trials and breakaways).
Short (Pure) Intervals	2.5-second to 1-minute effort at 100 percent, followed by rest period at least 3 × length of effort. Start next effort when pulse is between 65 and 70 percent of maximum.	Increase anaerobic capacity. Increase anaerobic threshold. Help build ability to make short, fast bursts and sustain intense effort during last kilometer of race.
Motor Pacing	Drafting close behind a small motorcycle, using bigger gears.	Increases anaerobic threshold. Can be used to help with sprints, intervals, and high-gear tempo riding.
Sprint Training	All-out effort for 150 to 300 meters.	Improves initial acceleration or "jump." Builds and sustains top end-speed, to improve final "kick."

The most widely used of all specialized training techniques is the *Interval.* A basic form of interval training is recommended from the earliest stages of serious cycling (see Chapter 7). The key to advanced interval training is understanding how and when it is most effectively employed.

A few important rules about interval training:

- Longer intervals are done at lower intensity and thus should be incorporated near the beginning of the preseason training phase, but only after a good mileage foundation has been built (at least 1,000 miles in one and one-half months).
- Short (pure) intervals are done at highest intensity and should always take the rider into an anaerobic state or beyond his AT. This level can and should usually be maintained for about forty-five seconds. More than that will be either impossible or ineffective.
- Intervals, whether short or long, can be classified as *power* intervals or as *speed* intervals. Power intervals are done using a big gear at lower cadence (between seventy and ninety revolutions per minute) and build the capacity to handle a tough pace going uphill. Speed intervals are done at a much higher cadence (100–120 rpm) and help improve the ability to accelerate quickly or sustain high speeds, as in a fast-moving breakaway. Comprehensive advanced conditioning requires a blend of all types of intervals.

Another standard form of training that virtually every pro makes use of at one time or another is *motor pacing*. This bizarre activity has been around since cyclists first realized that they could match the speed of almost anything that went faster, as long as they could tuck in behind it and ride the slipstream. Riding behind a small motorcycle and driver (about the same wind protection as a large Russian cyclist) is like training with a robot that never gets tired and can always go faster.

The training value of motor pacing is real. As LeMond puts it, "I find that when I go out alone on the flats, I can ride for only about ten minutes at a rate close to my anaerobic threshold, unless I have a tail wind. Mentally it's just too hard to keep going.

Even with a tail wind, I can ride at my anaerobic threshold only for twenty minutes, at most. Riding behind a motorcycle, I can ride at my anaerobic threshold for 30 minutes. And, of course, that's better training."

In addition to extending one's ability to ride longer distances at the anaerobic threshold, motor pacing can also help in interval training (the effort phase is exerted next to the motorcycle, with the recovery behind, in the slipstream) and in sprints (the motorcycle brings the rider up to a high speed and the rider tries to sprint around).

Top cyclists incorporate different types of motor-paced training

Davis Phinney is a talented sprinter who has won stages in the Tour de France, like this one in 1986. *Presse Sports photo*

into their year-round program. Generally, motor-paced sessions are used once or twice per week on a tempo day and/or on an interval day. Since motor-paced training is usually more intense, pros will normally motor-pace from one to two and one half hours per session. However, Jock Boyer, America's first entrant in the Tour de France, believed that motor pacing could be very effective at much higher levels. (See "Motor Pace Junkie.")

Far too many races have been lost in the final few meters for pro cyclists to ignore the critical importance of developing and refining a good finishing sprint. Davis Phinney, the king of American road sprinters, has fine-tuned this ability to the point where he has won several stages in the Tour de France, by mere inches.

Sprint training involves putting time and focus into honing the skill of the finishing kick. Even though the best sprinters seem to have been born with an uncanny talent for it, any rider's sprint can be improved. Phinney suggests devoting an hour to this exercise once or twice a week, throughout the entire training year.

Advanced conditioning for world-class cycling requires a commitment and focus few mortals possess. Maybe there is perverse comfort in knowing that even the superstars have their problems.

One such nemesis is the ever-elusive "staleness." Called "burnout" in the executive world, this is a form of psychological weariness and lack of motivation that is probably caused more by mental stress than anything else.

Jock Boyer following brother Winston, in one of his many motor-pacing sessions. *Presse Sports photo*

MOTOR-PACE JUNKIE

Jock Boyer pedaled to a different cadence. As America's top road rider, with nowhere to race but Europe, he had to. He was the first American ever to ride the Tour de France and he helped pave the way for Greg LeMond's first pro season, with the French Renault team.

In 1983, Boyer placed twelfth in the Tour de France, an outstanding performance. That year he also brought along an acupuncturist and encouraged his wife to sneak her way into the race caravan, by disguising herself as a man.

Boyer had different theories about preparation for races as well. In many cases he opted to train for European races alone, in the mountains of Colorado and the plains of Utah, his only companion being a motorcycle driven by a friend or brother Winston.

"It wasn't unusual for me to go for nine hours at a time," said Boyer, "sometimes I would do four or five mountain passes in a day. While a lot of racing was important, I often rather preferred the solitude of motor-pacing through the mountains."

Boyer would pile on the miles during his one-man training camps, usually doing at least 800 miles per week. To simulate racing conditions he would have the motorcycle vary its speed and lead him in long and short intervals.

"Riding behind the motor could really draw me out," said Boyer. "I never found another training partner who could do that."

Every pro admits to bouts of staleness from time to time. Although it may seem to the outsider that cyclists are always on vacation (what could be better than spending several hours a day riding a bike), the truth is that their daily grind can become quite boring—even debilitating—unless they can occasionally find a way to escape. Add to this the psychological demands of day-in, day-out race performance and it's no wonder that now and then a bike rider can be sickened by the sight of his bike.

The best cure for staleness is diversion. Greg LeMond plays golf, sometimes even taking a day off in peak season. Nineteen eighty-four Olympic Champion Alexi Grewal often takes a week-long "vacation" of mountain bike riding, right in the middle of the racing season. Taking one day a week off as a rule is a highly recommended hedge against staleness, as well as an aid to physical recovery.

The sports world is full of great stories of how its legends "blew off steam" before scoring their greatest triumph. Bob Beamon, for example, uncorked a bottle of wine and made love to his wife the night before he shattered the world long jump mark, in Mexico City in 1968. The very same year, ski champion Jean-Claude Killy spent a few days relaxing away from snow, in the South of France, before

Riding behind a motorcycle is like riding with a superstar.
Presse Sports photo

scoring his triple gold at the Winter Games in Grenoble. One must wonder whether there was also a bottle of wine involved in Killy's sojourn—and if so, whether it was the same vintage as Beamon's!

Very similar to staleness, in outward appearance and effect, is the affliction of *overtraining*. But there is one big difference: staleness can occur even if the physical demands of racing and training are low. Overtraining, on the other hand, is a deep-seated mental and physical fatigue caused by training (or racing) at a higher level than the body can handle. Staleness is usually a symptom of overtraining and can often lead to the diagnosis of overtraining, particularly if physical demands have been high (see chart on page 126).

Top athletes also fall victim to what we call the "*advanced conditioning myth,*" which holds that when the body is so strong and fit, it is impervious to the afflictions of mere mortals. Ironically, the reverse is more often true: well-conditioned athletes are highly susceptible to common illnesses.

Eddy Borysewicz, former U.S. National Team Coach, has worked with many of the nation's top cyclists, including such notables as LeMond, Andy Hampsten, Davis Phinney, Alexi Grewal, Ron Kiefel, and others. In his book, *Bicycle Road Racing,* he makes this observation: "When you are in good shape, you are strong on the

OVERTRAINING

SYMPTOMS:

- Staleness (lack of motivation)
- Fatigue (tired legs and body)
- High pulse rate (resting pulse is significantly higher than normal)
- Sleep loss (inability to sleep through the night)
- Irritability (short temper, inability to relax)
- Sickness (colds, flu, intestinal disorders)

CAUSES:

- Pushing too hard (longer and harder efforts than the body is conditioned for)
- Poor recovery (lack of recovery time between hard efforts)
- Poor diet (body is not receiving enough nourishment to fuel the effort)

REMEDIES:

- Physical check-up (blood test for anemia, other physiological problems or imbalances)
- Reduce program (cut back on hard racing and training)
- Rest (total change of pace, until strength and motivation return)

bike, but your body does not have good defenses. It has no fat, it looks like you've been in a concentration camp. All your energy is directed to doing one thing—pushing the pedals. The harder you work at that, the greater the chance your body will weaken in another respect."

Not only are finely honed athletes more vulnerable, they are more sensitive to changes in their body. They also lead a life-style that exposes them to many people and environments.

Bizarre medical problems can develop in highly conditioned athletes and be misdiagnosed, since the symptoms are attributed to a more probable cause.

For example, in the 1965 Tour de France, top British rider Tom Simpson seemed to be getting progressively weaker as the Tour wore on. "He is not strong enough for such a race and the mountains are killing him," said journalists and race watchers. But Simpson felt something else was wrong. After a personally disappointing finish, he went to the doctor and discovered that over the past month he had been sharing his food with an intestinal tape worm!

Similarly, in 1989, Greg LeMond was suffering miserably

through the Tour of Italy. It was starting to look like his comeback from a 1987 hunting accident and other maladies would never happen. Many thought he was washed up. He had been training and racing hard with no ill-effects, apart from mediocre results, but a former Tour de France winner and athlete of LeMond's caliber should have been performing better.

"I was getting dropped so easily," he said, "I just couldn't believe all the work and training I had been doing wasn't paying off."

Finally, with just a few days left in the race, he had his blood tested. Improbable as it may seem, this top athlete who had been doing everything right was diagnosed as severely anemic. Immediate injections of iron produced quick results. On the final day, LeMond was second in the individual time trial, the best result he had had in three years. Six weeks later, he won his second Tour de France.

SUMMARY

Advanced conditioning for the serious cyclist comes from greater time commitment, higher training intensity, and increased specialization.

It is characterized by a body that is fine-tuned and highly adapted to the rigors of cycling. Body fat drops to at least one-third of its normal level and cardiovascular efficiency is improved through a strengthened heart and more efficient breathing. Pulse rate drops to half that of a normal person and recovery time is greatly improved.

Pros achieve the highest levels of advanced conditioning through carefully planned training programs, and they race as many as 150 days per year. It's a full-time job.

The basic training principles for pros are the same as for beginners. Advanced training methods include intervals, motor pacing, and special sprint training.

But advanced conditioning sometimes comes at a price. Staleness, overtraining, and nagging ailments, such as frequent colds and even anemia, can hit the strongest and best-prepared athletes. It seems the finer the tuning, the more delicate the machine.

9 The Cyclist's First Aid Kit

Is cycling a high-risk sport? That depends on the kind of cycling you do and how you approach it. At the wild end of the spectrum is the "kamikaze downhill," at Mammoth Mountain, California. This event is just what its name implies. Screaming down gravel-strewn ski trails, in the summertime, at speeds of fifty mph, is not for the faint-hearted. Neither is falling off, without at least the benefit of a soft snow landing. Bring a first-aid kit and make sure your medical insurance is up to date if this is your favorite form of cycling.

Risk can be high in road and track racing as well. Sprint racing on the velodrome is not supposed to be a contact sport, but it often is. Blown tires and locked handlebars are part of the game. Races are frequently delayed until one or more combatants can return from the first-aid room.

The rush of skittering down alpine switchbacks is for high-risk personalities only. Jean-Claude Killy, a former Olympic and World Cup downhill champion, with a legendary penchant for derring-do, says descending a narrow mountain road at a high rate of speed on a bicycle is the only thing he has found that approaches the

Mark Whitehead's spill on the velodrome was more a case of wounded pride than serious injury. *Cor Vos photo*

exhilaration—and risk—of downhill ski racing. The difference is that in cycling, you often share the course with other racers, cars, and motorcycles.

In the 1961 Tour de France, race leader and defending champion Roger Riviera, of France, disappeared into the fog with chief rival Gastone Nencini, of Italy, as they careened down the side of a mountain at nearly sixty miles per hour. Only Nencini emerged. Riviera was found in the rocks at the bottom of the cliff, far below, with a broken back. He survived the crash, but never raced again.

If you are properly prepared and equipped, cycling need not be so great a risk. We have dramatized the perils of cycling's extremes, but in fact the most common dangers of the sport are on the public roadways. Those perils can be minimized greatly with the right equipment and some good old-fashioned common sense.

THE BIGGEST DANGER—FALLING

Depending on whose estimate you believe, there are 80 million to 100 million bicycle riders on America's roads, approximately 25 percent of whom ride at least once a week. With so many people pedaling at all different skill levels and under all different riding conditions, it is no wonder that there are a lot of accidental dismounts. Here are some crash statistics from the *Bicycle Institute of America's 1989 Bicycling Reference Book:*

- Number seeking treatment in doctor's office: 1,000,000 (1 percent)
- Number seeking treatment in emergency room: 570,000 (.57 percent)
- Serious head injuries: 70,000 (.07 percent)
- Deaths: 941 (1 per 100,000)

RISKS

	INJURY	DEATH
Car Accident	1/100 registered cars	1/10,000 registered cars
Bike Accident	1/100 cyclists	1/100,000 cyclists
Ski Accident	.7/100 skiers	—
Motorcycle Accident	1/100 registered motorcycles	9/10,000 registered motorcycles
Airplane Accident	—	6/10 million air travelers
Drowning	—	3/100,000 swimmers

Statistics from National Transportation Board, U.S. Consumer Product Division, Federal Aviation Administration, National Safety Council, and the Bicycle Institute of America.

Although these figures show that cycling certainly has its risks, the likelihood of getting hurt on a bicycle is about the same as from being injured in a car or motorcycle accident, with death being considerably less likely.

By far, the biggest contributor to serious cycling injuries and fatalities is the fact that most cycling is done on roadways that are shared with cars. Ninety percent of all deaths on bicycles results from collisions with motor vehicles, and half of all bicycling fatalities are of children under sixteen. It is for that reason that bicycle safety education is becoming a big topic among parents and educators.

With a fairly good chance of taking a tumble once in a while, it makes sense to practice a little risk management.

It also makes sense to teach yourself what to do in case the inevitable happens. The first step is learning to *relax* and not being overly fearful of what will happen if you fall. The vast majority of cycling tumbles are relatively minor, resulting only in minor cuts and scrapes. Here are some of the misadventures of coauthor, Dave Chauner:

TEN TIPS ON REDUCING THE RISK OF ACCIDENT

1. Go with the Flow. A widespread misconception is that cyclists should ride facing oncoming traffic (like pedestrians). The rule to remember is *"just like a car."* One out of five bike/car collisions results from riding on the wrong side of the road.

2. Obey Traffic Rules. Don't run stoplights, stop signs, or blind intersections.

3. Signal When Turning. Let motorists know where you're headed.

4. Avoid Busy Roads/Narrow Shoulders. Most cyclists quickly learn the back roads. Sometimes a heavily traveled road with wide-paved shoulders is safer than a winding, narrow secondary road. *Try to ride before or after rush hour.*

5. Avoid Night Riding. If it's necessary, wear reflective clothing, mount bike lights and stick to well-lighted roads.

6. Know How to Get in and out of Your Pedals. Practice this in a parking lot until it becomes second nature, before hitting the roads.

7. Develop Good Turning Technique. Take a corner in a smooth arc, with inside leg paused at the top of the pedal stroke to avoid scraping the inside pedal on the road or curb. In group rides, leave room for other cyclists on the inside.

8. Protect Your Front Wheel. This is the most vulnerable part of your bicycle for causing crashes—a slight knock from either side will put you in the ditch. Don't overlap wheels with a rider in front. Avoid potholes, sewer grates, railroad tracks, and pavement seams, particularly if they run parallel to your direction of travel.

9. Leave Your Walkman at Home. A key to preventing accidents is being on sensory alert. Music in your ears will put your mind on the music, not on the road.

10. Maintain Your Bicycle. Many falls result from blown tires, missed shifts, skipping chains, and other preventable equipment failures. Keep the bike maintained and adjusted. Quickly correct any developing problems with tires, brakes, chains, and gears.

In fifteen years of racing, I probably fell off my bike at least 30 times, and I have the scars to prove it. About half of these spills came in training, the rest during races.

My most memorable crash in training was when I smashed into the side of a car at about 40 miles per hour. I was leading a group down Stenton Avenue outside Philadelphia on a quiet Sunday morning. My light was yellow, turning to red, but I thought the driver pulling out would see me and slam on his brakes. He didn't. I skidded sideways, took the blow on my right hip and ended up flipping over the car and landing 20 feet on the other side. I was riding (somewhat gingerly) two days later and raced the next weekend.

My best racing crash was in Holland in 1969. I blasted out of the final turn in an all-out sprint for a special prime prize. A spectator stepped right in front of me and I plowed into him at about 35 miles an hour. Even though he was big and soft, we both took a pounding. I twisted my back and the pain lasted for a couple of weeks. I can still see the cinder that got embedded in my left arm in that one. My new friend walked away, but I bet he remembered to look both ways the next time he crossed the street.

Over the years, I fell off at slow speeds and fast speeds, awkwardly and with great panache. I've probably regenerated elbow and knee skin a dozen times but I never broke any bones or had a serious concussion, although many riders I know did.

The three things I remember about crashes are that they happen very fast, that pavement is a very hard and unforgiving surface, and that there is always one vivid moment or "snapshot" that becomes frozen in your mind. For example, I can still see the look on the driver's face in that car on Stenton Avenue. His mouth and eyes were wide open, he was wearing a fishing cap and he had gray hair around his temples. I can imagine what he remembers.

I honestly believe that some people, even though they may be well-coordinated, are accident prone, injury prone, or both. Some riders always seem to be covered with scabs and bandages. I knew one rider who broke his collarbone six times.

Apart from good luck, I believe the main reason I was never seriously hurt (although I often fell hard enough to) is that I cannot recall a sense of panic when the unthinkable became imminent. It was almost a sense of, "Oh well, here goes!" Instead of trying to fight the fall or break it with my hands, I tried to roll into a ball with arms protecting my head. Falling is apparently another instance where it pays to "go with the flow."

Fear makes one tense, and a tense person is not only more likely to fall, but also more apt to get hurt. The best way to prepare yourself for a crash is to build confidence on the bike. The more comfortable and agile you become, the more likely you will be able to ride in close quarters without panic and the better your chance of recovery if you are bumped or thrown off balance. Although most accidents happen so fast there is no time to think, there are some drills you can do to improve agility and develop a "second nature" reaction to falling (see "A Crash Course").

Preventive maintenance of yourself and your bicycle will help you hit the road with confidence. If you discover a front tire with a big bulge in it and depart without changing it, you will probably spend a good portion of your ride waiting for it to pop. You become tense and more likely to be hurt if you should fall.

Two other things that tend to help produce a worry-free ride are wearing a helmet and carrying an identification card. There is so much talk about bicycle head injuries these days (even though less than one per thousand cyclists will sustain such an injury) that it makes sense to wear a helmet, if only for the peace of mind. It's also wise to carry some kind of ID card, noting persons to contact in case of an emergency, as well as any special medical information (blood type, allergies to medicines, etc.) that would be helpful to those caring for you. There is certainly some comfort in knowing that your family would be notified and that an attending good Samaritan could save your life if the proper emergency information were readily available.

A CRASH COURSE

Learn To:

1. Feel confident and agile on bike
2. Relax (go limp) when falling
3. Tumble and roll rather than hit and bounce

Practice:

On grass on an old bike:

1. Doing wheelies
2. Riding on a 4-inch-wide board
3. Jumping over small logs
4. Standing still with feet on the pedals
5. Riding with a friend, in a figure eight, touching shoulders and elbows

On grass without a bike:

1. Shoulder rolls from kneeling, then standing positions
2. Shoulder rolls from a run until a 2- to 3-foot-high pole can be cleared. (Objective is to touch ground first with the shoulder, then tuck and roll to a sitting or standing position.)

BUILD CONFIDENCE—BE PREPARED

1. Wear a helmet every time you ride.
2. Tell your family or friends where you are going and when you will be back.
3. Double-check your bike.
4. Carry a laminated ID card in your jersey pocket or on a chain around your neck, with this information:
   - Full name, address, phone number
   - Next of kin or good friend (two contacts, with phone numbers)
   - Family physician, name and phone
   - Blood type
   - Any allergies to medications.

RECOVERING FROM A FALL

The most amazing thing about a pro falling off a bicycle is how quickly he gets back up and how anxious he seems to be to get back in the race. There is no shortage of published photos of the heroic cyclist carrying on with a bloodied arm and shorts ripped halfway off, exposing a hip that looks like raw hamburger.

As gruesome as this may seem, it usually doesn't hurt as bad as it looks. In fact, if a racer suffers a serious injury, it is rare that he can or will get back on his bike. In some cases, as with Davis Phinney in the Coors Classic one year, it's not only possible to race but to win with a serious injury.

The difference between how a novice and an experienced racer reacts to falling is really one of mental conditioning.

"You don't want to get up after a crash," says 1984 Olympic Gold Medalist, Alexi Grewal, "you do it because it's your job and you can't

It looks worse than it feels! *Press Sports photo*

afford to lose any time. All it takes is quitting once to realize that most injuries don't hurt enough to justify dropping out anyway."

Beginning riders need to be a bit more cautious. If you do fall off, it may be easier to ride than you initially think, but it is important to observe these rules:

1. Before getting up, do an inspection of head, shoulders, arms, legs, and feet. Stop any heavy bleeding immediately with a handkerchief or clothing.
2. Stand up slowly, if possible using something to support you. Any shooting pains means it's time to sit back down or keep your weight off the injured area. Find a position that is less painful. If the pain doesn't leave, stay still and wait for help.
3. Before getting back on the bike, check your body over again.
4. If all wounds are superficial (not bleeding profusely or accompanied by sharp pain), it's generally okay to get going again. Getting your blood circulating helps abrasions feel better and can shorten initial pain and discomfort.
5. If serious pain develops while riding, stop for help.

When you get home, make sure you take care in cleaning and covering all abrasions. The healing process will be quicker and a lot less painful if you follow the steps set forth below. If there is any severe pain, particularly in the head, it's a good idea to see a doctor right away.

PHINNEY CARRIES ON

Certainly the greatest crash victim among Americans is Davis Phinney, 7-Eleven team member and veteran Tour de France rider. One year his face plowed through the rear window of a team car, resulting in hundreds of facial stitches.

Only a few weeks later he was racing again and no less fearful of taking risks. "The scar gives my face character," he shrugged.

In 1983, Phinney landed underneath a six-man pileup at the Coors Classic in Colorado. His wrist immediately puffed up to the size of a tennis ball. "For the rest of the race I just rode mostly with one hand because it hurt to grip the bars," he said.

But Phinney not only carried on one-handedly, he won the final sprint and took the race. The crowd loved him on the podium, arm encased in ice packs and bandages. "Yeah, I almost passed out from that one," Phinney admits. "But my adrenalin always seems to keep me going."

Davis Phinney finished the 1983 Coors Classic with a badly sprained wrist.
Seth Goltzer photo

REMEDY FOR ROAD RASH

Abrasions are so common with cyclists, they have a name for them: Road Rash. Here's how to take care of it, so it will not get infected and will heal quickly.

1. Bite the bullet and clean wounds thoroughly:
   - Use soap and water or Betadine® solution (an over-the-counter iodine cleaning solution).
   - Scrub with a soft brush, removing all tar and road dirt. Screaming here is okay (the brush should be a small hand-washing brush, with soft bristles). If wounds are deep, have a doctor do it.
   - Ice can be applied, followed by a cold-water rinse, to reduce swelling and pain.
2. Smear cleaned wound with antiseptic (Bacitracin® or Neosporin® are recommended over-the-counter topical antibiotic ointments).
3. Bandage the wound:
   - Cover with nonstick dressing. (Spenco® "second skin" is excellent and Telfa® nonstick pads are also good.)
   - Use adhesive tape to hold bandage in place. (If wound is on arm or leg, "surgical mesh" is a great way to hold the bandage in place, without restricting movement.)
4. Clean and rebandage twice daily:
   - Softly scrub the wound during a morning and evening shower. Reapply antiseptic and dressings as above. (Scabs should not be allowed to form. They stiffen the area, crack and bleed with movement, and significantly prolong healing.)
5. Check for infection. Prolonged redness or swelling may mean infection. See a physician immediately.

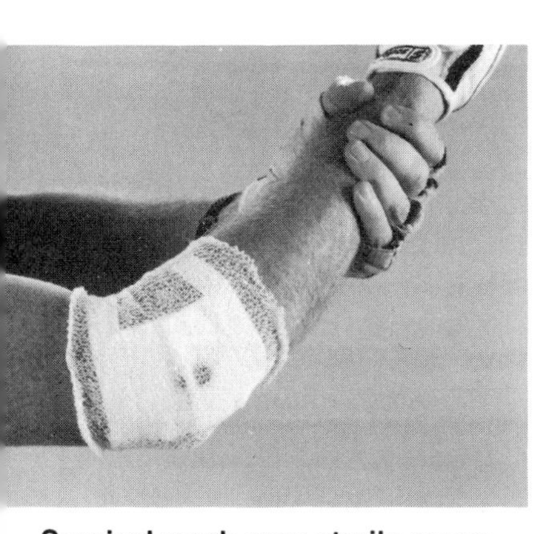

Surgical mesh over sterile gauze pads is the best way to cover road rash and promote faster healing (see text). *Seth Goltzer photo*

More serious injuries from falling, such as concussions and broken bones, cannot be ignored and should obviously be attended to immediately. The addicted cyclist should know, however, that depending on the nature and extent of the injury, it is often possible to continue riding (or at least training on a stationary bike) during the healing process, under the supervision of a knowledgeable sports doctor. It is not uncommon, for example, for racers to be outfitted with special wrist and elbow casts that permit near-normal training and racing.

The collarbone (the one most commonly broken by cyclists) generally heals within six weeks, with the fully healed bone stronger than the original equipment. Training during the recovery period from a broken collarbone should be under very controlled and forgiving conditions. An indoor trainer or flat, smooth roadways, to lessen road shock, are two oft-recommended techniques.

SADDLE SORES

Pain from falling off your bicycle is one thing. Pain from staying on is quite another. The more one rides, the more likely one will, at some time or another, meet up with "the trauma of the saddle."

Saddle soreness takes many forms, ranging from a simple red rash to nasty boils that can make grown men cry. Even the legends, such as Eddy Merckx and Bernard Hinault, have suffered this malady to the point that their performances have been affected. (Merckx' were once so painful that he felt the need to adjust his saddle while flying down a mountain at over fifty mph.)

The watchword for saddle trauma is prevention. In Chapter 3, we learned the wisdom of investing in a good seat ("better safe than saddle sorry"). Saddle trauma almost always stems from one of two things:

1. bacterial growth
2. broken skin, from chafing during constant pedaling.

The best way to guard against both of these is through proper care of what an old-timer we knew called "the stem end of your constitution" and everything it comes in contact with (see box).

Should problems still develop, there are several tried-and-true methods for cure. Rashes and minor skin breaks should be treated daily with antiinflammatory/antibacterial creams such as Cortaid®, Neosporin®, or Bacitracin®. Should the condition worsen or develop into boils (hard, round pimplelike sores under the skin), rest and a visit to the doctor are recommended. Severe boils need to be lanced and/or treated with oral antibiotics.

Pros who must keep racing with or without boils will be injected with an interlesional steroid to dry up the problem. An antiseptic, anesthetic skin cream called Nupercainal® is also often used to help lessen the pain.

CYCLIST'S LEG PROBLEMS

Despite the occasional occupational hazard of saddle trauma, having one's weight supported by a machine, with a certain amount of shock-absorbing ability, has real advantages in the strains and pulls department. Relatively common and often debilitating injuries suf-

HOW TO PREVENT SADDLE SORES

1. **Ride in proper cycling shorts.** Long, close-fitting legs; no inner seams and a quality chamois lining are essential. Chamois must be next to the skin.
2. **Clean shorts after every ride.** Warm water, mild antiseptic soap, thorough rinsing, and drying under ultraviolet light will beat back bacteria.
3. **Take care of your chamois.** When dried out after washing, chamois can be restored by rubbing it briskly by hand. Before each ride, the chamois should be lubricated to restore moisture and help lessen chafing. (Recommended chamois lubricants: Jecovital®, A & D Ointment®, Kucharik's Chamois Fat®, or Vaseline®.)
4. **Take care of yourself.** After a ride, never stand around in your riding shorts. Thoroughly clean crotch area after every ride (using alcohol will kill bacteria and help toughen the skin).
5. **Make sure it's not your bike.** Improper saddle height, tilt, shape, or overall position on the bike can cause saddle soreness. (Review Chapter 3 for correct positioning.)

fered by runners, such as shin splints, strained tendons, and pulled muscles are not nearly as prevalent among cyclists.

In fact, Jeff Galloway in his highly regarded book, *Galloway's Book on Running*, recommends cycling as good therapy for recovery from these kinds of running injuries: "Cycling doesn't produce the gravity stress (pounding) of running and therefore will not aggravate *most* injuries," he says.

But the constant, repetitive act of pedaling in the same position all the time can result in internal leg problems, particularly in the knees and other joints (see table on page 139).

The most common leg problems encountered by cyclists include bursitis, chondromalacia, several forms of tendinitis, and tenosynovitis. Virtually all of these problems stem from some imperfection in the pedal stroke that, when repeated over and over, leads to inflammation, possible swelling and, in all cases, pain. The onset of these problems can usually be traced to a recent crash, change of bicycle or bike position, or an unusually long or strenuous effort.

The number-one treatment for these injuries is immediate and total rest. Forcing oneself to "ride through" the problem can result in serious damage that could eventually lead to surgery. Both Bernard Hinault and Stephan Roche, the Tour de France winners in 1985 and 1987 respectively, each missed an entire season due to knee problems and ensuing operations to correct them. Application of ice, physical therapy, taking an antiinflammatory agent (like aspirin) and, in the extreme, cortisone shots are the generally prescribed treatments before an operation is recommended.

If these problems are caught early, treated quickly and completely, and their underlying causes eliminated, it is possible that a recurrence will never happen.

Since most cycling-related leg problems involve the knees, it helps to observe a few important rules for their avoidance:

HOW TO AVOID KNEE PROBLEMS

1. Use low gears, spinning at optimum cadence of 85–95 rpm.
2. Check saddle height for proper pedaling position (see Chapter 3).
3. Develop a smooth, fluid pedal stroke (see Chapter 6).
4. Check cleat/shoe/pedal relationship (see Chapters 3, 4, and 6).
5. Always keep knees warm (they should be covered when temperature is below 70°).
6. If pain starts, with or without swelling:
   - Stop riding immediately
   - Ice the knee
   - Take aspirin
   - Consult physician

LOWER-BACK PAIN

A most common affliction among cyclists is lower-back pain, and it usually results from one of the following:

1. *Poor cycling position* Usually the "reach" is too short, not allowing the back to stretch out enough and placing too much weight on the hips and lower back (see Chapter 3).

2. *Overwork* Pushing high gears and climbing big hills, before the body is in shape to do so, puts undue strain on the lumbosacral muscles (lower back).

3. *Anatomical problems* Chronic lower-back pain that won't go away through correcting riding position and/or conditioning the back through training could be due to a more serious problem, such as curvature of the spine or a herniated disk.

One of the ways for correcting most back problems is to strengthen the back through a program of regular exercise. Daily stretching and sit-ups are recommended.

When backache occurs during a ride, it is important to vary the riding position by standing up and stretching and, with back straight, rocking the back from side to side.

Obviously, persistent back pain that does not improve with equipment adjustments and/or conditioning should be discussed with a doctor.

CYCLISTS' LEG PROBLEMS

PROBLEM	SYMPTOMS	LOCATION	CAUSE	TREATMENT/CURE
Bursitis	Deep hip or knee pain develops during ride.	Hips, knees	Inflammation of bursar sacs from constant, repetitive motion of nearby joints	• Rest (off the bike) • Ice at first • Heat after 2 days • Modify position on bike
Chondromalacia	Deep knee pain and sensation of "grating" under the kneecap. Develops as ride progresses.	Underside of patella (kneecap)	Abnormal path is taken as the patella moves up and down with knee flexing during pedaling. Underside of kneecap begins to disintegrate along with cartilage.	• Rest (off the bike) • Stop ride as soon as pain is felt • Take aspirin (antiinflammatory) • Ice 5–7 minutes persistently • Check shoe and saddle positions
Tendinitis	Swelling and pain on and off bike	Around knee or above heel	• Irritating, repetitive movement causes tendons to pull away from their connection points on bones. • Overuse of quadriceps causes patellar tendinitis. • Bad pedaling, wrong saddle height causes Achilles tendonitis. • Too high saddle causes popliteal tendinitis.	• Rest (may ride below pain level) • Two aspirin with meals • Ice 10 min. each day, if swelling • Modify position on bike
Tenosynovitis	Sudden pain and discomfort, hard to pedal	Ankle area	Inflammation of synovial membrane of a tendon caused by bad foot placement on pedal, poor pedaling technique, or biomechanical foot defect.	• Rest • Insert orthopedic soles • Modify shoe placement on pedal

NUMBNESS

Many cyclists complain of numbness (or a tingling sensation), in the feet, hands, or crotch, developing during a ride. These are the contact points between rider and bicycle and undue pressure can pinch the nerves and blood vessels running through these areas. The resulting numbness is unnerving and can lead to bigger problems if not attended to immediately.

Here's what you do:

1. *Hand numbness:*
    - "Reach" may be too short. Check position and try fitting a longer stem.
    - Wear padded gloves and wrap handlebars with cushioned tape or special handlebar wrap (available at good bike stores).
    - Change hand position frequently while riding.

2. *Foot numbness:*
   - Check for proper shoe/cleat/pedal relationship.
   - Try looser-fitting shoes.
   - If using toe clips and straps, keep straps loose.
3. *Crotch numbness:*
   - Make sure saddle is level (nose tilting up or down is the most common cause of this).
   - Wear shorts with thick chamois padding.
   - Try a different-shaped saddle and sit further back (make sure you are sitting on pelvic bones, not soft tissue).

NECK PAIN

Nine times out of ten this is brought on by an improper riding position. Reach that is too short or a saddle that is too high in relation to the stem will "pitch" you too far forward and put undue strain on the shoulders. This will also force you to constantly arch your neck to see where you're headed. Add a heavy helmet and the whole thing will become a pain in the neck.

Check your position and do some neck-strengthening exercises.

CRAMPS

Leg cramps have lost races. They are usually brought on by an effort too great for the level of conditioning. Pushing that extra little bit is sometimes enough to seize up one or more tired muscles. A cramp is a sustained contraction that usually relaxes after a few seconds. For cyclists, it most often occurs in the calf muscle.

Amazingly, a calf-muscle cramp will lessen if you press the middle of the calf firmly with your thumb and hold for ten seconds or so.

The likelihood of cramps can also be lessened somewhat by increasing the intake of electrolyte replacement drinks, such as Gatorade.® These guard against depletion of potassium and magnesium, body salts that aid the normal contraction of muscles.

SUMMARY

Cycling, like any other sport, has a certain amount of risk associated with it. The biggest risk of injury from bicycling is from falling. One out of every 100 cyclists is treated for minor injuries each year. The most serious injuries occur when cyclists and automobiles come together. Ninety percent of all bicycle-related deaths come from collisions with motor vehicles, so choosing where and when one

rides and wearing a helmet can greatly reduce accidents and serious injuries.

Good hygiene and a proper saddle and shorts are the best remedy for unpleasant, but common, saddle sores.

Although trauma injuries to joints, tendons, and muscles are fewer and farther between in cycling than in running, the repetitive nature of pedaling can cause problems for the legs and knees. These include bursitis, chondromalacia, tendinitis, and tenosynovitis. Each should be treated immediately by rest, icing, aspirin, and, if they persist, consultation with a doctor.

Most knee and leg problems, back pain, neck pain, and numbness can be corrected or prevented by determining the proper fit on the bicycle and by ensuring that the feet are positioned properly on the pedals.

In a crash like this, bikes are usually hurt more than bodies.

10 Family Cycling

Bicycling has been promoted as a great family sport as long as we can remember, and never stronger in that regard than in the first full-color Schwinn catalogs of the 1950s. What could be more pleasant than a leisurely pedal around the neighborhood with Mom, Dad, and the kids riding single file, each on their own properly proportioned bicycles?

Today, however, Dad's slacks and cardigan have been exchanged for a Lycra skin suit and his bike has become a sophisticated piece of exercise equipment, compared to the balloon-tired coaster of yesteryear.

The baby boomers who appeared as kids in the fifties' Schwinn ads now have their own offspring and family cycling is experiencing a grand revival, albeit with more of a fitness orientation and a high-tech, modern flair.

The bicycle industry is of course delighted. The gear one can buy for keeping the family together on wheels can exceed a year's college tuition. The baby seat or trailer soon gives way to the starter bike, then BMX, Freestyle, and scaled-down adult models. The baby ATB cannot be far behind. Tandems (bicycles built for two) have even been custom-made with a third seat in the middle and special crank assemblies, so junior can be sandwiched between a panting and sweating parental pair during their daily workout.

Despite the rising costs and sophistication of equipping the whole family, surveys by the National Sporting Goods Association and Gallup indicate that cycling, like walking, softball, and volleyball is on the increase, partially due to the fact that two or more family members are likely to participate in these activities at the same time. This is consistent with the theory that time-pressed modern parents are streamlining their life-styles and eliminating solo activities from their schedules. It is no secret that less family-oriented sports like running, swimming, aerobics, racquetball, and calisthenics have declined markedly since 1984.

Studies have shown that cycling breeds togetherness, unless, of course, a family member goes off the deep end. A survey of *Bicycling Magazine* readers, in 1989, revealed that approximately half of all respondents felt cycling was helping their current relationships. However, when mileage levels reached 300 miles per week, 40 percent said the opposite. Some other interesting findings:

Cycling has been promoted as a family activity since the Schwinn catalogs of the fifties. (Shown are Dick and June [Allison] Powell and children.) *Courtesy of Schwinn Bicycle Company*

- Forty-two percent of women respondents met a sex partner through cycling, as compared to 24 percent of the men.
- Sixty-five percent of women respondents said cycling helps their relationship, as did 49 percent of the men.
- Respondents rode their bicycles an average of 4.41 times per week and had sex an average of 2.98 times per week.

Since this is the family chapter of a G-rated book, we will let you draw your own conclusion from that last statistic!

LIVING TOGETHER, TRAINING TOGETHER

For many couples who ride bikes, cycling is the tie that binds. But sweating together is not always bliss.

"Our biggest fight was over a steep hill," said Tracy, a twenty-one-year-old fitness consultant from Connecticut, who met her husband Jamie at a triathlon in which they were both entered. "Cycling together was the catalyst of our relationship. But one day Jamie picked a route that I knew went over a very steep hill. He went up it like nothing and I had to get off and walk. To make it worse, he just kept going. I was furious. It took me twenty minutes to catch up."

Jamie was a victim of the silent treatment until they got home. But the relationship survived and Jamie and Tracy discovered what so many other athletic couples admit to: it's very difficult to train together all the time, unless there is a close match in ability. Says Jamie: "I get frustrated when I feel like riding hard and have to slow down or wait a lot of the time."

Here are some tips on how to keep your cycling and the relationship on the same track:

- *Don't force the program.* No matter how close, two people do not feel the same way about everything at all times. When one wants to

Special tandems are made to take a child in the middle.
Dan Burden photo

stay in bed and the other wants to hit the road, work out a compromise and live with it or go your separate ways for a few hours. And don't feel guilty with the choice.

- *Agree on "together rides."* Pick one or more rides per week when both will accept the "stay together rule." The stronger rider must temper the urge to blast off, while the other demonstrates a cheerful willingness to try harder. (Good luck!)

- *Ride with others.* Group rides, like group therapy, relieve one-on-one tensions, particularly if the group has members with similar ability levels as you and your spouse. Such a group will motivate the slower riders to try harder, and it will be refreshing for them to meet others who have not yet hit the fast lane.

- *"See you back at the ranch."* Many couples are perfectly happy to suit up together, pump up tires together, and ride by themselves. A favorite technique is to choose a circuit or route where the faster rider can do more laps, during the same amount of time. Another is to ride an out-and-back course where the faster rider can pick up his or her mate on the way home. Each will get a satisfying workout and will still have a chance to ride together for at least part of the way.

- If all else fails, be prepared to accept that sometimes the best policy is no policy at all. Perhaps the "you take the high road, I'll take the low road" approach will provide some quiet time and space for you both. Also remember that one man's feast is often another man's poison. In that case, take a deep breath and say "Viva la différence!"

PREGNANCY AND CYCLING

Couples who enjoy cycling together or simply enjoy having their own time to ride each day face a whole new scenario when mother becomes heavy with child.

For those women who have made a commitment to regular cycling, pregnancy can mean many different things, not the least of which is fearing that one's cycling days are coming to an end.

Merideth Drake, a dedicated cyclist and triathlete, whose life and life-style revolve around spinning wheels (her husband Geoff also happens to be the assistant managing editor of *Bicycling Magazine*), found that cycling during the last half of her pregnancy was so uncomfortable that she had to give it up:

"It was ironic to think that cycling, which had always made me healthy, was now making me feel ill. It was frustrating to watch Geoff leave for a ride. I missed our time together, a shared meal at the end of a long ride, and the outdoors. I wanted to cry every time he left. Sometimes I did. When I saw a fit woman cycle past, I almost

EXERCISE DURING PREGNANCY*

The American College of Obstetricians and Gynecologists provides these recommendations for pregnant women who have engaged in regular exercise prior to becoming pregnant:

- Exercise three to five times per week for 15 to 60 minutes per session.
- Check pulse several times during each session. Pulse rate should fall within 65 and 90% of maximum, depending upon fitness level (see Chapter 7 for determining maximum pulse rate).
- Avoid dehydration and overheating.
- Stop immediately if severe pain is experienced.
- Always warm up and cool down for several minutes, before and after each workout.
- Wear a sports bra.

* Note that some conditions, such as heart disease, premature labor, a history of miscarriages, or ruptured membranes may preclude exercise. Consult your physician about any exercise program.

felt like sticking a pump in her spokes. I began to wonder if I'd ever be fit again."

Two and one-half months after giving birth to a healthy daughter, Drake was back cycling and had soon progressed to the fitness level she had prior to pregnancy. Her hiatus from cycling had lasted nearly a year, due to five months of severe winter weather, followed by four months of discomfort and nearly three months of recovery.

Is it possible to cycle throughout pregnancy? Absolutely. According to medical studies, vigorous exercise is possible right to the onset of labor, provided it is carefully monitored and approved by your physician. Obviously, it is important to consider added risk factors—like falling—before sticking with an intense program.

Perhaps the most infamous pregnant-cyclist story is that of Mary Jane "Miji" Reoch, eleven-time national champion, who delivered her first child at age thirty-five. Reoch actually won a race when she was five months pregnant, but the day she gave birth was even more unbelievable.

Her friend and nearby neighbor in Philadelphia, Julie Currie, recalls the incident: "Miji had wanted to ride her bike to the delivery room and I had told her I would ride with her. At first it was kind of a joke. But one evening she called and said she was starting labor and was ready to go. Well, it was raining cats and dogs and the hospital was twenty-five miles away, through rush hour traffic. It was crazy, so I said forget it!"

But Reoch was determined. "I was very fit," she said, "and I had

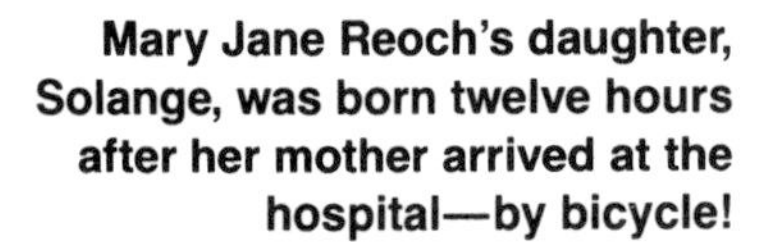

Mary Jane Reoch's daughter, Solange, was born twelve hours after her mother arrived at the hospital—by bicycle!

talked with doctors who said it could be done. And besides, I thought it would be a neat story to tell my daughter."

She made it to the hospital without incident. ("I even told a recreational rider I passed to use a lower gear," she said.) Reoch recalls that her biggest problem was getting her bike past the entrance to the emergency room. Twelve hours later, a healthy girl was born, with no ill effects suffered by mother or daughter.

Reoch's story is less a shining example than a proven point: With the right mindset, almost anything is doable.

Most of the stories of women cycling through pregnancy fall somewhere between Drake and Reoch. Audrey McElmury, 1969 World Champion, didn't go so far as to ride to the hospital, but she did calculate that her son Ian had about 4,000 miles behind him by the time he arrived. Sue Novara-Reber, a national and world sprint champion, rode until one week prior to delivery. "For me, it was the perfect exercise," she said.

Although the overall effects of cycling during pregnancy and after birth will probably never be accurately quantified, due to wide fluctuations among individuals, there are some interesting observations based on case histories:

1. Although exercise during pregnancy may help reduce morning sickness, lessen the likelihood of varicose veins, reduce excessive weight gain, and better prepare one for labor, the most important gain may be psychological. "It felt great to be active when others thought I should be lying down," says McElmury.

2. A high level of fitness is not necessarily helpful during labor but will pay off during recovery. It has been noted that exercise can stiffen the perineum and pelvic floor, making delivery harder. But a fit person with strong heart and lungs can recover quicker from the intense physical effort of labor than can someone who is not used to strenuous exercise.

3. Having children may make the female athlete stronger. Women cyclists who have been at least as strong postpartum include Sheila Young-Ochowicz who won national and world sprint titles after her first child; Maria Canins, of Italy, with three children, who won the Tour de France for women; and forty-three-year-old Casey Petterson, winner of the 1987 Race Across America, who is also the mother of three.

CARRYING BABY (ON THE BIKE)

Now that the bundle of joy has arrived, what do you do with it when you want to go for a ride?

The purist will call a babysitter or press the spouse or a relative into service until the ride is over. The more enlightened parent will figure out a way to bring the child along—at least some of the time.

There are two recommended ways of doing this. Both have their pluses and minuses.

The *baby seat* is intended for infants who are about nine months old (old enough to hold their head up) and may be used until they weigh about forty pounds (around age four). There are two types of baby seats, both of which must be fastened securely to the bicycle. The first is a simple plastic seat that is mounted on the top tube with a set of collapsible footpegs that mount on the down tube. The child holds the handlebars, puts his feet through straps on the footpegs, and is seated between the rider's arms and knees. About the only thing good about this design is that the child is enveloped by the parent. This design is *not* recommended for the following reasons:

- The child cannot be securely strapped in.
- The rider of the bike cannot pedal effectively with a child between the knees.
- Even if it's your own kid, no one else should be holding the handlebars but you.

The rear-mounted baby seat (bolted to the frame over the rear wheel) offers a better alternative. When shopping for one of these, take the advice of the Bicycle Institute of America:

- Shop for a bicycle-mounted child seat intended for use over the rear wheel.

THE REAR-MOUNTED BABY SEAT

ADVANTAGES:

- Child can be strapped in and well-protected
- Child's hands are free, without being able to touch handlebars or spokes
- Seat attaches firmly to frame, at three points

DRAWBACKS:

- Bike is less stable and harder to pedal
- Safe units add considerable weight
- Bike is harder to mount and dismount

COST RANGE: $25–$100

BEST BRANDS: Troxel®, Rhode Gear®

Photo courtesy of Rhode Gear

- Check with your bicycle dealer. Your bike may not be suitable for a rear-mounted child seat or may need special attention, to safely and securely mount the seat.

- Look for a seat that provides your child with a protected place to rest his or her feet. The seat should also have spoke guards.

- If your own seat has exposed springs, make sure you fit it with a rear "spring guard," to keep small fingers from getting into places they don't belong.

- A seat with a high back supports your child's head, especially as children often fall asleep during a ride.

- A seat should have a sturdy lap and shoulder seat belt much like the one on your child's car seat. Keep it buckled whenever your child is in the seat.

- For comfort's sake, choose a seat with a shock-absorbing cushion. But don't add extra cushions. This could raise your child too high in the seat to be safe.

- Think of a bicycle helmet too. Get your child a helmet and use it every time you ride.

As ludicrous as it may seem at first glance, the *best* way to carry a child is in a specially designed *trailer* (see below.) Common charac-

teristics of trailers are a lightweight aluminum frame, a molded plastic "bucket," to hold children and/or cargo, and a pair of twenty-four-inch wheels. Trailers are secured to the bicycle by a flexible hitch that attaches to the seatpost or rear fork and allows the bike to lean over without tipping the trailer. Trailer options include forward-facing or rear-facing child positions and a variety of coverings, ranging from polyurethane windshields to nylon screening. Here's what to look for when shopping for a trailer:

- Load capacity up to one hundred pounds.
- Light overall weight, without sacrificing strength
- Narrow wheels and tires, to reduce rolling resistance
- Seat comfort and security features, such as built-in harness and protective sidewalls
- Adaptability for multiuse, such as carrying luggage or yard work.

Trailers are the preferred accessory among dedicated cyclists who believe that bringing the kids along is a great experience for them. Says serious trailer puller, Tim Grieco, of Tommy's Inc., a bike shop in Torrington, Connecticut: "Knowing that the child is wrapped in a security blanket and would be protected in case of an accident provides peace of mind for the adult pulling the trailer. You may have to go a little slower and use lower gears, but it's worth it."

THE TRAILER

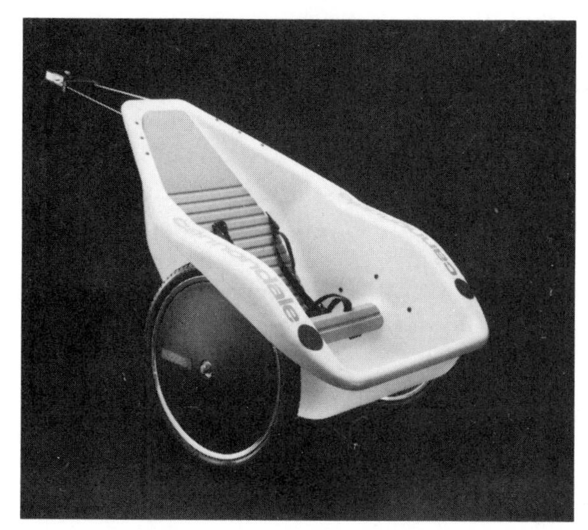

Photo courtesy of Cannondale

ADVANTAGES:
- Child(ren) can be strapped in and well-protected
- Additional gear can be brought along
- Bike remains stable
- Less wear on rear tire than with baby seat
- Trailer attaches and detaches easily
- Option for multi-use

DRAWBACKS:
- Substantially increases rolling resistance
- Cost is high

COST RANGE: $150–$400

BEST BRANDS:
Cannondale® and Kiddie Kart® (rear facing), Burley®, Blue Sky Cycle Cart®, Equinox®, and Winchester® (front facing)

ON THEIR OWN

No topic is closer to a cycling parent's heart than when a son or daughter is ready for that first solo ride. To children, mastering a bicycle is a real step toward independence. Having mobility and total control of a vehicle for the first time are big steps. How parents handle this is particularly crucial in making a child love or hate cycling. Also, understanding what the child is capable of at various stages of development is critical in making sure the learning process is accomplished the best way possible. Here are some pointers adapted from the Bicycle Institute of America:

- *Make sure the first bike fits.* The simple rule of thumb is that the child be able to straddle the bicycle's top tube with feet firmly on the ground. About an inch of clearance between the child's crotch and the top tube is ideal. Buying a bike that is too big, with the idea that the child will "grow into it," is a big mistake. Not only is such a bike dangerous, it may dampen enthusiasm for riding. Seat height should be adjusted so that there is only a slight bend in the knee at the bottom of the pedal stroke.

- *Buy the right bike.* Bicycle dealerships are your best bet for a safe, sturdy starter bike. A single-speed, coaster-brake model is the best type to learn on. Training wheels help teach turning and braking and are recommended as confidence builders until the child shows he has mastered the basic skills.

  Most children's starter bikes come equipped with "high rise" or BMX-style handlebars. This is unfortunate. For a four-, five-, or six-year-old to turn such a bike they must be in the "sit up and beg position," which goes against the principles of good bike handling. In a right turn, for example, the right end of the handlebar will poke the child's chest, while he has to lean and stretch with his left arm to hold the other side. This is particularly true with training wheels attached (without them, turning is as much a function of leaning and shifting body weight as turning the handlebars). Defy the manufacturer and ask your dealer to swap the BMX-style bar for a narrower and flatter or even a children's dropped bar—at least until it is time to remove the training wheels.

- *Know what a child can handle.* Most four-year-olds have developed sufficient coordination and motor skills to ride a bicycle with training wheels. The balance needed for handling a two-wheeler generally comes between ages four and six, well before a child is capable of riding in traffic. At the early ages, adult supervision is critical. Here are the guidelines suggested by the Bicycle Institute of America:

TEACHING BASIC RIDING SKILLS

BALANCE AND CONTROL

- Learn on a one-speed bike (with coaster brake) that fits properly (see text).
- Fit training wheels, until braking and steering are mastered.
- Teach two-wheel riding on a flat field of grass:
    - —Walk next to the child, holding under the seat, until balance is mastered.
    - —Encourage longer and longer distances of "solo" riding, from a few feet between one parent and another, to across the field, etc.
    - —Don't push the child too soon and always end each session on a high note.

SAFETY RULES TO MASTER

- Ride *with* traffic at all times. It's not only the law, but wrong-way riders get hit by cars (it's the cause of one out of five bike accidents).
- Stop before entering any street. One in three accidents result from riding into a street without looking, often from the child's own driveway.
- Obey all traffic signs and signals, particularly stop signs and red lights.
- Don't turn left without looking back first. If oncoming traffic is heavy, dismount and wait until road is clear before turning.
- Avoid busy streets. Establish acceptable routes and roads for children and make dangerous streets off limits.
- Don't play games on the roads.
- Follow-the-leader, trick riding, and jumping obstacles are for safe off-road places only.
- Don't ride at night—it's twenty times more dangerous, even with lights and special clothing.
- Wear a helmet. Children's models are available at all good bike stores. Look for the ANSI sticker of approval for protection insurance.

— Children age six and under should ride under adult supervision at all times.

— Children ages seven and eight may ride unsupervised, but not in the street.

— Children ages nine and older may, with proper training, ride on their own, but should be restricted to certain streets. Nine- and ten-year-olds can learn specific rules and safe riding skills, but are not always good judges of vehicle speeds nor understanding of concepts like "right-of-way."

- Make sure that safe skills are learned from the beginning.

START YOUNG BUT KEEP IT FUN

A ten-year study released by the Chrysler Fund/AAU Physical Fitness Program, in 1989, tested 9.7 million students nationwide and revealed that children's sedentary life-styles are making them fatter and less fit than their counterparts ten years earlier.

Program director, Dr. Wynn F. Updike, said that the lower scores on basic physical fitness tests partly result from youngsters' reliance on transportation and emphasis on technological games.

Other studies, like those conducted by Professor Thomas Gillian of the University of Michigan, indicate that eight- and nine-year-olds participating in twenty-five minutes of vigorous exercise, four days a week, can significantly reduce health problems (such as high blood-lipid levels, a contributor to heart ailments). Other studies have proven that an individual's cardiovascular *potential* can be improved by exercise only up until about age fifteen.

These findings tell us that strenuous activity is good for young people. It will help them live longer and healthier lives and become better potential athletes. And racing around on bicycles (safely, of course) is one of the best ways for children to get the kind of vigorous exercise they need.

This does not mean that kids with an interest in cycling should be channeled into a serious program of training and racing: Cycling is not like swimming, where world records can be broken by fifteen-year-olds. In fact, fifteen is about when youngsters first start to develop the muscle strength to handle the power demands of serious bicycle racing.

BMX is a great way for kids to get into racing.

THE TOUR DE YOUTH (MINI-CLASSICS, USA)

A colorful banner stretches across the road. A photo-timing camera sits poised for action high above the finish line. Nervous racers, mustered for the start, adjust their helmets and make last-minute equipment checks. As the announcer begins the countdown the crowd strains forward. . . . BANG, THEY'RE OFF!

Forty pair of little legs churn away from the starting line looking like a swarm of whirling windmills they disappear around the first turn. This is flat-out, high-speed racing at its best. There's no holding back, no complicated strategies, just a desperate urge to pedal as furiously as possible, until the race is over.

"This is no day camp," says Christy Rosen, mother of two and race director for the decade-old Red Zinger Mini-Classic, a nine-day stage race for 10- to 16-year-old children in and around Boulder, Colorado. "These kids take their racing very seriously and they're out for blood."

But Rosen is quick to point out that there is a lot more to the nation's best-organized series of youth races than cutthroat competition. To begin with, the Red Zinger Mini-Classic is the cornerstone of a summer-long series of youth races, collectively known as "Mini-Classics, USA." Organized by Youth Bicycle Racing Promotions, a non-profit company, the entire series is run by volunteers, most of whom are parents or graduates of the program. According to Rosen, the main objective is to provide children with a training ground for safe racing. Heavy emphasis is given to good sportsmanship, safety, and complete family involvement. Although gratification from participating is a big reward, many graduates go on to become amateur racers and even Olympic team candidates. The program's most successful graduate: Roy Knickman, 7-Eleven team member and Tour de France rider.

For more information contact: Youth Bicycle Promotions (Mini Classics, USA), Box 18356, Boulder, CO 80308

Photo © S. C. Reuman/Conundrum Designs

Before then, cycling should be fun and competition a healthy diversion only if the motivation is there. BMX racing can be a great first step. Most kids like the flash and the acrobatics in this kind of racing. The races are short, fast, and exciting, but do not require the participant to be a highly trained endurance athlete. BMX is of particular value in the development of good bike handling skills. Several top racers, including Olympian John Tomac, got their start in cycling as BMXers.

The best event for aspiring road racers, though, has to be the Red Zinger Mini Classic, in Colorado. Started as a local kid's event in 1977, it's now a summer-long series for youngsters, starting at age ten.

Interestingly, some of the world's best cyclists started much later:

- Eddy Merckx, five-time Tour de France Winner: First race, age fifteen
- Bernard Hinault, five-time Tour de France winner: First race, age sixteen
- Jeanne Longo, 1989 world champion and women's Tour de France winner: First race, age seventeen
- Greg LeMond, two-time Tour de France winner and America's top-ranked cyclist: First race, age fourteen.

HOW OLD IS TOO OLD?

A forty-year-old man finishing third in the Tour de France? One Frenchman, Raymond Poulidor, did it in 1976. What an example! What a specimen! What Poulidor proved, and what hundreds of thousands of masters-category racers confirm every year, is that it is possible to beat back father time.

Unsurprising to the gray underground of older cyclists, bicycling has long been one of the three favorite sports of the over-fifty set, ranked only behind swimming and "general exercise."

Dr. Kenneth Cooper, renowned author and exercise physiologist, has concluded that cycling and other similar cardiovascular exercises actually retard the aging process: "The body thrives on use and tends to age prematurely only when we stop using it."

Benefits of cycling that are of particular importance to older people:

- No inherent joint trauma
- Reduced blood pressure
- Reduced risk of heart disease
- Improved muscle tone
- Burns calories

Moreover, for the former or aspiring middle- to old-aged athlete, cycling's skyrocketing masters program offers everything from local age-category racing to World Cup competition.

Skip Cutting, a 1964 and 1968 Olympic Team member, returned to competitive cycling several years after ending his pro sprint-racing career, in 1975. By the mid-eighties, Cutting was competing regularly in veterans and masters events around the U.S. In 1987, Cutting traveled to Austria and won the World Cup Masters in his age category.

For Cutting, it was a great achievement, considering that cycling had become more a hobby than the focus of his career. He readily admits that cycling is an important part of his life-style, but one that does not close him off to other sports and interests.

Performing well again is extremely gratifying for a past champion, even if personal performance cannot match the glory days of one's youth. As Cutting puts it: "It's great to be 43, fit and sassy, and feeling the wind in my face. I don't mind getting older, I'm just not going to give it any recognition."

SUMMARY

Cycling has always been a great family sport and can be enjoyed by couples and families with children. With today's equipment options, the kids can come along before they can pedal, or for that matter, walk. The towed trailer is the best way for small children to experience the fun of cycling.

Women need not fear that having a child will end their cycling days. Many women have pedaled right up to the delivery day and have come back stronger than ever.

Teaching children to ride is a combination of attention to safety and not pushing too hard too soon. The same is true of getting into racing. Greg LeMond, for example, did not enter his first race until he was fourteen.

On the other side of life, one is never too old to ride a bike or even race. Frenchman Raymond Poulidor placed third in the Tour de France, when he was forty. Others, like former Olympian, Skip Cutting, look forward to competing in Masters races as long as they can.

11

Touring

Ray Benton was president of ProServ, Inc., a successful sports management company. He made a great living, regularly traveled the world, and was friend and confidant to many household names in sports, including Arthur Ashe, Jimmie Connors, and Michael Jordan.

To the outsider, sports management may seem like a fun and glamorous field. In some ways it is, but it is also fiercely competitive, and like any other profession it can be a real grind, particularly if, as in Benton's case, it is pursued year after year on an intense and professional basis, at the highest level.

At age forty-seven, Benton decided that he needed a break and a new direction. He stepped down as president and began what he hoped would be a lengthy sabbatical in which he could recharge his batteries and define his goals and priorities, for the next stage of his life. As a first step in "decompressing," Benton, a casual cyclist at best, took his son on a leisurely bicycle tour through France. Not only did he have one of the best experiences of his life, he returned from that two-week sojourn with the fire back in his belly. Within weeks he was acquiring small bicycle-touring companies in the United States and Europe and combining them into Travent, Ltd., now a leading packager of luxury bicycle vacations, with the slogan "Unusual adventure in uncommon comfort."

Benton, an experienced and savvy marketer, was quick to recognize a golden business opportunity resulting from the coming together of several trends, including the bicycle boom among adults, increased leisure time and discretionary dollars, and a growing boredom with crowded and confining destination resorts. He perceived a desire on the part of many to combine a healthy fitness activity with a more intimate experience, involving people and countryside, than is possible on jet planes, freeways, theme parks, and tourist traps.

Although Travent represents the Rolls Royce of the bicycle-tour movement, it is the mere tip of the iceberg. Bicycle touring has been around as long as the bike itself. The beauty of it is that it can be custom-tailored to suit the tastes, budget, and the time constraints

Cycling tours are one of the best ways to see the countryside. They "put back all those spaces that disappeared between places." *(Greg Siple) Travent International Photo*

of anyone who can ride a bike and who has an inclination to venture beyond their block.

A bicycle tour can be anything from a loop around New York's Central Park to the legendary Race Across AMerica. One usually starts bicycle touring by taking the bike, finding a good road, and pushing off. The next step is riding with a relative, friend, or mate, and then with a group. From there, the challenges relate to sharpening skills and broadening horizons, both in terms of distance and finding new and exciting places to ride. The ultimate benefit of bicycle touring is that most of the fun is in getting there.

ROOTS AND ROUTES

Bicycle clubs and tours began to proliferate during the first bicycle boom, in the late 1800s. These outings ran the gamut from Sunday picnics and rides around the park to one-day century (one hundred mile) rides and the first cross-country ride by Tom Stevens, on a high-wheeled Ordinary, in 1884.

No discussion of the origins of U.S. touring, or for that matter bicycling, is complete, without a look at the first and still largest touring organization, the League of American Wheelmen.

The L.A.W. was formed in 1880, at a three-day meeting in Newport, Rhode Island. Its founding fathers were Charles E. Pratt, C.

L.A.W. Clubs held big touring rides all across the U.S. This one started in Hagerstown, Maryland, in the early 1890s. *Pennsylvania Historical and Museum Commission*

Kirk Monroe, and Frank W. Weston. Weston, known for many years as "The Father of American Cycling," had founded the first bicycle exporting firm in 1877 and, during the same year, the first bicycling newspaper, the *American Cycling Journal.*

Cycling in those early days had a very rough road, in more ways than one. Public prejudice, dating back to the "Boneshaker" craze of 1868–69, was reflected in laws prohibiting use of the streets by cyclists, in most jurisdictions. Cyclists were considered a nuisance, particularly by the horse-and-buggy set, who claimed the bikes caused the horses to shy. Early cycling enthusiasts were pelted with tomatoes and even run off the roads by irate carriage drivers.

Through a well-organized lobbying effort and some dramatic public demonstrations involving parades of cyclists, the L.A.W. succeeded in rolling back the discriminatory legislation and opening many of the streets, parks, and highways of America to the bicycle.

The L.A.W. also instigated the "good roads" movement that resulted in the paving of America's highways. To this end, it published a monthly *Good Roads* magazine, which it ran at a loss for ten years.

Thanks to the innovative and adaptable new sport-rack systems, such as the Thule model shown, it is now easy to bring your bikes with you, along with your luggage and other sports gear. *Photo courtesy of Thule System*

Sterling Elliott, the magazine's editor in 1984 remarked: "It was the wheelmen who started the good roads movement, for the reason that the carriage makers didn't know about it. The horse knew about it, but he couldn't talk."

The L.A.W. is also credited with first organizing rules to govern amateur bicycle racing in this country, and they governed the sport during its first twenty years.

The L.A.W.'s ranks took a dramatic upsurge toward the end of the century, with the introduction of the Safety cycle. Nearly two million bicycles were produced in 1897, female membership grew, and, as a result of this bicycle boom, League membership reached an all-time high of 102,636 in 1898.

In Europe, the evolution of organized clubs and tours also closely followed the development of the bicycle itself. In France, for example, the UVF, the first bicycle federation in that country, launched its *brevets* of fifty and one hundred kilometers, around 1890.

TOURING TODAY

Today's bicycle touring options are limited only by the breadth of the imagination and the depth of the pocketbook. Touring is often categorized in two basic types: Fully loaded and light.

In fully loaded touring, the cyclist, like a hiker with a backpack, is pretty well self-contained. Instead of the backpack, the touring cyclist uses saddlebags, or "panniers," and other smaller bags that are distributed about the bicycle, in such a way as to least interfere with the bike's balance and performance. The extent to which you load up your bike depends on the type of trip you are taking. Obviously, you will need less for a day trip or overnight than for a week and you can greatly reduce the load if you intend to stay in motels, hostels, or friends' homes, rather than "rough it" beneath Mother Nature's shining canopy.

Touring light is possible in the case of a day or overnight trip or on longer trips, if you or your group are fortunate enough to travel with a "sag wagon," a van that accompanies the group, carrying their baggage as well as extra parts and tools for their bicycles. When traveling with a sag wagon, one needs only those items necessary for a one-day ride, such as light food, additional clothing for weather changes, water bottles, air pump, patch kit, and tube.

TYPES OF TOURS

DAY TRIPS

These can be free-form or structured, depending on your style. Day trips are great because you can travel so lightly. The key is to remember not to "bite off more than you can chew," particularly when you are a novice cyclist. It is not uncommon for one to get caught up in the excitement of a beautiful day and the curiosity of what's around the next bend and forget that for every mile and hour traveled out, you must do the same coming back. You can avoid this pitfall by planning your route so you hit your driveway before the "bonk" hits you. It makes sense to plan your trip in advance and to carry a map, some change for the telephone, and some personal and medical information in case of an emergency.

If you enjoy riding with others, nearly every community has a bike club that organizes several day trips over the course of the season. These may be found through your friendly, local bike shop or the organizations listed at the end of this chapter.

OVERNIGHTS

The overnight is a good second step that will help you test whether you are cut out to be a long-distance touring cyclist. The overnight can be a camping trip, a visit to some friends in a nearby town, or perhaps a round trip to a motel or bed and breakfast. In addition to the items listed above, for light touring and day trips, you will probably want to bring along a change of cycling shorts, whatever clothing you will need for the evening's activities, and an abbreviated kit of toiletries.

BICYCLING MAGAZINE'S 25 BEST TOURING AREAS IN NORTH AMERICA

- Nova Scotia, Canada
- Cape Cod, Massachusetts
- New York's Finger Lakes
- DelMarVa (Coastal Delaware, Maryland, and Virginia)
- Northwestern Coastal Florida
- Michigan's Upper Peninsula
- Minnesota's Lake Country
- Wisconsin's Door County
- Puget Sound, Washington State, and British Columbia, Canada
- Northwest Coast, California, and Washington
- Lancaster County, Pennsylvania
- Central Kentucky
- Natchez Trace Parkway, Mississippi and Tennessee
- Santa Fe and Oregon Trails, Kansas
- Texas Hill Country (Austin area)
- Yellowstone National Park, Wyoming
- Bryce/Zion/Grand Canyon National Parks, Utah and Arizona
- Napa Valley, California
- San Diego, California
- Green Mountains, Vermont
- Blue Ridge Parkway, Virginia and North Carolina
- San Juan National Forest, Colorado
- Rocky Mountain National Park, Colorado
- Oak Creek Canyon, Arizona
- Icefield Parkway, Alberta, Canada

EXTENDED TOURS

These take a variety of forms and the watchwords are *planning* and *preparation.* In planning your tour, you should decide in advance just what kind of experience you are seeking. Are you out to prove a point, escape from civilization, view beautiful scenery, lose weight, visit vineyards, raise money for a favorite charity, or link two nations in a symbolic gesture of peace and goodwill? All these have been done through cycling. The options are yours, and you are only limited by your vision, time, energy, and bank balance.

Before you leave, however, you should give some thought to getting into reasonable shape. It is conceivable that you can ride yourself into shape, but your trip will certainly be more fun if you can focus on the lovely scenery, rather than your sore bottom or burning thighs. Being reasonably physically fit is particularly important when touring with a full load, since it will take more strength and endurance to power and control the heavier bike, hour after hour.

If you are a fairly frequent rider, e.g., averaging one hundred miles per week for a couple of months prior to your trip, you should be in reasonable shape for a trip involving shorter daily distances (sixty miles or less). If, however, your quest is more ambitious, you should take a look at the training program set forth in Chapter 7, and if you are out to break any records, consult Chapter 8.

If you are a first-time, long-distance cycling tourist and will be traveling with a full load, an average of fifty miles per day is a realistic target to shoot for. When planning a trip, multiply the number of days you have by fifty miles and plot your route accordingly. It is not uncommon for more seasoned tourists to cover eighty or even one hundred or more miles per day. On a longer trip, it is probably a good idea to allow for at least one rain, laundry, or "goofing off" day.

One of the best-known and most accomplished long-distance touring cyclists is Greg Siple. In 1973, Siple, his wife, and some friends cycled from Alaska to Argentina—an 18,272-mile jaunt he dubbed "Hemistour." Siple captures the essence of bicycle touring with the following sage observation: "Our modern technology of transportation has made the world smaller and smaller until there's nothing left to see. What a bicycle does is make the world big again . . . [it] puts back all those spaces that disappeared between places." Siple is now a member of a nonprofit organization for touring cyclists known as Bikecentennial, created to map a 4,450-mile bicycle trail (the TransAmerica Trail) across the United States. More than 4,000 cyclists rode part or all of this trail, as part of the bicentennial celebration in 1976.

THE CENTURY RIDE

The century ride, now over a century old, is a rite of passage for the serious and more athletic cycling tourist, much like a marathon or a triathon for athletes in those sports. A century ride is a single-day ride of one hundred miles. Like a marathon, the primary objective is to finish and to do so with dignity. Anyone who can pedal a bike can complete a century, provided they prepare for it. Like the marathon, there is also the issue of *how* you finish it. Do you want to cross the finish line with a smile on your face and celebrate later that evening with your comrades . . . or rather, crawl across and limp directly to the first aid station? The difference is simply a matter of doing the homework—spending the necessary time in the saddle. See Chapter 8, for a training regimen for your first century.

THE BREVETS

The French version of the century is the *brevet.* There are two kinds of *brevets,* the *Randonneurs,* in which the cyclists establish their own speed and the objective is to comfortably finish the distance, and the *Audex,* in which the riders stay in a pack, at a set pace (average is 22.5 kph), controlled by a road captain. The classic

TYPES OF *CYCLOTOURISTS*

Jacques Faizant, a well-known French political cartoonist and an avid touring cyclist, divides the world of touring cyclists into three categories:

"A *cyclotourist* cycles leisurely. He visits churches, castles, and so on. He is also often a photographer, and stops every two miles to get a snapshot, which considerably bothers any *randonneur* who happens to be with him.

"A *randonneur* cycles for the sake of cycling. Being on a bike is the main part of his fun. Of course, he looks at the scenery, and appreciates the sights, but he doesn't stop every now and then to pick flowers or look at a little birdie.

"A *cyclosportif* is a guy who, deep in the bottom of his heart, regrets not having become a racer when he was still young enough. Accordingly, he dresses himself in a racer's outfit (even if his belly is a little bulging), uses a racing bike, and pedals at full speed as long as he can. (And some of them can go far and fast!)

"The *cyclosportif* despises the cyclotourist, whom he mockingly calls '*conemplatif.*' In turn, the cyclotourist despises the *cyclosportif,* whom he calls '*couraillon,*' which is a very disreputable word for racer . . . The *randonneur* is the sensible fellow in the middle. He seldom stops, seldom races, but nevertheless can do both when he feels like it.

"Actually, the word '*randonneur*' is used for both cyclotourists and *randonneurs.* There are so many jokes about people loitering in the fields with their bikes at their sides, that cyclotourists prefer to call themselves *randonneurs* to keep their morale high. Human nature you know!

"The cyclotourist uses a rather heavy bike with 650c tires, the *randonneur* uses a '*randonneuse*' which is a lightweight bike with 700c tires (clinchers) and fenders. The *cyclosportif* uses a racing bike with tubulars and no fenders. When it rains he is covered with mud from head to toe, but he loves it."

distances for *brevets,* which increase in length as the season progresses, are 200, 300, 400, 600, 1,000, and 1,200 km, each distance to be completed within a set number of hours. The best-known *brevet* is Paris–Brest–Paris, a 1,200-mile annual affair involving 2,000 or so riders from ten countries.

OTHER RIDES

Most every town that has a strong cycling club has some kind of annual long-distance group ride. San Francisco has "The Tour de France in San Francisco," Palm Springs the "Desert Classic," and New York the "Five-Boro Bike Tour," which involves a field of over

10,000 riders. Over the past few years, a series of "Challenge Rides" have emerged, incorporating the element of machismo, as men and women on bicycles tackle awesome distances, steep mountains, high winds, and triple-digit desert heat, to determine who can absorb the most agony and still keep smiling.

THE LUXURY BICYCLE VACATION

As Ray Benton and his associates at Travent and others have discovered, there is a growing market for hassle-free luxury vacations that combine the exhilaration and fitness benefits of cycling with first-class amenities and exotic ports of call. These trips are particularly popular in a hectic, high-tech age where many have seen the world's great monuments and yearn to do something special—to get off the beaten path and experience the exotic. Most of these operations involve the close personal attention of a guide, expert both in cycling and the region visited. Some even combine cycling with one or more additional activities, such as island-hopping aboard a chartered yacht, wine tasting, skiing, ballooning, white-water rafting, and even elephant and camel riding! The new breed of bicycle-tour operator has redesigned the traditional bicycle-tour experience to appeal to a broader, if not more affluent audience. They are not selling cycling, per se, but rather a "happening" or life-style, and they stress that you do not have to be a physical wonder to enjoy a bicycle vacation.

TOURING PACE

Your pace depends on your level of fitness and what you are trying to accomplish. In a leisurely day tour involving eight hours of riding, the pace during your time in the saddle should not be that brisk. Most reasonably fit riders can manage a cadence of 75–80 in a gear of 42 × 17 or 18, for hours on end in rolling terrain, provided they are not fighting heavy winds. An occasional stop to rest or enjoy the scenery will help you keep up the pace, when you're on the road. If you are in reasonably good condition you will be able to cover 50 to 150 miles, depending on how hard you want to push it and whether your objective is to smell the flowers or log the miles.

Long, steady distance training or century rides require a different pace altogether. In these instances, the rider tries to maintain a consistently high cadence. The point in a century ride is not to finish in any particular time, but to maintain a strong, consistent pace through the entire distance. Serious century riders stop only when they have to.

CHALLENGE RIDES

An increasing number of fun and serious rides have emerged over the past few years, to challenge those with a sense of adventure and a desire for a good workout. *Bicycle Guide* magazine recently listed eight:

ALMOST ACROSS ARIZONA
500 miles and 15,000 feet of elevation, in eight days; from the rim of the Grand Canyon to Nogales, Mexico; "Scenery so captivating it has actually caused cyclists to veer off the road and crash"; late September/early October; contact: Richard Corbett, Grand Canyon to Mexico–Almost Across Arizona Bicycle Tour, P.O. Box 40814, Tucson, AZ 85733; (602) 791-9599.

A GRAND MESS
150 mile, two-day event through beautiful and historic Civil War battlefield country; from Harrisburg to Gettysburg, Pa., across Delaware to Harper's Ferry, West Virginia; for the benefit of Multiple Sclerosis; contact: Dianne Mordecai, National Multiple Sclerosis Society, Central Pennsylvania Chapter, 1 Ararat Blvd., Harrisburg, PA 17110-9720; (717) 652-2108.

TO HEL'EN BACK
Three-day event, with 205-mile loop around Oregon's Mount St. Helens, with a hike on the volcano; for the benefit of the Cancer Society; end of June; Contact Roger Humphrey, 2011 Main Street, Vancouver, WA 98660; (206) 254-3934.

PACIFIC–ATLANTIC CYCLING TOUR
19-day ride, from San Diego, California, to Jacksonville, Florida; created by Race Across America participants, Lon and Susan Haldeman; June; contact: PAC Tour, P.O. Box 73, Harvard, IL 60033; (815) 943-3171.

HOTTER 'N HELL 100
One of the country's most popular century rides; ride around Wichita Falls, Texas, with 12,000 cyclists, in desert winds and triple-digit temperatures; used as a fundraiser for local causes; late August; contact: Hotter 'n Hell Hundred, P.O. Box 3241, Wichita Falls, TX 76309; (817) 692-2925.

THE KENNEBEC PASS RIDE
Separates the mountain (bike) men from the boys; 50-mile loop over Durango, Colorado's 11,426-foot Kennebec Pass; part of the annual Big Jim Classic Stage Race; August; contact Chuck Taylor, Hassle-Free Sports, 2615 Main Avenue, Durango, CO 81301; (303) 259-3874.

THE DEATH RIDE
Five Sierra mountain passes (150 miles, 15,000 feet of climbing); 1,200 participants; mid-July; contact: Alpine Chamber of Commerce, Attention: Death Ride, P.O. Box 265, Markleeville, CA 96120; (916) 694-2475.

MOUNT WASHINGTON HILL CLIMB
The ultimate hill climb; 4,000 vertical feet with average grade of 10%; high winds, nasty weather; good ol' New England fun; mid-September; for benefit of Cancer Society; contact: David Goucher, P.O. Box 882, Wolfeboro, NH 08394; (603) 569-3635.

Courtesy of Bicycle Guide *Magazine*

FIVE LUXURY TOURS—DOMESTIC

CALIFORNIA WINE COUNTRY

Unique country inns, wine tastings, and gourmet dining in the Napa, Sonoma, Alexander, and Russian River valleys. Five days. Around $800. Backroads Bicycle Touring, Box 1626, San Leandro, CA 94577; (415) 895-1783.

CHAMPLAIN SALE & CYCLE

Sail and live aboard a 77-foot schooner on New England's Lake Champlain. Four days, around $550; six days, around $675. Vermont Bicycle Touring, Box 711, Bristol, VT 05443; (802) 453-4811.

VERMONT COUNTRY CYCLERS

Weekend adventures and longer (5 day) breakaways in the mountains and beautiful country inns of Vermont, Virginia, and Nova Scotia. $250 to $1,000. Vermont Country Cyclers, P.O. Box 145, Waterbury Center, Vermont 05677-0145; (802) 244-8751.

ALASKAN ADVENTURE

Cycling, white-water rafting, flying, horseback riding. Seven and one-half days. Around $1,400. Backroads Bicycle Touring.

HAWAII

Cycling in the twin paradises of Maui (around $760) and the Big Island (around $685). Five days. Island Bicycle Adventures, 569 Kapahulu Ave., Honolulu, HI 96815; (800) 233-2226.

FIVE LUXURY TOURS—INTERNATIONAL

FRENCH WINE COUNTRY

Tour the great chateaus and vineyards of France's famous Loire, Provence, Burgundy, Dordogne, and Alsace regions. Tours also available to the Venetian heartland and Tuscany, in Italy; Ireland; the Swiss Lakes; as well as island hopping on a luxury yacht in the British Virgin Islands. One-week tours. Around $2,000. Travent, International, P.O. Box 305, Waterbury Center, Vermont 05677-0305; (800) 235-3009, and Travent International, La Grange au Vager, 21190, Mersault, France.

SOUTH PACIFIC PARADISE

Sail and cycle around the five islands of French Polynesia, including Tahiti and Bora Bora. Fourteen days. Around $950 to $1,350. Off the Deep End Travels, Box 7511, Jackson, Wyoming 83001; (800) 223-6833.

NEPAL AND INDIA

Cycling, river rafting, trekking, biking, and elephant and camel riding. Thirty-three days. Around $2,400. World Expeditions, 690 Market Street, Suite 1206, San Francisco, CA 94104; (800) 541-3600 (in California (415) 362-1046).

CHAMPAGNE REGION, FRANCE

Private tastings at such famous champagne houses as Dom Perignon and Moet Chandon. Eight days. Around $2,200. Butterfield & Robinson, 70 Bond Street, Toronto, Ontario M5B 1X3; (800) 387-1147.

ITALIAN RIVIERA

No more than 36 miles per day from Monte Carlo to Pisa. Eleven days. Around $1,600. McBride's Earth Adventures, 6608 St. James Drive., Indianapolis, IN 46217; (317) 783-9449.

TOURING EQUIPMENT

Choice of the proper equipment is perhaps the most important aspect of planning a bicycle tour. You may be able to limp along if your physical condition is wanting, but you will be stopped dead in your tracks by a serious equipment failure. Here are some notes on special equipment considerations that apply to touring:

THE BIKE

Touring with a lightweight racing bicycle is practical only if you have a sag wagon or support vehicle to carry your clothes and equipment. A racing bike does not have the mountings for racks or the brazed-on eyelets, needed for attaching panniers. It will be strong enough to carry luggage, but a racing bike is designed to be stiff and responsive, not forgiving and comfortable. A touring bike is the better way to go (see Chapter 2). Bikes made specifically for touring are designed to remain stable when carrying front and rear loads. They generally have a longer wheel base (forty inches or more), chain stays, and fork rakes. This provides more shock absorption and comfort. They also have brazed-on fittings, for extra water-bottle cages, and front and rear racks and panniers. Since tight cornering is not crucial, touring bikes also have a lower bottom bracket, to provide a lower center of gravity and consequently more stability under load. The more deluxe sport/touring models have cantilever-style brakes, for added stopping power, and a third chainring, for extra-low gearing. Touring bikes tend to be less expensive than racing bikes, due to the heavier materials used in their frames, but a good touring bike, fully loaded, can cost well over $1,000.

WHEELS AND TIRES

When touring, particularly in the case of longer rides, use alloy, 27 × 1¼ rims, and a wider gauge (27 × 1⅛ or 27 × 1¼), clincher tire, instead of a thinner tire. Avoid racing tubulars. More rubber on the road will create increased rolling resistance, but it will be worth it in terms of increased riding comfort and fewer flats. When on the road, keep your tires fully inflated (recommended pressure should be printed on the tire), to keep the rolling resistance to a minimum (see Chapter 4). If your bike has tubular wheels or the new 27 × 1 clinchers, have them rebuilt or get a second set of wheels for touring. The standard 27 × 1¼ wheels are not only stronger, they have a much wider availability of replacement rims, tires, tubes, and spokes, and this can be important if you break down in a town with no state-of-the-art bike shop.

RAYMOND LAMIRE ON HOW TO PREPARE FOR A BICYCLE TOURING VACATION

BEFORE YOU GO:

1. Get on a bike: you should condition the part of your anatomy that meets the bicycle.
2. Get used to a hard seat (the soft bed/hard bed analogy is fitting: the soft bed is nice at first but causes problems later).
3. Read about the country and region you will be visiting.

TO BRING:

1. Padded cycling gloves.
2. Cycling Shorts with padding (either tight-fitting or baggy).
3. Rain Gear; depending on the season bring:
   a. Rain jacket (not a poncho)
   b. Tights, to put over your shorts on cool mornings.
   c. Rain pants, only in cool weather.
4. Stiff-soled shoes: preferably cycling shoes, designed for touring, but not with cleats.

Courtesy, Travent International

SPOKES

Experienced tourists recommend use of heavier (14 gauge) spokes, used in a cross-4 pattern to maximize wheel durability. Popping spokes in the middle of nowhere is no fun.

GEARING

Gear ratios should be designed to accommodate hills with extra weight (unless, of course, you are traveling light). The front chainrings should be 52/36; 52 for flats and downhills and 36 for climbing steep hills. The freewheel should have gears ranging from 13 teeth to 28 or 32; 13 for speed and the latter two for climbing. As noted above, some of the new sport/touring models have triple chainrings, for an even wider gear range and lower lows.

SADDLE

Make sure it's a good one and that you're used to it, because you'll spend plenty of time there. For more information, see Chapter 4.

PACKS AND PANNIERS

These are essential for fully loaded touring. Don't try to strap a suitcase or backpack on your bike. Panniers are designed to fit like saddlebags on either side of your front and back wheels. In addition, there are handlebar bags and bags that fit within the triangular space between the tubes of your frame. The most common arrangement is two back panniers and a handlebar bag. These

SOME TIPS ON PACKING YOUR PANNIERS

- Load heavier objects first (bottom of bags). This will lower the bike's center of gravity and make it more stable.
- Weight should always be equal on both sides.
- Position as much weight as possible over wheel axles.
- If you are using rear panniers only, average weight should be around 35 pounds. Once weight exceeds 35 pounds, at least 1/3 of total weight should be on the front of the bike.
- With front and rear panniers, distribution should be 45% on the front of the bike and 55% on the rear.
- Don't overload the handlebar bag (over 6 pounds). It will destabilize your steering.
- Less is more. Don't bring more than you really need.

A fully loaded touring bike has weight evenly distributed between front and back. A low center of gravity is important.
Photo by Bruce Alexander, courtesy of Cannondale

THE HYBRIDS

The increasing popularity of various kinds of bicycle touring has spawned a new generation of models known as Sport/Touring bikes. This category spans a spectrum from heavy-duty land cruisers to near-racing bikes and are a good choice for a person interested in an occasional century ride and more frequent high-speed recreational riding. These tend to have lower gearing than racing bikes and braze-ons to accommodate racks. They can also be adapted with fenders for foul-weather riding. This group has recently spun off yet another new subcategory known as "hybrids," which are mostly ATB but with some road-bike characteristics. The hybrids can handle rugged off-road terrain and yet offer dropped handlebars for better on-road control and a more aerodynamic position. They feature wider (up to 1.5 inch) tires on 26- or 27-inch wheels, and other ATB features such as triple chainrings, cantilever brakes, and shift levers on the handlebar ends. Leading brands in this new category include Specialized, Miyata, Fisher Serotta, and Bianchi. *Photo courtesy of Specialized Bicycle Components*

panniers and bags are usually made of lightweight but sturdy nylon, dyed with reflective colors. Panniers are supported by special touring racks. Blackburn is the leader in America, and perhaps the world, in production of quality, lightweight racks. Rear racks cost around twenty-five to thirty dollars and front racks around thirty to thirty-five dollars. Panniers are made by many independent companies. Cannondale and Rhode Gear make high-quality products. Larger handlebar bags cost between thirty and sixty dollars, front panniers between fifty and seventy dollars, and rear panniers between seventy-five and one hundred thirty dollars.

WHERE TO FIND OUT

The most comprehensive source of information regarding bicycle touring in North America is: *Bikecentennial,* P.O. Box 8308, Missoula, MT 59807; (406) 721-1776. Bikecentennial is a nonprofit service organization, for recreational touring bicyclists. Since its incorporation in 1974, Bikecentennial has developed and mapped a nationwide network of bicycle-touring routes and has produced a variety of publications and services for bicyclists, including: *The Cyclist's Yellow Pages,* a complete trip-planning resource; *The Cyclosource Catalog,* a collection of books, maps, and specialty products; and a Trips Program that offers a wide variety of organized tours ranging from six to ninety days in length. Individual membership costs twenty-two dollars yearly, and includes a subscription to *Bike-Report, The Cyclist's Yellow Pages,* and discounts on Bikecentennial maps and products.

A second, good general source of information, particularly regarding touring clubs and rides, including century rides, is the *League Of American Wheelmen,* Suite 209, 6707 Whitestone Road, Baltimore, MD 21207; (301) 944-3399. The League, founded in 1880, is the original national organization for bicyclists and has become well known for its advocacy efforts. It also has a number of services for touring cyclists, including touring-information sources in each state, homes where cyclists can stay overnight, and a special magazine, the *TourFinder.*

MAPS AND ROUTE PLANNING

A good state map is an excellent source of information in planning your route. In addition to a comprehensive diagram of the roads, they include information on parks, elevations, and towns and their sizes. It is often good to stay on the secondary roads, marked in blue or gray on the state maps, since they are often more scenic and less congested. Roads along rivers are usually a good bet, because they tend to be flat and scenic. Population figures are helpful, since towns with populations over 1,000 usually have such services as grocery stores, motels, and restaurants. If you want more detail on the smaller roads, use a county map, which may be obtained through better bookstores, as well as auto clubs, state highway departments, and the county itself. Bikecentennial is one of the best sources of touring maps and where to find them.

CHEAP LODGING

In addition to private homes open to members of the League of American Wheelmen, The *American Youth Hostels* organization is

A CHECKLIST FOR THE FULLY LOADED TOURIST

Shelter: Ground cloth, tent with rain fly, tent stakes and guy lines, sleeping bag in waterproof covering, pad or air mattress.

Food: Cooking and eating utensils, aluminum foil, can opener, stove and fuel, water purification tablets, food supply.

Bike Repair: Tire pump, patch kit, chain remover, spoke wrench, spokes, spare tube, tool assortment.

Clothing: 2 pairs riding shorts (chamois or terrycloth crotch), tights or leg warmers, 2 jerseys, sweater/sweatshirt, underwear, 3 pairs socks, bike shoes, bike socks, walking shoes, rain gear (breathable), windbreaker, 1 pair long pants, 1 pair short pants or swimsuit, 2 t-shirts, one long-sleeved shirt, belt.

Personal: Toilet kit, towel, washcloth, soap, first aid kit, sunglasses, suntan lotion.

Other: Matches in waterproof container, hat, insect repellent, toilet paper, pocket knife (Swiss Army is recommended), camera and film, maps, compass, water bottles, bike locks.

---

very cycling-oriented and has networks of dormitorylike hostels throughout Europe and in New England, Pennsylvania Dutch Country, and the Colorado Rockies, which are listed in their annual handbook. Contact American Youth Hostels, National Campus, Delaplane, VA 22025. Bikecentennial has also developed a network of cyclists who accommodate others in their private homes. These number over 500 and are listed in the *Touring Cyclist's Hospitality Directory.* Other good sources of lodging for cyclists are found in the *Campground and Trailer Park Guide,* by Rand McNally, and for indoor accommodations, *The Cyclist's Guide to Overnight Stops,* by Ballantine Books.

Some *good books* on bicycle touring:

- *Bicycle Touring,* Bicycling Magazine, 1985, Rodale Press, Emmaus, PA. Information on equipment, accessories, offbeat repairs, race training for tourists, plus anecdotes.
- *Biking Through Europe,* Dennis and Tina Jaffee, 1987, available from Bikecentennial (see address above). Seventeen tours in France, West Germany, Denmark, Great Britain, Holland, Austria, Belgium, and Switzerland. General information is given about these countries as well.

- *The CTC Route Guide,* Christa Gausden and Nicholas Crane, 1984, published in England, available through Bikecentennial. A detailed guide to planning tours in England, Scotland, and Wales. Compiled by the Cyclist's Touring Club.
- *Freewheeling: Bicycling the Open Road,* Gary Ferguson, 1985, The Mountaineers, Seattle, WA. An introduction to bicycle touring.

SUMMARY

There is a form of bicycle touring to suit almost every taste and budget and there are excellent organizations and resources in place to provide the necessary information.

An exciting new trend in recreation is the luxury bicycle vacation that incorporates the health benefits and exhilaration of cycling with the ability to see the countryside in a more intimate and meaningful way. The options range from weekends at quaint New England bed and breakfasts to multiday treks through the Himalayas.

Fully loaded bicycle touring requires specialized equipment, such as wider tires, special gear ratios, and packs and panniers to carry one's gear. One need not go overboard, however, since manufacturers are now producing bicycles that, with minor modifications, can serve a variety of uses.

12 Racing

Bicycle racing is fun, but it is not easy. Like any serious sport, it involves challenge and a certain degree of risk. To be good, even at the level of citizens' or recreational racing, one must make a serious commitment, not only to training but to studying the sport's subtle techniques and strategies. Cycling competition is not for the timid or fainthearted. It requires intestinal fortitude.

Despite this, millions of people around the world compete regularly in bicycle races, ranging from kid's backyard BMX races to "Le Tour" itself. While the challenges are great, so too are the rewards.

Bike racing is fun and exciting, and it's a great way to stay fit and to meet new people who share a common interest. Although the "thrill of victory and the agony of defeat" have been experienced by cyclists of all ages and both sexes, most experience a certain fulfillment, from the mere act of participation. Of course, if you have the talent and the persistence, you can build a very respectable career as a bike racer. The very best spin their pedals to fame and fortune, retiring wealthy, yet with long, healthy lives before them.

However, as most bike racers, from weekend warriors to winners of the Tour de France, will quickly tell you, the value of the experience is rooted in the basic joy of riding a bicycle.

French superstar, five-time Tour De France winner, Bernard Hinault, put it this way in his book, *Road Racing, Technique and Training,* which he wrote on the eve of his final season: "Cycling has given me the good fortune to live in the open air and to train on all kinds of terrain, from the plains to the mountain passes. No other sport offers the same opportunities, and this suits me very well. After all the years I've spent cranking out the miles in the pack, I still take pleasure in the countryside as it rolls by and I always look at it, even in the toughest moments."

GETTING STARTED

It is easy to understand why baseball is the great American pastime. Nearly every school fields a team and nearly every community has a Little League program. Not so in cycling.

Bicycle racing in America is organized somewhat haphazardly, on a local club level. Unfortunately, there is not yet a well-structured, nationwide program for young cyclists, at the grass roots level.

Races, for the most part, are run by amateur promoters. Although some school programs do exist, they are not yet a serious part of the interscholastic sports system. Varsity letters are rarely awarded in cycling and, in light of today's tight budgets, funding for a team's expensive equipment is often out of the question.

The focal point of bicycle racing in America is the local bicycle shop. Many of the two thousand or so "pro level" bicycle dealers scattered around the country (see Appendix for the top one hundred) are responsible for helping most active racers get started. Bike racers tend to work in bike shops, or at least hang out there, when they are not at school, at work, or in the saddle. Information on local rides, races, and clubs is usually available.

There are approximately one thousand organized bicycle clubs around the U.S., most of which have some sort of affiliation with at least one shop. Like any kind of special-interest organization, a bicycle club moves in the direction of its most active members. Some clubs are small and "elite," while others offer a broad program for every type of cycling interest. Some of the larger clubs organize a hundred or more events per year.

Bicycle racing takes four basic forms in the United States: BMX, Club Level, Amateur (USCF), and Professional (USPRO).

BMX (Bicycle Motocross) racing is done on short dirt tracks, full

WHAT TO LOOK FOR IN A BIKE CLUB

FOCUS

Most clubs have a strong orientation—either toward racing or touring.

RANGE OF ACTIVITIES

A good club will organize regular group training sessions, trips to races, one or two big events (such as a local race or century ride), and off-season social activities, like dinners and dances. A newsletter sent to members is the best source of such information. Most racing clubs have members who provide coaching. Some actually pay an experienced coach to work with the club's serious racers. A good club will also help organize coaching clinics and special workshops, throughout the year.

BIKE-SHOP AFFILIATION

Most clubs have a very close association with a particular bike dealer or even several in the area. A side benefit of club membership is often "member discount" at these shops.

SPONSORSHIP

More serious racing clubs often field sponsored teams that compete in regional races. Benefits of sponsorship, such as free uniforms and equipment, free entry into races, travel support, etc., usually accrue exclusively to the club's top few racers. Check on club policy and what you have to do to get on its "A" team, before joining.

MEMBERSHIP

Cyclists come from diverse backgrounds, and from all socioeconomic groups. Attend a few club events to make sure you fit in.

WHERE TO GET RACING INFORMATION

BMX

AMERICAN BICYCLE ASSOCIATION (ABA)
Address: P.O. Box 718, Chandler, AZ 85244
Phone: (602) 961-1903
Dues: $25.
Purpose: Sanctions races
President: Clayton John

NATIONAL BICYCLE LEAGUE (NBL)
Address: 211 Bradenton Ave., Suite 100, Dublin, OH 43017
Phone: (614) 766-1625
Dues: $30.
Purpose: Sanctions races, affiliated with the USCF, fields US Team for international competition
Exec. Director: Lawrie Burnette

AMATEUR RACING

UNITED STATES CYCLING FEDERATION (USCF)
Address: 1750 E. Boulder St., Colorado Springs, CO 80909
Phone: (719) 578-4581
Dues: $16 to $32 depending on category
Purpose: Issues amateur licenses and sanctions amateur races, develops talent and fields U.S. Olympic Cycling team
Executive Director: Jerry Lace

OFF-ROAD RACING

NATIONAL OFF-ROAD BICYCLE RACING ASSOCIATION (NORBA)
Address: 1750 E. Boulder St., Colorado Springs, CO 80909
Phone: (719) 578-4581
Dues: $25
Purpose: Sanctions races, issues licenses
Principal Contact: Duann Hall

PROFESSIONAL RACING

UNITED STATES PROFESSIONAL CYCLING FEDERATION
Address: RD1 Box 1650, New Tripoli, PA 18066
Phone: (215) 298-3262
Dues: Vary with classification
Purpose: Issues professional licenses and sanctions pro races. Selects U.S.A. professional team for the annual World Championships
Executive Director: Jack W. Simes, III

of bumps, dips, jumps, and curves, using a special bike with twenty-inch wheels, knobby tires, and motorcycle-style seat and handlebars. Although the "moto" in the title is a misnomer, BMX racing is perhaps inspired more by dirt-bike motorcycle racing than by any form of bicycling competition.

BMX has been chiefly the domain of kids, with most moving on to other pursuits, in their early to midteens. However, this segment of cycling has evolved to the point that there is actually a "tour" of professionally organized competitions. Some are even televised and offer enough prize money, which, along with cycling industry endorsements, supports a class of pro BMXers, some well into their twenties.

An offshoot of the BMX movement is the so-called Formula One class. Formula One bikes are similar to BMX bikes, but are more aerodynamic and have smoother tires, more suitable for the hard tracks and other surfaces, such as parking lots, on which the races take place.

The growth curve of BMX and Formula One has recently taken a downturn. It is thought that this is due to a defection, at an earlier age, to the new sport of ATB (mountain biking) and road racing, the latter as the result of recent accomplishments of American role models, such as Hampsten and LeMond, on the international level. Another form of cycling competition, and one that seems to be growing in popularity with youngsters, is Freestyle.

Club races are those which do not require entrants to have an official racing license, issued from one of cycling's three recognized governing bodies: the United States Cycling Federation (USCF), the National Off-Road Bicycle Racing Association (NORBA, now part of the USCF), or the United States Professional Cycling Federation (US PRO).

The following is an overview of organized cycling competition in the United States, in 1988:

BMX: 80,000 racers/700 events
Club: 128,000 racers/2,000+ events
USCF: 32,000 racers/1,000 events
USPRO: 200 racers/3 events

Competitions organized by age and sex categories are possible in all of these forms of racing, with the exception of the professional class, which is only for men (a women's pro class may be on the horizon).

Within each age division, *USCF amateur racing* is broken into categories (or "cats," in the vernacular of the amateur cyclist), with the assignment of category based upon experience and performance:

Philadelphia's CoreStates Championship is America's richest single-day race and the annual U.S. Professional National Championship. *Seth Goltzer photo*

Category IV: beginner/novice. Can be upgraded to
Category III, after completing eight Cat IV events. Can be upgraded to
Category II, after placing in top three of three Cat III events.
Category I: elite racer, national, international, and Olympic level.

Category II events are generally longer and more difficult, with more prize money, and the best ones, for reasons explained below, are open to professionals. The most common elite-level cycling competitions in the U.S. are the "pro-am" races open to "Pros, I and II".

Of course, with the "graying of America," veterans and masters racing (thirty-five and over), in virtually all categories (with the exception of BMX and Formula One), is one of the fastest growing segments of the sport and it spans the spectrum as far as seriousness and intensity is concerned.

AMATEUR VS. PRO

The dividing line between pro and amateur cycling is a fuzzy one indeed. The world governing body of cycling is the Unione Cycliste International (UCI), located in Switzerland. Most countries have one cycling federation or national governing body (NGB) that governs both pro and amateur cycling. One of the rare exceptions is the United States, where amateurs are governed by the USCF and pros by USPRO.

Under the rules of the two groups, a minority of top amateurs can compete in pro events (except the USPRO Championship) and vice-versa. Prize money is awarded in both. The "amateurs" are entitled to engage in commercial endorsements (with restrictions as to how much they can receive personally and the balance put into a trust fund, until they retire or turn pro) and they are limited to two thousand dollars per day in prize money.

From a global perspective, pro cycling is clearly the pinnacle of the sport—the "NFL" of cycling so to speak. All the major tours and classics are pro events. In the United States, the trend is in that direction. The nation's premier all-pro event, the CoreStates Championship, carries a USPRO sanction, and it is expected that other major U.S. events, such as the Tour de Trump, will soon be all pro as well. The most recognized names in American cycling (LeMond, Hampsten, Phinney, Grewal, and so on) hold professional licenses.

AMERICA'S BIKE RACE

The catalyst for professional cycling in the United States is its flagship event, the CoreStates USPRO Cycling Championship.

Introduced in 1985, this 156-mile, all-pro road race is held through the streets of Philadelphia each year and is the U.S. official national and professional road-racing championship. The winner becomes the US Pro Champion for the year, and the top three American finishers automatically earn spots on the U.S. pro road-racing team, to represent the country at the annual UCI World Championships.

Beyond its importance to pro cyclists, the CoreStates (so named for its primary sponsor, CoreStates Financial Corp) has proven that a bike race can achieve the same stature and widespread popularity, in the United States, as major classics in tennis, marathon running, car racing, or golf.

The Championship and its surrounding activities has become a key annual happening on the calendars of Philadelphians. The race is covered by both local and national television, and draws over 300,000 spectators around its now legendary fourteen-mile circuit (the racers pedal ten laps, plus opening and closing loops on the Benjamin Franklin Parkway, to reach 156 miles). A week-long series of parties, special athletic events, and street festivals builds to the invasion of the pro cyclists, who come from all corners of the world, and for six hours paralyze the nation's fourth largest city.

Nowhere is the race more exciting than in the hillside neighborhood of Manayunk. Here, on an incredibly steep half-mile stretch of residential street, lined with one-hundred-year-old row houses, the Championship can be won or lost. It's the "Manayunk Wall," and the racers must climb it ten times. The "Wall" is a combination of the Roman coliseum, spring break at Fort Lauderdale, and the fifty

yard line at the Super Bowl. "It really gets to you," says Eric Heiden, America's speed-skating hero, and winner of the inaugural event. "But the people cheer you on. Their enthusiasm is so great. It's better than being in a European race."

Although the U.S. professional class has grown to 200, from less than a handful in 1982, the number of all-professional races in the country has not kept pace, largely because many amateur-sanctioned races are also open to pros. Also, until just recently, many American pros have felt it necessary to spend most of their time racing in Europe where there is more and better competition. In fact, several top North American pros, such as LeMond, and Steve Bauer of Canada, maintain second homes in such places as the Netherlands and Belgium, so they may have a convenient place to rest between the stops on the lengthy European circuit.

Until more pro events evolve in this country, or until the merger of the two organizations (now in the works) is effected, it is likely that we will see pros and amateurs competing "on the same field," for some time to come. There is no question, however, that cycling, like many other Olympic sports, is headed toward open status and that the distinction between amateur and professional will continue to blur.

In any case, there should always be the opportunity for cyclists to race with others on the same level.

ROAD RACING

There is no question that the most popular form of bicycle racing around the world today is road racing.

Road racing requires a carefully designed route—a course or circuit that is protected from traffic and suitable for cycling. Park roadways, city streets, country roads, and even parking lots are frequently used for road races, which can take several forms:

TIME TRIAL

One rider against the clock. The strategy is simple: Go as fast as possible over the distance. This can vary from less than a mile to over a hundred, on flat or hilly courses. In the U.S., the most popular distance is twenty-five miles.

CRITERIUM

America's most popular form of racing, because it is relatively easy to organize and offers good viewing for spectators. Distances vary from ten miles to around one hundred kilometers (sixty-two and one-half miles), on a circuit of usually less than two miles per lap. Talented criterium riders have a lot of speed and aren't intimidated by flying around tight turns in the middle of a large pack.

ROAD RACES

These can be held from point to point, over a circuit (usually more than three miles per lap) or on a route that combines the two. Road races are longer than criteriums and can be up to one hundred seventy-five miles for pros. They usually feature courses with challenging terrain, like steep hills or mountain passes.

STAGE RACE

This, the ultimate form of road racing, includes time trials, road races, and sometimes criteriums. A stage race can be as short as two days or as long as twenty-one consecutive days. Each day of racing is called a stage. Each rider's time is recorded for each stage. Adding together all the rider's stage times gives his total time for the entire race. The rider with the lowest cumulative time at the end of each stage wears a special leader's jersey during the next stage. Final overall placings (called general classification or "G.C.") are determined by ranking each rider's cumulative time. The four "monuments of cycling," the tours of France, Italy, Spain, and Switzerland are all stage races.

Road-racing rules are fairly straightforward. The first one across the finish line at the end of the race is the winner (unless, of course, there is a disqualification). The exceptions are in time trials where the fastest time wins, in multiday stage races where the best cumulative time wins, and in a points race, where special sprint laps score points, with the highest overall point scorer declared the winner.

Unlike in the film *Breaking Away,* a rider is not allowed to make intentional contact with another rider or impede another's forward progress, particularly in the final sprint. Intentional fouls, like running a rider into the curb (a "hook"), deliberately crossing over another's front wheel (a "chop"), punching, spitting, or jamming a pump into the other rider's spokes are all grounds for instant disqualification, possible long-term suspension, and (depending upon the perception of the wronged party) assault charges.

THE CONTROVERSIAL CALL

There were 500 meters to go in the 1988 World Professional Road Championship, in Rhonse, Belgium. After 170 miles and seven hours of incredibly hard racing, it looked as if the World Champion would be one of two men: Maurizio Fondriest, of Italy, or Belgium's own Claude Criquielion, winner of the title in 1984.

The vast majority of the 100,000 fans jamming the fences on the gradual climb to the finish line were united behind the Belgian. In unison they chanted: "cri-qui-on, cri-qui-on!"

With seventy-five meters to go at the 1988 World Championships, Maurizio Fondriest (far right) starts his move around Steve Bauer. An instant before, Bauer and Claude Criquielion collided, leaving the Belgian sprawled on the pavement. *Photosport International*

While Criquielion walked his bike to the finish (left). . . . *Presse Sports photo*

Bauer, after receiving news of his disqualification, was consoled by friend Greg LeMond. *Cor Vos photo*

But suddenly, and seemingly out of nowhere, the two leaders were joined by the flying Canadian, Steve Bauer. In a phenomenal last-lap effort, Bauer had closed their twenty-second gap. Not only was Bauer a feared sprinter, on this day he was as strong and as powerful as any racer in the field.

With the finish line banner looming closer, Bauer chose to blast by his opponents, without a pause in his pedaling. Criquielion and Fondriest seemed caught by surprise, their reactions appearing too slow, with the finish barely 200 meters away.

But the roadway was getting steeper. Bauer may have attacked too soon. Criquielion fought back and chose to try to move by on Bauer's right side, even though the Canadian was drifting in that direction and gradually narrowing the alley between himself and the cement signpost bases and steel crowd-control barriers, on the edge of the road.

As Criquielion drew closer, the Canadian stuck out his right elbow and moved noticeably closer to the barriers. Criquielion had nowhere to go and crashed violently into the fence. Bauer's momentum plummeted and the seemingly written-off Fondriest shot by to cross the line first, hands thrown jubilantly in the air.

What had happened?

Criquielion claimed foul, charging Bauer with deliberately blocking him to prevent his passing. Criquielion said, "It's unfortunate for me that Bauer played hockey when he was younger. When he saw that I was going to pass him in the sprint, his reflex was one of a hockey player to force me into the barriers."

Bauer said he was reaching down to shift gears and that Criquielion should have known better than to pass on the inside, anyway.

Fondriest claimed his victory was legitimate, that he was just starting his sprint from the left and would have passed both of them in any case.

After five minutes of tension-filled confusion underscored by thousands of Belgian fans booing and even threatening Bauer, the officials made their ruling:

Fondriest, World Champion; Criquielion, 2nd; Bauer, disqualified.

Within hours, Criquielion filed a lawsuit against Bauer, claiming assault and battery. For the next couple of days, Belgian police put a round-the-clock guard around Bauer's nearby second home, and Bauer appealed the judges' decision, seeking reinstatement to second place.

Fondriest, proudly sporting his rainbow-striped World Champion's jersey started the 1989 season with a new team and a big salary increase.

The ruling stood.

At the height of its popularity, six-day bike races drew sellout crowds to New York's Madison Square Garden. This one was in 1934.

VELODROME RACING

For sheer hair-raising excitement, few sports compare to bicycle racing on a steeply banked velodrome. Speed, bike-handling skill, tactics, superb athletic power, and the ever-present threat of spectacular crashes are the ingredients that should fill the grandstands with screaming fans. But velodrome, or track racing as it is more commonly called, is just not where it should be, either in Europe or in the U.S.

As we learned in Chapter 1, that was not always the case. From the turn of the century to the eve of World War II, track racers, particularly short-distance sprint specialists, drew huge crowds around the world, and nowhere was the sport more popular than in the United States, especially up and down the eastern seaboard.

In his well-researched book on the history of cycling, *Hearts Of Lions,* Peter Nye captured the era like this:

> The races were fiercely competitive. In the open events, fields of fifty to sixty went hard and fast around the velodromes, which were only twenty-two feet wide. The riders zipped around these narrow tracks at speeds approaching forty miles an hour, and there was a lot of body

> contact through the turns. Bike races on the boards were like hockey on wheels. Riders slammed each other into the boards of the outside railing and crunched together in mass pileups that twisted wooden wheel rims and steel frames like pretzels. Falls could be serious. Dan Pischione of Providence was killed by a splinter that drove into his abdomen when he fell. Reggie McNamara of Australia, called Old Ironman for the punishment he endured, left a tooth embedded in the track boards after one crash.

But by the beginning of World War II, the sport had all but died in the U.S. (see Chapter 1).

In Europe, the big money flowed into road racing. Heroes were men who could endure against all odds, men with great courage and stamina. Sprinters with quick reflexes and crafty tactics just didn't have the same marquee value as before.

The only form of velodrome racing that continued to flourish in Europe was the "Six-Day," winter indoor grinds that often featured the great road-racing stars. Today, the winter indoor six-day circuit has at least fourteen stops, in cities throughout Europe. They draw large crowds, particularly if a Tour de France champion is entered.

Although it hardly approximates the hoopla, fanfare, and sheer popularity of its golden age, velodrome racing is by no means dead, even in the United States. In fact, velodromes continue to be built and used, particularly as a result of heavy emphasis on the nation's Olympic program.

The most successful U.S. velodromes (like Pennsylvania's Lehigh County Velodrome, just west of Allentown) have come at least part way in reviving the excitement and spectator appeal of track racing. A good evening at the velodrome offers a mixed card of fast-paced events drawn from track racing's full repertoire, without the less spectacular fare, such as Olympic-style time trials and long waits between races.

The bottom line on velodrome racing is that it will take a colorful promoter to bring it back to its former glory. Today, that requires major governmental and private-sector support, television exposure, an aggressive publicity and public relations campaign, a valid league format with support in major cities, and a particular brand of promotional savvy that will play on personality as well as business acumen. After all, the most successful velodrome racing always had a good sprinkle of vaudeville.

The following are the categories of track racing:

OLYMPICS

Gold medals are awarded to men in five velodrome races, and in two events for women:

VELODROMES

as of April 1, 1989

ALKEK VELODROME
Houston, TX
Alkek Velodrome Racing Assoc.
Kathy Volski
11300 Regency Green Drive, #3108
Cypress, TX 77429
(713) 578-0858

ALPENROSE VELODROME
Portland, OR
Mike Murray
1632 Birdsdale
Gresham, OR 97030

BATON ROUGE VELODROME
Baton Rouge, LA
Baton Rouge Velodrome
3140 North Sherwood Forest Blvd.
Baton Rouge, LA 70809
(504) 272-9200

BROWN DEER VELODROME
Milwaukee, WI
Brown Deer Velodrome
c/o Erv Ochowicz
1505 Coachlight Drive #21
New Berlin, WI 53151
(414) 786-0623

DICK LANE VELODROME
East Point, GA
Dick Lane Velodrome
1431 Norman Berry Drive
East Point, GA 30344
(404) 765-1085

DORIAS VELODROME
Detroit, MI
Wolverine Sports Club
Box 63
Royal Oak, MI 48068

ENCINO VELODROME
Encino, CA
Southern CA Cycling Federation
Box 713
Torrance, CA 90508-0713
(818) 881-7441

KISSENA VELODROME
Flushing, NY
New York Bicycling Federation
87-66 256th Street
Floral Park, NY 11001
(718) 347-8195

LEHIGH COUNTY VELODROME
Trexlertown, PA
Lehigh County Velodrome
217 Main
Emmaus, PA 18049
(215) 965-6930

MAJOR TAYLOR VELODROME
Indianapolis, IN
Major Taylor Velodrome
3649 Cold Spring Road
Indianapolis, IN 46222
(317) 926-8350

MARYMOOR VELODROME
Redmond, WA
Washington State Bicycling Assoc.
P.O. Box 15633
Seattle, WA 98115
(206) 633-5274

MEADOWHILL PARK
Northbrook, IL
Northbrook Cycling Committee
422 South Gibbons
Arlington Heights, IL 60004

ST. LOUIS VELODROME
St. Louis, MO
St. Louis Velodrome
P.O. Box 15102
St. Louis, MO 63110
(314) 481-1120

SAN DIEGO VELODROME
San Diego, CA
San Diego Velodrome Committee
2221 Morley Field Drive
San Diego, CA 92104

SANTA CLARA COUNTY VELODROME
San Jose, CA
Northern California Cycling Assoc.
845 Juanita Drive
Walnut Creek, CA 94595
(415) 287-SJBC

7-ELEVEN VELODROME
Colorado Springs, CO
7-Eleven Velodrome
Bruce Svihus
1776 East Boulder
Colorado Springs, CO 80909
(303) 634-VELO

7-ELEVEN OLYMPIC VELODROME
Carson, Ca
Dominguez Hills
CSUDH–Velodrome
Greg Wright
1000 East Victoria
Carson, CA 90747
(213) 516-4000

WASHINGTON PARK BOWL
Kenosha, WI
Washington Bowl
P.O. Box 836
Kenosha, WI 53141
(414) 656-8066

- *Kilometer:* One man against the clock, from a standing start, for 1,000 meters (men only).
- *Individual Pursuit:* One rider starts on the opposite side of the track from his or her opponent. The one who gains the advantage, by the end of the distance, wins (men 4,000 meters, women 3,000 meters).
- *Team Pursuit:* Same as above, but four-man teams ride against each other. Riding in single file, the lead rider rotates to the back of the line every lap. Three riders must finish (men only).
- *Sprints:* A highly tactical battle between two combatants who get to the finals through several rounds of eliminations. The race length is 1,000 meters, but a time is taken only for the last 200 meters (men's and women's).
- *Points Race:* A 50-kilometer race with sprints for points, every 5 laps. Final placing is determined by adding up the total number of points won throughout the race (men only).

Indoor six-day racing (right) is still very popular in Europe. Partners relay each other into the race, which keeps the speed high and adds to the spectacle. *Presse Sports photo*

The sprint event is characterized by high-speed maneuvering and close finishes. Here Nelson Vails takes a close one. *Presse Sports photo*

WORLD CHAMPIONSHIPS

- *Tandem Sprints:* The same as sprints, but with two riders, together on a tandem sprint bike, going against another pair for over 2,000 meters. (Amateur men only.)
- *Kierin:* Nine riders on the track are paced by a small motorcycle (derney), until the last lap, when the derney swings out of the way and the racers sprint to the line. (Adapted from Japanese racing, pros only.)
- *Motor Paced:* Up to ten motorcycles and drivers each pace a cyclist, in a race that generally lasts one hour. Speeds average over fifty mph and cyclists (amateurs and pros) ride bikes with small front wheels and a huge gear.

OTHER POPULAR RACES

- *Madison:* Two-man teams relay each other in and out of the race by way of a special handsling-type of pickup. One man actually races while the other slowly circles the track riding "relief." Named after Madison Square Garden where it originated, this is the most spectacular form of track racing and is the main element in six-day racing.
- *Miss-and-Out:* The last rider across the line after each lap is withdrawn, until there are only a few riders left to sprint for the finish.
- *Six-Day Races:* The "stage race" of velodrome racing, the "Six" lasts for six days and nights and combines sprints, madisons, pursuits, miss-and-outs, and other events, into an entertaining mix of racing, usually conducted during two racing sessions per day and featuring two- or three-man teams. Race is scored first on farthest distance pedaled (number of laps) and second on points accumulated in specialty races.

OFF-ROAD RACING

Today, the fastest-growing segment of competitive cycling, and for that matter, cycling as a whole, is a form of racing that surfaced as recently as 1980, in California. Since then, off-road, all-terrain, or mountain, bike racing (ATB) has taken the world by storm. Already, 700 sanctioned events per year have emerged in the U.S. alone.

The Mammoth Cycling Classic, at Mammoth Mountain, California, is the "grandaddy" of mountain bike competitions and was both the first unofficial and official world championship.

Although the sport is still developing, the events contested at Mammoth include:

- *The Observed Trials:* A skill test where the rider must ride, climb, and hop his bicycle over a variety of obstacles without falling off. A foot touched to the ground for balance is called a "dab." The competitor with the fewest dabs, after making it through the entire course, is the winner.

- *The Climb:* An endurance test in which the riders race each other to the top of the mountain.

- *The Kamikaze Downhill:* A full-out, timed run down the side of the mountain, usually on a gravel access road or cat track. Fastest time to the bottom wins.

- *The Cross-Country:* Similar to a road race, all riders start together and race over a set course or multilap circuit, over rolling terrain, through the mountains.

Mountain biking was first organized, on a formal basis, by a group called the North American Off-Road Bicycling Association (NORBA). In 1989, NORBA was merged into the United States Cycling Federation, which recognized the Mammoth Cycling Classic as the first official world championship. The same year, the Unione Cycliste International (UCI) declared that mountain bike racing was an important enough form of cycling competition to be organized and promoted by countries around the world. The UCI declared that, starting in 1990, the annual World Championships will be put out to worldwide bid. The UCI recognizes the cross-country as the event that determines the World Champion.

Many road racers have taken to mountain bike racing with considerable success, the most notable to date being Ned Overend and John Tomac. It is predicted that the sport will continue to grow, particularly as public roadways become increasingly congested. The mountain bikers must, however, make peace with the environmentalists. This is being accomplished in some areas through the use of specially designated mountain bike trails and in others through multi-use trails, with various rules concerning right of way between cyclists, horses, and pedestrians.

There is another, rather arcane, form of off-road cycling that predated mountain bike racing, yet hasn't captured the public's imagination, particularly in North America. *Cyclocross* is very popular in Europe, and is a preferred form of off-season competition for many top road racers.

Cyclocross resembles the cross-country discipline of mountain biking, with the exception that a cyclocross competitor is required to dismount and run with his bike over certain barely negotiable parts of the course. Also, since some reasonably good stretches of road are also always included, cyclocross bikes are lightweight and

Mountain Men. The first two stars to emerge from mountain bike racing are Ned Overend (left) and John Tomac. Overend has won more national titles, but Tomac has also successfully competed in BMX and amateur road racing. *Photos courtesy of Specialized Bicycle Components and Mongoose*

thin-tired (see photo on page 190) and otherwise much closer to a road bike than a mountain bike. The cyclocross rider must be a good cyclist, runner, and a bit of an acrobat. Cyclocross races in the U.S. are sanctioned by the USCF and are run in the November-to-March winter season.

A PRIMER ON RACING TACTICS

The first thing to know about bike-racing tactics is that there is a lot to know. Learning the subtleties comes through careful observation and a lot of trial and error, both in training and in races.

Since most races are run on the road with many other cyclists of similar ability, riding in close quarters with others becomes one of the most important fundamentals to master. It requires balance, coordination, timing, confidence, and sometimes a dash of gymnastics.

Riding in a pack is probably the most intimidating hurdle to a

Cyclocross combines running with cycling, and is very popular in Europe. *Cor Vos photo*

first-time racer. That first elbow-to-elbow contact can be enough to scare the fight out of you, but take comfort in knowing that once you progress into the more advanced categories of racing, life in the pack becomes far less hair-raising. It's not unlike learning to drive a car in traffic. Once you master it, the intimidation will diminish, and the best way to acquire the skill is through practice, practice, and more practice. Here are some tips:

1. *Ride with more experienced cyclists* whenever you can. They will give you pointers and be safer to ride with.

2. *Do plenty of group rides before you race.* The pressures of competition can do strange things to people, like make them nervous and shaky. The more experience you have, the more likely you'll be able to anticipate and/or deal with someone else's erratic moves.

3. *Learn pace-line etiquette.* Learn how to "sit on a wheel," on the proper side of the rider in front of you, without overlapping dan-

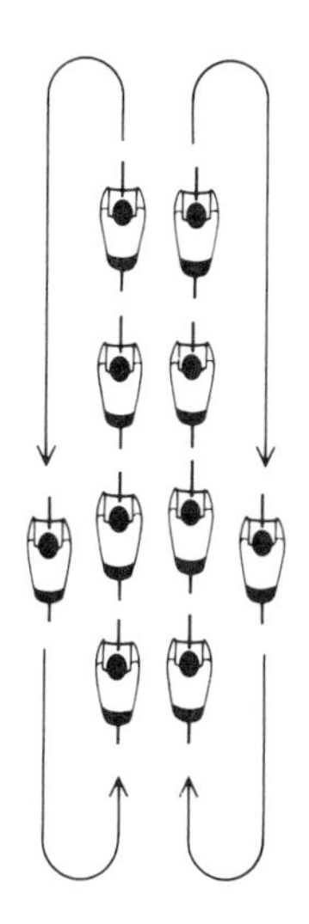

Double-file pace line, used in training. After lead riders finish their "pull" at the front, they peel off at the same time and drift back to the end of the line.

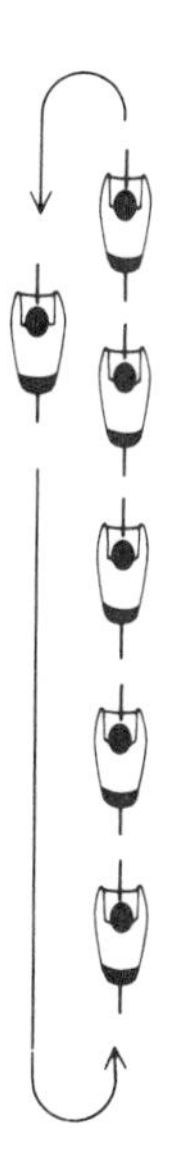

Single-file pace line, used in training or when wind is directly in the face. Lead rider ends his "pull" by swinging off and drifting back to the end.

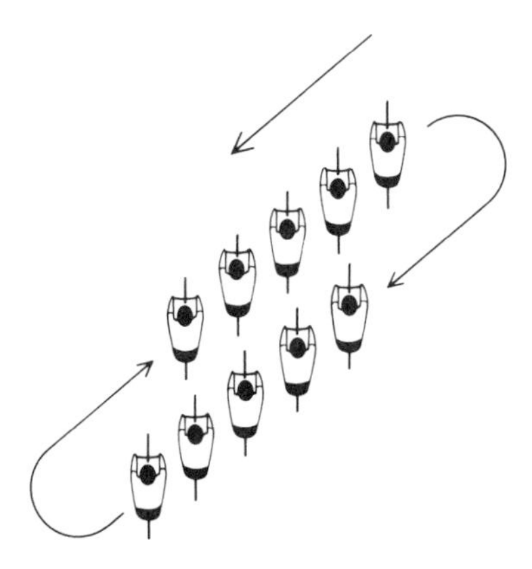

The high-speed pace line or rotating echelon. As soon as the lead rider makes it to the front, he peels off into the wind. Since rotation is continuous, no one rider is burdened with setting the pace for more than a few pedal strokes.

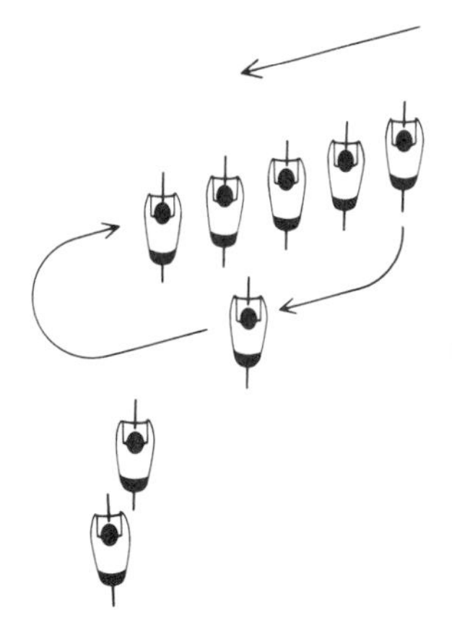

In high crosswinds, the echelon can stretch only as far as the width of the road. Because the speed is so high, riders who are squeezed out of the echelon either get dropped or form a second echelon a few yards behind.

gerously. If the wind is coming from the left, the following rider should be positioned slightly behind and to the right of the rider in front (see illustration). When it is time to "pull through" and "take pace," you should do so smoothly.

4. *Find a good coach.* The subtleties of group riding technique need to be discussed and practiced under the supervision of a critical eye, not just read about. Look for a club with a good coach or experienced rider who will spend time on the road with you.

TACTICAL TERMS

Attack: An aggressive acceleration usually used to start or in an attempt to break away.

Breakaway: When one rider or a group of riders has gotten ahead of the pack by more than a few seconds.

Bridge the Gap: Ride from the pack to the breakaway, usually a very difficult thing to do if the breakaway is moving fast.

Chaser(s): Rider or riders who are trying to bridge the gap or catch a rider or group ahead of them.

Dropped: Loss of contact with the group in which one is riding, usually due to fatigue.

Echelon: A formation of riders, drafting each other, that spreads across the road to get maximum protection in a crosswind.

Field Sprint: The final burst to the finish line, contested by the main pack of riders (always assumes that a breakaway has already finished).

Final Sprint: The final burst to the finish line (usually assumes that there is no breakaway ahead).

Jam: A period of fast riding within the race. Usually applied to a fast-moving rider or group, as in, "The chasers had to jam for twenty minutes before they caught the breakaway."

Jump: A quick acceleration, usually to catch other riders off guard (e.g., to start the final sprint or make a sudden attack).

Lead out: When a teammate or competitor paces a following rider to maximum speed in a sprint. As the lead rider fades, the paced rider sprints by, at a much faster speed, for a "slingshot" effect.

Pace line: Riders in single or double file, where the lead rider(s) will systematically "swing off" the front and drift to the back of the line, until it is time to "pull" again.

Pack: The main cluster of riders. Synonymous with bunch, field, group, or peloton.

Pull: To set the pace at the front of a pace line. When a rider "takes a pull," he is taking his turn breaking the wind at the front.

Pull through: Move to the front of a pace line, from second spot, after the lead rider swings off the front.

Push: To ride in a big gear, at low cadence, for more speed.

Sit in: To stay tucked in another rider's draft or comfortably in the pack.

Soft pedal: To turn the pedals without applying real power (usually an energy-saving tactic that attempts to fool other riders).

Sprint: An all-out maximum effort to the finish line that can usually be sustained for no more than twenty-five seconds.

Swing off: Move to one side after taking a pull.

Wind up: Gradual acceleration to get to top speed.

Wheel Sucker: A derogatory term, referring to a rider who always sits in and never expends any energy by taking a pull at the front.

A beginning racer will improve more quickly if he or she understands the above tactical vernacular and learns the basic principles governing cycling strategy. It also helps to have a hunger to excel. With those things in mind, here are the basics:

1. *Stay in the Race.* Begin with one simple tactic: Stay with the field and finish the race. Until this becomes routine, the enjoyment of a real tactical race cannot be experienced.

2. *Observe Everything.* Bernard Hinault estimates that only 10 to 15 percent of a top field of pros really concentrates on the subtleties of what is happening in a race at any given moment (i.e., who feels good, who feels bad, who's bluffing and when, shifts in the wind, why someone is eating a rice cake instead of a fig newton, and so on). A blatant example of being out of touch in a race (and one that happens all too frequently) is beating the pack in the final sprint, only to discover you placed fourth, because three riders had broken away.

3. *Conserve Energy.* In Chapter 5, we saw that a drafting rider can maintain the speed of his pacemaker, while exerting 15 to 20 percent less energy. That's equivalent to starting a one-hundred-mile race at the twenty-mile mark! The rider who "sits-in" the longest will be freshest at the finish. Many a race has been lost by the strong, well-trained rider who rides ahead and breaks the wind too long, only to see the fresher rider sprint by at a crucial moment, near the end of the race.

4. *Use the Faster Wheels.* Conserving energy by resting all day will keep you relatively fresh at the finish, but it won't ensure victory. A bike race is a dynamic thing. Riders are always trying to break away. Use the back wheels (slipstream) of the faster riders, as they come by, to stay near the front of the action. Conversely, avoid making tiring efforts just to get to the front.

5. *Make Decisive Efforts.* The best tacticians initiate few moves during the race, but when they do it usually results in getting in or initiating a winning breakaway. Pick your shots carefully: Decisive efforts are intense and therefore should be saved for the right tactical moments in the race.

6. *Sprint All-Out.* As you close in on the finish line, time your final sprint so that you can give maximum effort to the end. If possible, use another racer to "slingshot" you across the line (see "lead out" above). Put every ounce of energy into the pedals and concentrate totally on going fast. Don't let up, sit up, or relax until *after* you have crossed the line. High fives and bows are best taken on the podium, not at the finish.

This may seem like mumbo jumbo, but will make increasing sense after a few months of serious training, group rides with local racers, and entry into a race or two. It is also a good idea to take advantage of some of the excellent writings available on the subject of racing tactics. Best bets:

Greg LeMond's Complete Book of Bicycling; Greg LeMond and Kent Gordis; Putnam Publishing, 1987; Chapter Five.
Road Racing Technique and Training; Bernard Hinault and Claude Genzling; VeloNews, 1988; pp. 116–131.
Bicycle Road Racing; Edward Borysewicz; VeloNews, 1985.

SUMMARY

While bicycle racing is not for the timid, it has a variety of kinds and categories that offer fun and excitement for both sexes and most ages. The best starting point is the bicycle shop. There are roughly two thousand specialty pro shops nationwide, which can usually provide local club information and access to serious racers and competitions.

Throughout the world, road racing (which includes criteriums, point-to-point races, circuit races, and stage races) is by far the most popular form of competition. Off-road racing or mountain biking is growing rapidly, and the increasing number of velodromes being built indicates that track cycling may regain at least some of the status it had during "cycling's golden age," earlier in the century.

Racing strategy and tactics take a long time to learn and require years of seasoning to master. The best way to learn and improve is to ride with, pay attention to, and emulate the faster and more experienced racers. Understand the principles, make yourself "go the distance," and seek good coaching, to help with on-the-road practice, particularly in group riding situations.

13 Cycling's Holy Grail: The Tour de France

"There are people who claim that bike racing is dying and perhaps it is. Fewer Europeans ride bikes every year, and increasing traffic is forcing the races off highways on to back roads where fewer people watch.

"But to Europe, bike racing is still the most grueling sport, the most dramatic, the most glorious. There is so much suffering in it, so much courage and strength, so much effort, so much of the scenery it pedals through and over, that it is still the supreme sport, the supreme spectacle, the supreme test of athletic might. Across the mountains await money, fame, rest for aching legs. But first the riders must sweat the big drops."

Those words are from *The Bizarre World European Sports,* written by Robert Daley, European sports correspondent for *The New York Times.* They are as true today as when they first appeared in 1963.

Bicycle racing is an epic sport that has become big business, and there is no event in cycling more epic than the Tour de France. It is a timeless classic that has carried on for nearly a century, interrupted only by the two world wars.

The Tour is a three-week-long bicycle race that is beamed to one billion television viewers around the world—twice the audience for America's Super Bowl. An estimated 14.6 million people stand by the roadside for a glimpse of the racers as they flash by on route each day, to some distant mountain pass or picturesque French village.

The Tour generates millions of dollars of revenues each year for its organizer—the Société du Tour de France, a company owned in part by the popular French sporting paper, *L'Equipe,* and the publishing conglomerate, Hachette, both under the ultimate control of French industrialist, Philippe Amaury.

Perhaps the biggest financial beneficiaries of the Tour are the star racers themselves. Superstar cyclists have retired as wealthy and famous public figures, capitalizing on the fame they earned by trying harder and pedaling faster.

In the 1980s, Americans cashed in for the first time in Tour history. And nobody in cycling history has been able to do that better than Greg LeMond, who after his 1989 comeback victory,

(opposite and above)
Millions line the Tour's route each year, from Alpine summits to the Champs Elysée, in Paris.
Presse Sports photos

signed cycling's richest sponsorship deal, a three-year, $5.5 million contract to ride for a French team sponsored by "Z," a children's clothing company, comparable to The Gap in the United States.

This contract seemed like a steal to Roger Zannier, Z's president, who outbid all other suitors, including 7-Eleven and several other powerhouse teams of international cycling: "I'm a pragmatist," Zannier was quoted as saying in *Velo-News*, the journal that broke the news on LeMond's contract. "Last year we calculated that our team's exposure on television was worth about 55 million francs (over $9 million) in terms of traditional publicity . . . (cycling is) too good a publicity opportunity to ignore."

The publicity caravan is a parade of eye-catching, moving advertisements that precedes the racers and entertains the crowds. *Presse Sports photo*

Sometimes the blatant commercialism surrounding the Tour seems to overshadow the event itself. But in the final analysis, this is only true with respect to the hoopla that ensues after new heroes are made each year. During the twenty-plus days of racing, the news is about the drama on the road. Sponsors get fantastic on-site television and print exposure at the event, but that just seems to add to the color. Each and every July, Le Tour is a riveting story of willpower, intrigue, danger, and courage played out on a canvas of spectacular mountains, medieval cobblestones, lush farmlands, and bustling cities.

In the words of renowned American sports columnist Red Smith: "There is nothing in America even remotely comparable with it. We think the World Series claims the undivided attention of the United States, but there is a saying here that an army from Mars could invade France, the government could fall, and even the recipe for sauce Bearnaise be lost, but if it happened during the Tour de France nobody would notice."

Part of the Tour's magic is the countryside it traverses. *Presse Sports photo*

HOW IT BEGAN

The first Tour de France was born as a publicity stunt. As we know from earlier chapters, bicycle racing was one of the world's biggest sports and already a passion among Frenchmen by the start of this century. *Le Velo,* a popular French newspaper, had done well by devoting itself to chronicling the exploits and derring-do of the early wheelmen. By 1902, *Le Velo* had been sponsoring, organizing, and writing about Bordeaux–Paris, cycling's first real annual classic, for eleven years. Other races like Paris–Roubaix and Paris–Tours had also become immensely popular.

Enter *L'Auto* (subtitled *Automobile Cyclisme*), a scrappy competitor run by an ambitious ex-bike racer named Henri Desgranges. Frustrated by failed attempts to stage a bigger and better race than those that his competitor Pierre Giffard of *Le Velo* had promoted, Desgranges hit upon his destiny. From a half-kidding suggestion by a *L'Auto* staffer named Leo Lefevre, Desgranges evolved and launched his vision for the "greatest bike race in the whole world."

This was an event that would scoop *Le Velo* once and for all. The challenge was thrown out to all comers: A race lasting nineteen days consisting of six 400-km legs, or "stages," with one to four days of rest between each. Prize money: a whopping 2,000 francs (about $40.00). For a racer to win, he had to complete all six legs, in the fastest overall time.

Desgranges and his staff at *L'Auto* attacked the project with mercenary zeal. Think of the coverage! Think of the new readership! Think of the blow to *Le Velo!*

On July 1, 1903, sixty hale-and-hearty wheelmen started the first Tour de France from the Alarm Clock Cafe, on the outskirts of Paris. The first stage was 467 kilometers to Lyon, and at an average speed of twenty-five km per hour, took the riders nearly twenty hours to complete.

These pioneers finished in darkness and without much fanfare, except for *L'Auto*'s own fervent and extensive coverage. But, by the time the first Tour de France finished, back in Paris, nearly three weeks later, enthusiasm for this new, almost diabolical endurance test had captured the nation's imagination. It certainly didn't hurt that thirty-two-year-old Maurice Garin, the most popular racer of the day and a naturalized Frenchman, claimed the first victory.

Garin's time of ninety-four hours, thirty-three minutes, for the

L'Auto

HENRI DESGRANGE

AUTOMOBILE — CYCLISME

LE TOUR DE FRANCE — LE DÉPART

Organisé par L'AUTO du 1er au 19 Juillet 1903

LA SEMENCE

PARIS
NANTES
LYON
BORDEAUX
TOULOUSE
MARSEILLE
ESPAGNE

L'ITINÉRAIRE DU TOUR DE FRANCE

QUI ?

The first Tour de France was big news, particularly for *L'Auto,* the newspaper that sponsored it.
Presse Sports photo

2,428-km distance, was three hours faster than the best of the remaining twenty finishers. *L'Auto* made Garin larger than life. Dubbed the "little chimney sweep," because of his prior vocation, Garin's star quality did not escape the eyes of Desgranges, the consummate promoter, who described him this way in his daily diary on the Tour: "To me he was a little devil. Small he was indeed (5′3″, 138 lbs.), but he was the toughest of them all. Very powerful, a human dynamo, full of incredible resistance and endurance. He was a brute of a fellow, very provocative and high-handed."

Maurice Garin, first winner of the Tour, was called a human dynamo—and he even smoked cigarettes! *Presse Sports photo*

And so the legendary heroes of the Tour were born. But the early years of the race suffered serious growing pains, the worst of which almost got the best of Desgranges, in 1904.

In the second Tour de France, the event came close to dying at the hands of hooliganism. So partisan were the fans that they barricaded the route after their favorites passed by, clubbed the opposition, and spread tacks at critical places on the route. Add the dangers of riding long distances through the night and repeated threats of sabotage, and one can understand why Desgranges announced in *L'Auto*: "The Tour is finished; the second edition is the last. . . ."

But fate would not have it. The French Cycling Union intervened, and after an investigation, they disqualified the top-four finishers of 1904, officially for acts of "corruption." Garin, who had again reached Paris before the others was implicated and suspended from competition for two years, leaving nineteen-year-old Henri Carnet the winner.

Henri Desgranges was a bike racer before he founded the Tour de France. *Presse Sports photo*

Garin never returned to the winners podium and Desgranges, vindicated by the ruling, emerged with a better format that set the Tour on the right track for the future. In 1905, night racing was eliminated and, for the first time, mountain passes were included in the route. "*Le Grande Boucle*" (the big loop), as it was called, had become a midsummer institution for the French nation.

HOW THE TOUR IS WON

Asking the average American to explain a bicycle stage race is like asking the average Frenchman to describe the rules of baseball. Despite the Tour's popularity and increasing interest on the American side of the Atlantic, basic understanding of the game is just not part of our heritage. Here are some basics that will help the novice fan understand how the Tour is scored:

A PRESCRIBED ROUTE

The Tour de France is a stage race or multiday bicycle race that follows a prescribed route. To make it interesting, the route is changed from year to year, although some cities and most mountain passes have become traditional and are visited nearly every year.

A RACE IN STAGES

The route, usually about 2,200 miles in length (the distance from Chicago to Los Angeles), is broken into daily legs, or stages, of different distances. Each stage will usually start at one point and finish at another. The longest stages are most often through flat countryside, a good example being the 161-mile stage from Poitiers to Bordeaux, in 1989. Except in time-trial stages, where men race the clock, rather than each other, all racers start each stage together, regardless of where they finished on prior days.

LOWEST TIME LEADS

Each rider's finishing time for each stage is recorded and added to the previous total, on a daily basis. Thus, if a rider has completed stage one in two hours, ten minutes, stage two in three hours, ten minutes, and stage three in two hours, twenty minutes, his cumulative or overall time after three stages is seven hours, forty minutes. If that is the lowest overall time, the rider starts stage four as the overall race leader.

SYMBOLS OF THE TOUR

YELLOW JERSEY

Worn by the overall race leader (the rider with the lowest elapsed time after each stage). First offered in 1919.

GREEN JERSEY

Second most coveted jersey on the Tour. The first 25 riders to finish each stage score points. The rider with the current highest point tally wears green. The winner at the end is the best sprinter of the Tour. Introduced in 1953.

POLKA DOT JERSEY

"King of the mountain" jersey. Every climb in the Tour is classified for its severity, from category four (easiest) to the "hors" category (so tough it is beyond classification). The top riders to reach each summit (from three to fifteen, depending upon the climb's category) score points. Begun in 1933.

RED JERSEY

Worn by the rider who has scored the most points awarded at designated places along the route, usually in villages or special points of interest. Sometimes "time bonuses" are awarded (a deduction of as much as ten seconds for the winner, which will be subtracted from his actual time for that day's stage).

YELLOW CAP

The members of the leading team, determined by combining the elapsed times of the three best team members, all get to wear yellow caps. The team competition began in 1903. The yellow caps came later. If the overall leader of the Tour is also leading in one or more of the other competitions, he wears yellow and the rider who is second on points wears the special jersey.

A team time trial stage in the Tour is the rare chance an entire squad gets to ride as fast as they can, together. *Presse Sports photo*

CYCLING: A TEAM SPORT

"In cycling, you only get a great individual result when you are supported by a great team."—Laurent Fignon, winner of the 1983 and 1984 Tours de France.

Contrary to first impressions, cycling is very much a team sport, particularly in the Tour de France. A team usually has ten members for the Tour, although in some years there have been fewer and in some years more. Each team is formed around one or two "*stars,*" men who—possessed of uncommon talent and monumental ambition—are capable of winning the big one.

The rest of the team members play a support role and are called "*domestiques*" (helpers), because their job is to do the dirty work for the stars. This may consist of chasing down rivals, carrying food and drink, and even sometimes giving up a bike. *Domestiques* must be very good racers because they often have to work twice as hard as a star. The difference between a star and a *domestique* is that a team leader must be able to do *everything* well (climb, sprint, time trial), while a *domestique,* although generally strong in most areas, tends to be lacking in at least one.

Although teams are registered in one country or another and must contract most members from the country of registery, team title and first allegiance belongs to a commercial sponsor.

Sponsors pay handsomely for the privilege of backing a Tour de France squad. To be accepted into the Tour and to be able to perform well, a team must campaign year round. Salaries of racers, travel costs, a year-round "front office" staff, mechanics, vehicles, equipment, trainers, masseurs, and directors push a top team's annual budget well into seven figures.

Nevertheless, as noted by Jim Ochowicz, director of the top U.S.–based pro team, 7-Eleven, "When you consider the cost of advertising against the amount of air time a good team will generate through the Tour and other major races, it's a good deal."

THE YELLOW JERSEY

In 1919, Desgranges began to single out and honor the overall race leader by awarding the "*maillot jaune*" or yellow jersey, the color chosen to match the pages of *L'Auto*. The jersey was and is given to the racer with the lowest elapsed time at the end of each day. The right to start the new stage in yellow quickly became the most coveted symbol in bike racing. The one who keeps it after the final stage, in Paris, is obviously the overall Tour winner. Over the years, additional jerseys have been added to honor various other talents exhibited during the Tour.

Like American baseball, bicycle racing, beyond its basic scoring rules, involves a unique fabric of strategy, far more complex and interesting than is apparent to the novice observer. Just getting through the race requires a level of fitness, stamina, and experience, beyond the realm of most mortals. Winning requires an acute sense of one's limits, the strengths and weaknesses of other top contenders, near-perfect physical and mental health, and an experienced, resolute support team.

It is no wonder that only half of the racers who enter the Tour finish and that only 2 percent will ever wear the yellow jersey, even for one day. Despite that, every cyclist who races a bike sometime, somewhere, has dreamed of riding the Tour. As five-time winner, Jacques Anquetil put it, "Wherever you go, if they want to know if you are a real cyclist, they will ask: 'Have you ever raced in the Tour?' If the answer is 'yes,' then you are a real cyclist."

GREAT MEN OF THE TOUR

THE CANNIBAL

"I didn't feel the pedals that day. I wanted to win the Tour, but I didn't feel safe. That's why I planned to widen the gap. I attacked on the Tourmalet, 140 km from the finish. A very long way to go, I know. But I had no choice. Lomme Driessens, my team manager, told me Raymond Poulidor was organizing a pursuit. I was lucky to have my domestique Martin Vandenbossche up there to keep everything under control. A stupid attack of mine? No it wasn't. At the finish I was eight minutes ahead. The Tour de France was mine."

So spoke Eddy Merckx, eighteen years after he had won his first Tour de France, in 1969. Not only is Merckx one of three men in history to win the Tour de France five times, he is, by many accounts, the greatest of them all. Merckx is to cycling as Palmer is to golf, Laver to tennis, and Ruth to baseball.

EDDY MERCKX—
CAREER RECORD

Born: Meensel-Kiezegem, Belgium, 6/17/45
Professional: 1965–78
Principal Victories:
Five Tours de France. He competed seven times, winning 35 stages.
Five Tours of Italy (1968, 1970, 1972, 1973, 1974). Won 25 stages.
Tour of Switzerland (1974). Won five stages.
Tour of Spain (1973). Won six stages.
Tour of Belgium (1970, 1971). Won six stages.
Paris–Nice (1969, 1970, 1971).
World Road Champion (1967, 1971, 1974).
World Hour Record holder (1972).
Champion of Belgium (1970).
The Classic single-day races.
Paris–Roubaix (1968, 1970, 1973).
Milan–San Remo (1966, 1967, 1969, 1971, 1972, 1975, 1976).
Tour of Lombardy (1971, 1972).
Liège–Bastogne–Liège (1969, 1971, 1972, 1973, 1975).
Tour of Flanders (1969, 1975).
Flèche–Wallonne (1967, 1970, 1972).
Amstel Gold Race (1973, 1975).
Merckx competed in 1,800 races, of which he won an amazing 525.

Eddy Merckx, in 1969, on his way to winning his first of five Tours.
Presse Sports photo

By winning that stage in the Pyrenees, in 1969, Merckx became the first Belgian in thirty years to claim a Tour victory. He also displayed such will to win and superhuman ambition that he was soon nicknamed "The Cannibal."

But what is most remarkable about Merckx' first Tour victory is that he rode with the single-minded purpose of clearing his name of a doping scandal that had resulted in his disqualification from the Tour of Italy, a month before the Tour de France was to start.

After making it clear that he intended to win the three-week-long Italian Tour, Merckx talked about the consequences. "A bad thing for Italian cycling, of course. A couple of people came to see me and offered a tremendous amount of money to sell the race and let an Italian win. I refused, of course. I was honest, I didn't want to play games. The best rider must win, it's as simple as that."

A few days later, Merckx tested positive in a routine drug check and was forced to quit the race. Sure that someone had slipped a forbidden substance in his water bottle, he had something to prove: ". . . it nearly killed my reputation," he said. "That's why I desperately wanted to win the 1969 Tour de France. I wanted to prove I was honest."

He went on to become a true legend and remains, to this day, the sport's most prolific winner.

THE BADGER

The most recent Tour de France superstar is a man known less for crushing dominance than for his constant willingness to fight. The man from Brittany, Bernard Hinault, like Eddy Merckx, won five Tours de France (1978, '79, '81, '82, and '85).

Hinault was dubbed "*Le Blaireau*" (the Badger). Like the animal, Hinault seemed calm and peace-loving but, when cornered, no one could fight more fiercely. On more than one occasion he let his fists fly, out of frustration from being trapped by the media or blocked from going up the road by a political protest.

Hinault's five Tour victories were won in every way possible, although his forte was always his incredible speed in the time trial. His biggest margin of victory was fourteen minutes, thirty-four seconds, over the great Belgian climber, Lucian Von Impe, in 1981; and his narrowest, one minute, forty-two seconds, over Greg LeMond, in 1985.

In fact, Hinault's rivalry with the young, up-and-coming LeMond says as much about his character as any of the other episodes of his great career. In both 1985 and 1986, the two were teammates riding for the powerful Look La Vie Claire team. LeMond and Hinault had, until the 1985 Tour, enjoyed the relationship of pupil and mentor. Hinault had made it clear that one day he would turn the reins of Tour dominance over to LeMond.

But when? In the 1985 race, LeMond felt he had the opportunity and the desire to take over the yellow jersey from Hinault who was struggling through the Alps. But heeding instructions from his team manager to protect Hinault's lead, not challenge it, LeMond eased up on the tough climb to Luz Ardiden. As a result, Hinault went on to win the 1985 Tour and, with a good-natured smile, thanked LeMond and pledged to help the American win, the following year.

In 1986, the two again started as the stars of the strongest team on the Tour. But there was little talk about the pledge made a year earlier, and it soon became clear that Hinault was not willing to throw his talent behind a victory for LeMond. He had a shot at winning his sixth Tour and *domestique* was not a word that described

Bernard ("the Badger") Hinault's fighting spirit enabled him to win the Tour five times.
Presse Sports photo

Hinault. And who could blame him? A sixth victory would make him the champion of champions.

This was particularly evident when LeMond, sporting the yellow jersey well into the crucial final days of the Tour, found himself defending it against Hinault's seemingly unnecessary attacks and pointed references to the Tour not being over until after the final time trial.

LeMond felt let down, betrayed, and bewildered. He was clearly riding better than his teammates, Hinault included, yet not enjoying the traditional team support the *maillot jaune* commands. Would LeMond crumble? Would Hinault crush him?

What then happened made both men heroes. LeMond lost the critical final week's time trial to Hinault—but only by twenty-five seconds (and after a crash, at that!).

Although teammates LeMond and Hinault fought during the 1986 Tour, they both emerged as heroes. *Presse Sports photo*

The margin was insufficient for Hinault to take over the yellow jersey. Importantly, LeMond had not crumbled under the enormous pressure mounted by Hinault and several other members of his own team.

And the Badger? His refusal to throw himself behind LeMond made the 1986 Tour one of the most intriguing ever. He was right, in that he was true to his own character and made LeMond's win a worthy one, and perhaps, as LeMond angrily pointed out during the heated battle, he was wrong to break the rule of challenging a teammate.

It was in Hinault's nature to break the unwritten rules, when it made the difference between victory and defeat, but he was also by nature a realist. When LeMond mounted the podium after that all-important time trial, in 1986 (with several days to go to the finish), Hinault was quickly at his side. "Greg, it's over," he said, "You won the Tour."

Frenchman Jacques Anquetil was better known for stylish time-trialing than pleasing the crowds.
Presse Sports photo

LE NORMAND AND POU POU

Cycling experts usually agree on one thing: the Tour de France legend with the most style of all was Frenchman Jacques Anquetil, from Normandy. Known as "*Le Normand*" or simply "*Maitre,*" Anquetil was cool, calculating, and composed. His five Tour de France wins (1952, '61, '62, '63, and '64) were strategically engineered to take advantage of his phenomenal ability to time trial, although in one of his best wins, in 1963, he beat all the mountain-climbing specialists at their own game.

Largely as a result of Anquetil's cerebral and calculated approach, he never achieved the grass roots popularity he deserved.

But as is the case with many great athletes, the legends are often defined by their chief competitors, the men who push them to their greatest performance.

Although Anquetil's rivals were many, the one who most often stole the spotlight was Raymond Poulidor. "Pou Pou," as he was affectionately called by his legions of fans, was a great rider with the ability to time trial, climb, and sprint. But Pou Pou lacked what every real champion must have: the ability to put it all together consistently enough to finish first. He was nicknamed "The Eternal Second": In fourteen Tours de France spanning a seventeen-year career, Poulidor finished second three times, third five times, and seventh, eighth, ninth, and nineteenth once each. Despite such an impact on the record book, Poulidor never once—not even for one day—wore the yellow jersey.

Yet no racer has ever been as popular (nor pushed Jacques Anquetil harder) than this archetypal, "never say die" challenger. In the 1964 Tour, Poulidor lost to Anquetil by a mere fifty-five seconds, the narrowest margin of *Le Normand's* five wins.

During that amazing Tour, Poulidor suffered enough misfortune to last a lifetime. At the stage finish at the velodrome in Monaco, Poulidor sprinted a lap too early and lost a minute time bonus. Later, in the mountains, Poulidor was primed to take advantage of one of the worst days of Anquetil's career. *Le Normand* had lost four minutes on the Col d'Envalira climb. But with thirteen miles to go in the stage, Poulidor broke a wheel, and during the ensuing repair, which should have been routine, Poulidor's own mechanic pushed him off too hard, causing him to crash and costing nearly all the time he had gained on Anquetil.

But the real showdown came on the infamous Puy de Dome climb a few days later. Poulidor and Anquetil battled up the slope shoulder-to-shoulder. Two hundred thousand fans gave them only a narrow tunnel to the summit. Anquetil, eyes glazed with fatigue and hanging on for dear life, could scarcely hear the deafening chant "Pou Pou," "Pou Pou!" rising from the throng.

Finally, near the summit, Anquetil could fight no more. Poulidor, knowing this could be his moment in history, lunged over his bike, stomping the pedals with every bit of force in his body. At the finish he had gained forty-two seconds on his nemesis. But poor Pou Pou needed fifteen more to take over the yellow jersey. With a time trial soon to come, it was the closest Poulidor ever came to removing *le maillot jaune* from Anquetil's shoulders.

After Anquetil retired from the Tour, in 1966, he actually gained in popularity, often reporting favorably for the French media on Poulidor's continuing career. But in November of 1987 the great rivalry ended. Anquetil, fifty-three, died of cancer. On his deathbed, Anquetil said to Poulidor: "Well, Raymond it looks as if you have finally beaten me."

Raymond Poulidor finished in the top three eight times, but never once wore the yellow jersey.
Presse Sports photo

THE RAT

The stories of the stars and exploits of the Tour de France fill volumes. Some have been told and retold, no doubt over endless bottles of Beaujolais or Cognac, in small villages across Europe.

These tales range from great heroics to tragic deaths to endless debates about who deserved to win and who didn't. Most agree that Raymond Poulidor gets the title of most loved, Eddy Merckx of most dominant, and Joop Zoetemelk of most enduring.

Zoetemelk, a Dutchman who turned professional in 1970, has ridden more Tours than any other cyclist in history. He entered sixteen, finished them all, and no less than eleven times finished in the top five. He had six second-place finishes and one victory.

Was Zoetemelk a great cyclist in his own right or was he an unaggressive opportunist who depended on the mistakes of others to give him high placings? His unflattering nicknames, "The Rat" and "The Sucker," indicate that many fans felt the latter to be true, and to Joop's misfortune, his career spanned those of none other than Merckx and Hinault.

But Joop was always there, never quitting and always making the best of his circumstances. He lived for the bike and he loved the Tour. The only year he did not ride it during his long career was in 1974. After beating Merckx in Paris–Nice (an early season preparation race for the Tour), the Dutchman was almost killed in a head-on collision with a car. Defying the doctors who said he would never regain his abilities, Zoetemelk took eight months to recover before finishing a brilliant fourth, in the 1975 Tour (Merckx was second).

Of his sixteen Tour rides and sixteen finishes, Zoetemelk's only one to end in yellow was in 1980, when Hinault, leading by one minute, eight seconds, abruptly withdrew with severe tendinitis.

DEATH ON THE VENTOUX

Only one racer has actually died while racing in the Tour, although many have come close. This seems strange for such a risky sport where men plunge down mountainsides at 60 miles per hour, often on greasy rain-slicked roads.

But on July 13, the thirteenth day of the 1967 Tour, 29-year-old Tom Simpson, a popular British rider, stopped pedaling for good. It happened not far from the summit of Mt. Ventoux, a barren and desolate ash heap of a mountain in Provence.

It was a nasty hot day—110 degrees on the mountain—and Simpson, who in 1962 had been the first British rider to wear the yellow jersey, was determined to stay with the leaders. But as the riders struggled upward, Simpson began to fade. He looked uncomfortable, his face uncharacteristically ashen, and he began to wobble. Several spectators rushed from the sidelines to push him along. A little farther along he fell off his bicycle only to be helped back on. When he fell a second time, race officials were there to help him. "Put me back on my bike" were reportedly his last words. He lapsed into unconsciousness and was pronounced dead at a hospital in Avignon at 5:40 P.M.

Simpson's death sent shock waves through the sport. He officially died of heart failure, but a healthy supply of amphetamines was found in his jersey pockets and an autopsy revealed traces in his system.

Simpson's death was the catalyst for an extensive drug clean-up program, previously unknown to professional sports. The dark side of cycling had come out of the closet. Thorough testing soon became routine. As a result, more than a few cyclists were disqualified, suspended, or banned from the sport.

The most notable dope scandal came in 1978 when Belgian Michel Pollentier was found with a plastic tube running down his arm, from a concealed flask containing a drug-free urine sample. Sadly, Pollentier had just won the difficult stage to Alpe d'Huez and had earned the right to wear the yellow jersey. He was immediately disqualified.

Dutchman Joop Zoetemelk holds the record for the most Tours ridden and finished: sixteen between 1970 and 1986.
Presse Sports photo

Phil Liggett, British commentator and author of *The Tour de France,* had this to say about Zoetemelk's victory: "Naturally, Zoetemelk has his detractors—people who said that if Hinault had not retired he would not have won—but he pointed out that the Tour was the toughest of all races and Hinault's body had cried 'enough.' His hadn't."

Zoetemelk's last Tour ride was in 1986, at age forty. He finished twenty-fourth.

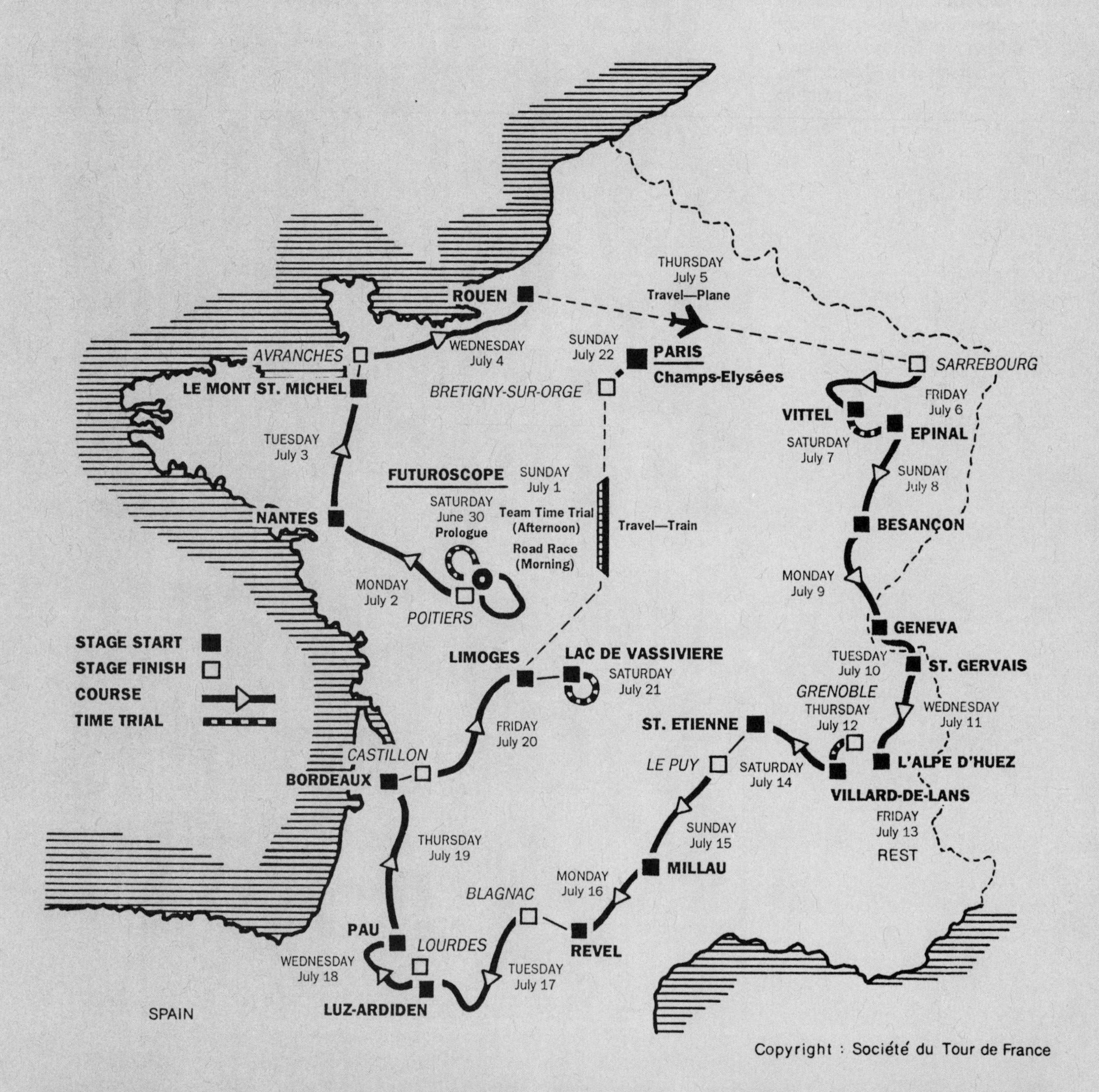

1990 TOUR DE FRANCE

THE TRAVELING ROAD SHOW

The Tour de France is accurately called the biggest single sporting event in the world. Although the Olympics and soccer's World Cup draw a larger number of participants and a bigger global audience, the logistics of staging a three-week-long competition that changes its venue day after day is unique to the sport of cycling.

The annual budget for the Tour is well over $10 million and pulls together a massive cast of characters who are involved in the race throughout its roughly 3,500-kilometer odyssey (approximately 2,000 miles):

- 4,000 in the race entourage
  - —200 racers
  - —600 support people
  - —44 full-time Tour employees
  - —600 accredited press
  - —600 TV and radio production staff
  - —1,650 workers associated with the publicity caravan
- 15,000 gendarmes
- 35 escort motorcycles
- 1,500 official Tour vehicles

The massive logistics needed to move, feed, and sleep this many race followers (not including the millions of fans!) is a year-round, militarylike operation run from the Société du Tour de France command center, on the outskirts of Paris. On the top floor of a five-story office building, also housing the offices of *L'Equipe* (newspaper), *Presse Sport* (photo services), and *Velo,* a cycling magazine, is the inner sanctum of the officials that run the Tour. Chief among these are two men, Director General Jean-Pierre Carenso (a veteran advertising and marketing executive), and Competition Director Jean-Marie LeBlanc (a former Tour rider and journalist).

Between 1987 and 1988, the business side of the Tour underwent a complete makeover. Ousted for alleged improprieties involving payments made to cover the shortfall from a Société du Tour–backed race in the U.S., in 1983, was seventy-six-year-old Félix Levitan, one of the Tour's patriarchs, since World War II. Jacques Goddett, his popular codirector retired with honor from the Tour, in 1988, at the age of eighty-two.

Streamlined and modern, the new Tour organization is committed to building on tradition, without any big departures from the Tour's successful format. As Carenso is quick to point out, "The Tour succeeded because of a unique formula. It has captured the nation because it is held in the month of July and does not interfere with France's traditional holiday shut-down in August. The terrain of France is perfect for this race with just the right mixture of extremely tough mountain passes and beautiful countryside. Those who would like to see the Tour expand out of France's borders would play with its essential character. We wish to keep the Tour what it has always been."

THE TOUR FEMININ

Perhaps the most radical departure from Tour de France tradition took place in 1984, when a special women's race was added. This came as a complete shock to many observers, since women had previously not been allowed to come near the Tour—not even as riders in cars in the race caravan. (In 1982, Jock Boyer's wife had to disguise herself as a man in order to sneak into one of the official vehicles.) Jacques Anquetil (known also as quite a ladies' man) summarized the French attitude about women racing the Tour, in his newspaper column: "I have absolutely nothing against women's sports, but I find that cycling is far too difficult for a woman. They're not made for the sport. I prefer to see women in a short white skirt rather than racing shorts. In fact, I like women a lot and am really sorry to see them suffer. On a bicycle, there's always a lot of suffering."

But the Tour Feminin, like the Tour itself, when it first began, is beginning to overcome it's initial growing pains. Won in its first year by an American, Marianne Martin, the race has since been dominated, much to the boredom of the media, by Italian Maria Canins (a mother of three, in her forties), and France's superstar, Jeanne Longo.

The format of the women's race has now stabilized as a stage race of roughly 1,000 kilometers, run concurrently with the final two weeks of the men's Tour. Although the stages are shorter, many of the tough climbs are included. Since Longo retired after 1989 and Canins will soon follow, the door is now open for new blood and more spirited competition.

A strong American squad is now developing. They won the team prize in 1989, anchored by Inga Thompson (third in 1989), and with potential future contenders like Susan Elias, Bunki Bunkaitis-Davis, Katrin Tobin, Sally Zack, and Phyliss Hines, it is likely that the U.S. will soon emerge as a powerhouse. Also, with stronger teams being fielded by eastern and western European countries, North and South America, and even Australia, the Tour Feminin could do for women cyclists what the Tour de France has done for the men—act as a catalyst to build the sport and provide a coveted annual classic.

AN AMERICAN PIONEER

American Marianne Martin rode into the Tour's record books by winning the first Tour Feminin, in 1984. *Presse Sports photo*

Whoever thought that Marianne Martin, from Fenton, Michigan, would forever be listed on the first line in a Tour de France record book?

But there she is: 1,051 kilometers in 29 hours, 39 minutes, 25 seconds, as winner of the historic inaugural Tour de France Feminin, in 1984. The first women's race lasted almost as long as the men's: 18 stages in 21 days. It was hard on the 36 entrants because they rode the last 50 to 70 kilometers of the men's route every day and had to get to the starts by car, often driving for hours early in the morning to stay ahead of the men's Tour.

What's more, in a theretofore male-dominated sport, the sight of 36 women huffing and puffing up roads and pistes, made famous by men like "The Cannibal," seemed out of place.

"It was pretty bizarre," said Martin, now working in advertising sales for *VeloNews,* in Boulder, Colorado. "The photographers wanted to take shots of us doing strange things like eating or doing our hair."

But those things didn't bother Martin. Riding the first women's Tour de France was a big adventure. She had only been racing for three years and had decided to quit after the 1983 season, but at a cyclist's party in Denver, Martin heard talk of a women's Tour being planned for the next year. It was the impetus she needed to get going again.

Two weeks before the squad was scheduled to leave for France, Martin traveled to the U.S. National Team headquarters in Colorado Springs to lobby for the last spot on the U.S. team. Partially because the women's Olympic team riders were bypassing the Tour de France in order to focus on the L.A. Olympic Games and partially because Martin was considered an endurance rider capable of going the distance, she got the spot.

In many ways that first Tour Feminin had surprising similarities with Desgranges' first Tour, in 1903. Martin, like Maurice Garin, had little in the way of support: no coach, no mechanic, and a public that greeted the race's passage more with curiosity than avid support.

But Martin pushed on. Conservatively at first and then, on the 11th stage, with more confidence in the mountains where she found she had more climbing power than most of her rivals. By the end of the Tour she had beaten her nearest challenger, H. Hage from Holland, by 3 minutes, 17 seconds.

In Paris, she stood on the podium with Laurent Fignon, winner of the men's Tour. Her name and photo were seen by an estimated 200 million people around the world. But Marianne Martin never rode the Tour again.

In 1985, an early season illness knocked her out for the year. "I was broke and I was in debt," she said, "I had to start earning an income. That meant no more cycling."

The Tour Feminin has since grown but Martin has no regrets. "I just thought it was the greatest thing in the world to be in France doing that," she said, "I was really fortunate to have the experience."

Under different circumstances, Martin may have developed into a great champion. But cycling is full of ifs. Only the record book lists the facts.

Italy's Maria Canins (left) and France's Jeanne Longo have dominated the Tour Feminin since 1985. *Presse Sports photo*

SUMMARY

The Tour de France is legendary among sporting events. It is a commercial success and unquestionably the premier event in professional cycling.

Legendary heroes and spellbinding tales of adventure and courage have emerged from the Tour. Three men have won five times: Jacques Anquetil, Eddy Merckx, and Bernard Hinault. Each of these men has contributed significantly to the interest and intrigue in the race, Anquetil because he stylishly and cerebrally engineered each of his victories, Merckx because he could annihilate his competition, and Hinault because he was always ready for a fight. Great also-rans like Raymond Poulidor and Joop Zoetemelk have given the Tour a more human dimension and its fans a continuing opportunity to root for the underdog.

Tragedy has also stalked the Tour. Tom Simpson's death on Mt. Ventoux, in 1967, stimulated a drug-control program that has made cycling a model for such efforts in other sports.

Appendix

I—TOP 100 BICYCLE DEALERS

ALABAMA
Cahaba Cycles

ARIZONA
Tempe Bicycle Shop
Full Cycle
Bicycle Harbor
Bicycles West
Dominic's Cycling
Speedway Bicycles

CALIFORNIA
Sausalito Cyclery
Jax Bicycle Center
Two Wheel Transit
Pro Bike, Inc.
T. Martin Imports
Mulrooney, Inc.
Budget Bikes
Criterium Cycle Sport
Simi Cycling Center
Summerland Bicycle

COLORADO
Criterium Bicycle Shop
Cycle Logic
The Outdoorsman
Bicycle Village
Bike Lovers Place

CONNECTICUT
Stamford Cycle Center
Newington Bicycle
Greenwich Bicycles, Inc.
Bicycle Cellar

FLORIDA
Orange Cycle Works
Benjamin Cyclery
Mack Cycle
ABC Bicycle Shop

GEORGIA
Bicycle South
Vinnings Schwinn
Bike Town U.S.A.

IOWA
Northtown Schwinn
Bike World

IDAHO
George's Lightweight Cycles

ILLINOIS
Village Cyclery
RRB Bicycles
Bikes Plus Ltd.
Kozy's Cycle
Oak Park Cyclery

INDIANA
Bicycle Garage, Inc.

KANSAS
Harley's Cycle Supply
Rick's Bike Shop, Inc.
Bicycle Pedaler

KENTUCKY
Bicycle Sport, Inc.

MASSACHUSETTS
Belmont Wheel Works
International Bike Center
Bicycle Alley
Plaine's Bike & Ski

MARYLAND
Century Bicycles, Inc.
Potomac Push Bikes

MICHIGAN
Alfred E. Bike
Village Cyclery

MINNESOTA
Now Sports, Inc.
Cycle Goods

MISSOURI
Maplewood Bicycle Sales & Service
Wheeler's Schwinn Cyclery
Touring Cyclist
Bike Center

NEBRASKA
Bike Rack, Inc.

NEVADA
Bicycle World

NEW JERSEY
Cyclesport
Beacon Cycling / Fitness
Beacon Pro Bike
Brielle Cyclery
Bicycle World

NEW MEXICO
Albuquerque Schwinn
Cycle Cave
Bikes Plus

NEW YORK
Stuyvesant Cycle
Brand's Cycle Center
Cycling Center of Westchester

(continued)

NORTH CAROLINA
Two Wheeler Dealer

OHIO
Montgomery Cyclery

OKLAHOMA
Collins Cycle Shop
Bicycle Gallery
Bob's Bicycle Shop

PENNSYLVANIA
Bicycle Technology
Cycles Bikyle
Bicycle World
Bike Line
Guy's Bicycles

RHODE ISLAND
East Providence Cycle

TEXAS
Richardson Bike Mart
Wheels in Motion
Freewheeling Bicycles
Bicycle Sport Shop
Daniel Boone Cyclery
El Paso Schwinn

VIRGINIA
Bicycle Exchange
Metropolis Bike
Nova Cycle

WASHINGTON
R & E Cycles
Gregg's Greenlake Cycle

WISCONSIN
Wheel & Sprocket

The above is the result of a Bicycle Dealer Showcase survey of bicycle industry representatives. Shops were judged according to the following criteria:

- Product Selection/Mix
- Store Presentation
  (cleanliness, organization, signage)
- Merchandising Display
- Productivity
- Personnel Training
- Credit Worthiness
- Standing Among Peers
- Integrity

Source: Bicycle Dealer Showcase 1990 top 100 list

II—SUGGESTED READING

PERIODICALS

Bicycle Guide, 711 Boylston St., Boston, MA 02116, (617) 236-1885. General interest.

Bicycling, 33 E. Minor St., Emmaus, PA 18049, (215) 967-5171. General interest.

BMX Action, Wizard Publications, 3162 Kashiwa St., Torrance, CA 90505, (213) 539-9213. Bicycle motocross news.

Cycling USA, 1750 E. Boulder St., Colorado Springs, CO 80909, (719) 578-4581. The U.S. Cycling Federation's membership publication.

Mountain Bike, Rodale Press, 33 E. Minor St., Emmaus, PA 18049, (215) 967-5171. All-terrain bicycle news.

VeloNews, 5595 Arapahoe Ave., Suite G, Boulder, Co 80303, (303) 440-0601. Racing newspaper.

Winning, 1127 Hamilton St., Allentown, PA 18102, (215) 821-6864. Racing magazine.

MOUNTAIN BIKING—ATB

Richard's Mountain Bike Book, Charles Kelly, 1988, Ballantine Books, New York. Covers equipment, technique, touring, competition, and land access.

HEALTH, FITNESS, AND NUTRITION

Fitness Through Cycling, Bicycling Magazine, 1985, Rodale Press, Emmaus, PA. A collection of articles on basic conditioning, racing, injury prevention, and cross-training.

The Two-wheeled Athlete, Ed. Burke, 1986, VeloNews, Boulder, CO. A collection of articles offering practical advice and explaining the philosophy and biology of exercise.

RACING

Beginning Bicycle Racing, Fred Matheny, 1983, VeloNews, Boulder, CO. Information on training methods and goals, clothes, nutrition, and injuries.

Bicycle Road Racing: The Complete Program for Training and Competition, Eddie Borysewicz and Ed Pavelka, 1985, VeloNews, Boulder, CO. A review of a year-round program used by the U.S. national cycling team, with information on preparation, strategy, clothes, nutrition, and equipment.

Greg LeMond's Complete Book of Cycling, Greg LeMond and Kent Gordis, 1988, Putnam Publishing Company, New York. Covers history, technique, racing, diet, bike selection, and maintenance.

Hearts of Lions: The History of American Bicycle Racing, Peter Nye, 1988, W. W. Norton & Co., New York. A definitive and entertaining history of American participation in the sport.

Road Racing: Training & Technique, Bernard Hinault and Claude Genzling, 1988, VeloNews, Boulder, CO. A look at equipment, preparation, skills, and tactics.

Tour de France, Phil Liggett, 1989, Harrap Books Ltd., London. History and evolution of the Tour de France.

REPAIR AND MAINTENANCE

Bicycling Magazine's Complete Guide to Bicycle Maintenance and Repair, 1986, Rodale Press, Emmaus, PA.

Bicycle Mechanics in Workshop and Competition, Steve Snowling and Ken Evans, 1986, Springfield Books Ltd., England.

The Bike Bag Book, Tom Cuthbertson, 1981, Ten Speed Press, Berkeley, CA. Concentrates on on-road maintenance.

CREDIT
LYONNAIS
WONDER

Index

Page numbers in italics refer to illustrations

Y

Z

ABOUT THE AUTHORS

David M. Chauner (left) and Michael W. Halstead

DAVID M. CHAUNER, *forty-one, is the founder and chairman of International Cycling Productions, America's leading packager, producer, and marketer of bicycling-oriented events and promotions. A former two-time Olympic cyclist (1968 and 1972), Mr. Chauner has been active in the production and packaging of cycling events since 1975, including the Yoplait 50K Bicycle Challenge Series (1979–1982), US Pro National Championship in Baltimore (1982–1983), Cititour, Bicycle Race of New York (1986), Citi-Circuit Bicycle Challenge in Chicago (1987), and CoreStates NJNB Classic (1989). In 1985, Mr. Chauner founded the CoreStates USPro Championship in Philadelphia and annually serves as the event's Executive Director. In addition to successful event production and management, Mr. Chauner has done extensive television commentary on the sport (NBC, CBS, ESPN, and others) and has written articles on cycling for* The New York Times *and* Sports Illustrated *as well as for numerous cycling publications.*

MICHAEL W. HALSTEAD, *forty-three, is president of International Cycling Productions. Prior to his association with ICP, Mr. Halstead spent twelve years with Mark McCormack's International Management Group, where he gained extensive insight and experience in virtually all aspects of sports marketing, management, and television. During his tenure at IMG, Mr. Halstead was instrumental in forming and managing its profit centers in the areas of Winter Sports, Broadcaster Management, General Merchandising, International Television Distribution, and Business Development. Mr. Halstead was a senior vice president when he left IMG to pursue his own ventures. In addition to being an equal partner with Mr. Chauner in ICP and the CoreStates Championship, Mr. Halstead is president and CEO of Sports & Company, the parent organization of ICP and an international sports marketing, television, and video company that packages properties and provides advice in these areas to a number of individuals, federations, and other entities in the world of sports and sports television. Mr. Halstead is an attorney, author, and former professional ski racer.*